Selling and Designing Wedding Flowers

Selling and Designing Wedding Flowers

Selling and Designing Wedding Flowers

Second Edition

First edition published 1991
Second printing 1992

Library of Congress Catalog Card Number: 93-83789
International Standard Book Number: 1-56963-010-0

Printed by:
Teleflora
Leachville, Arkansas

Other textbooks in Teleflora's Encycloflora™ series:

Purchasing and Handling Fresh Flowers and Foliage

Basic Floral Design

Green and Blooming Plants

Retail Flower Shop Operation

Visual Merchandising for the Retail Florist

Marketing and Promoting Floral Products

Floral Design for the Holidays

Designing with Balloons and Flowers

Selling and Designing Party Flowers

Selling and Designing Sympathy Flowers

Advanced Floral Design

Acknowledgments

Teleflora gives special thanks to the individuals who participated in the creation and development of this comprehensive floral training manual.

Frances Porterfield, AAF	Topeka, KS
Terry Lanker, M.Ed.	Wooster, OH
Richard Paul Salvaggio, AIFD, AAF, PFCI	Los Angeles, CA
Christy Holstead-Klink, M.S.	Nazareth, PA
Carl Lemanski, AIFD	Berkeley Heights, NJ
Pamela Linder, AIFD	Harbor City, CA
Harvey Pope, AIFD	Toronto, Ontario, Canada
Frankie Shelton, AIFD, AAF, PFCI	Houston, TX
Janice Stutters, AIFD	Littleton, CO
Gary Wells, AIFD	Kentwood, MI

Please note that Redbook Florist Services has been acquired by Teleflora effective June 9, 1997. All references made in this publication to Redbook and Redbook Florist Services are transferred to Teleflora.

Contents

Preface

Selling and Designing Wedding Flowers has been prepared for the person who seeks knowledge and professionalism in the floral industry as specifically related to weddings.

The book is a comprehensive source of information concerning mechanics and construction techniques for wedding flowers. A detailed discussion of marketing and selling wedding services and flowers and specific information about wedding customs and traditions, religious requirements, etiquette, and fashion is also included.

The ideas, methods, and conclusions presented in this book were drawn from the personal and combined experiences of a select group of retail florists and floral industry professionals. Any information drawn from other sources has been noted.

Selling and Designing Wedding Flowers has been written for use as a reference and training manual and will prove beneficial to individuals at all levels and in all areas of the floral industry. The concise text contains practical solutions to common problems, and illustrations provide step-by-step instructions for designing wedding flowers of varying degrees of difficulty.

List of Illustrations

List of Illustrations

List of Illustrations

List of Illustrations

List of Tables

Introduction

The contemporary bride has more options than ever when planning the wedding of her dreams. Individuality is of key importance to the bride as she strives to create an overall wedding mood which reflects her own personality. Currently, many weddings are planned around themes, such as a nautical wedding or an old fashioned garden party.

As a general rule, most couples are older and better educated when they decide to "tie the knot." Often these couples have established careers which provide dual incomes with which to plan their weddings. Brides and grooms typically know precisely what they want and will insist on following their own ceremony and reception ideas.

In order to coordinate every detail of their special day, the busy couple often engages the services of a wedding consultant. This consultant assists the couple in arranging for music, invitations, caterers, etc. Often, the knowledgeable florist is also able to provide many of these services to the couple for an agreed upon fee.

Wedding formality runs the gamut from lavish and luxurious cathedral weddings to simple, yet sophisticated, civil ceremonies. While many brides choose to have multiple bridesmaids, flower girls, and train bearers, others prefer the quiet elegance of a single honor attendant. This is also true for "encore weddings," in which the bridal party often consists largely of the couple's children.

Wedding fashions continue to favor elegant, feminine styles. Traditional ball gowns with rich embellishments and lengthy trains are perennial favorites. Although white and ivory have long been the standard bridal gown colors, brides are now choosing gowns in pastel shades or with colored accents. Tea length and floor length gowns are popular for bridesmaids and flower girls. Texture and detailing are evident in gowns of printed cotton, metallic lace, and sequined taffeta. Men's tuxedos are more fashionable than ever with a wider variety of colors, patterns, and styles available.

2

Selling and Designing Wedding Flowers

The trend in wedding flowers has followed the changes in wedding styles. Today's opulent weddings require a lavish use of flowers, while smaller, more discreet weddings call for simpler, yet distinctive, floral decorations. The weekend wedding, consisting of two or three days of wedding activities, provides additional needs for floral decorations.

Bouquets continue to favor romantic styles. The classical look of roses, baby's breath, and ivy is timeless. Abundant, gathered garden bouquets are natural choices for many brides. Stylized bouquets with an emphasis on a few select botanical specimens are preferred by brides who want something "different."

Ceremony and reception decorations are also receiving more attention than ever. Floral decorations of all types are used to create a wedding atmosphere and to continue the wedding style and theme.

As wedding styles and trends change, so must the florist. The competitive florist must strive to create new and unique floral decorations for the very specific needs of each wedding client. Whatever style or mood the bride selects for her wedding day, the florist should provide the highest quality product possible in order to enhance the wedding atmosphere. The true floral artist is able to translate the bride's wedding dreams into a vision of floral excellence.

Chapter 1

Wedding Etiquette

It is important for the retail florist to understand basic etiquette and ceremonial customs, as well as wedding forms and styles. Brides are overwhelmed by the multitude of wedding choices and situations. Along with the florist, other retailers and service companies compete for the bride's business, thus the florist must be a wedding professional who is able to offer guidance to bridal customers. The florist's knowledge will make the bride and her family feel more comfortable with their choices and will certainly help to enhance the shop's reputation.

Wedding etiquette involves five C's: change, constancy, combination, courtesy, and common sense. *Change* indicates the evolution of new attitudes and social trends that challenge traditional rules and regulations. There are new ideas of equality and individuality and newly expanded family structures as a result of multiple marriages, all of which affect wedding etiquette. At the same time, there is *constancy*, a sense of continuity that stems from a bride's desire to maintain the beauty and dignity of tradition. Brides also may choose whether to maintain certain elements of, or completely adhere to, tradition. These changes and choices have resulted in *combination* - a mixture of traditional and contemporary choices. Personal touches are added to existing liturgy and scripture. Joint ceremonies for interfaith marriages interlace important parts from two different religions. The possibilities are almost limitless. In a sense, there is no standard way to be married anymore! There are no hard and fast rules of etiquette as once was the case. This is why wedding etiquette involves *courtesy* and *common sense*. It means using the established rules of etiquette as guidelines. These guidelines are combined with courtesy and common sense to help make decisions about style, seating, and other wedding procedures for the challenging situations and creative ceremonies of many brides.

Selling and Designing Wedding Flowers

Weddings consist of two key elements: style and form. *Style* refers to traditional customs and rules developed over a period of time, such as rituals, ceremonial events, or symbolic acts. This is part of what we refer to as "the rules of etiquette." Style also includes the formality, mood, and tone of the ceremony, such as ornateness or lavishness. *Form* refers to the way in which vows are exchanged. For example, the type of ceremony that is chosen might be civil, religious, or self-written.

The illustrations and tables included in this chapter summarize some of the stylistic elements of weddings, including symbolism and traditional procedures. Specific information about etiquette for wedding ceremonies of different religious denominations is provided in Chapter 7, "Ceremonial Decorations".

Notes

Traditional Wedding Customs

Wedding customs and beliefs have been maintained throughout generations. These traditions can add beautiful touches to a wedding that all will enjoy. Understanding the origins of these traditions can make a wedding more meaningful and can influence a bride's decision about following such traditions. Some brides may choose to print the meanings of certain traditions which they utilize in the wedding program or a separate booklet.

Bridal Kiss

At the conclusion of the ceremony, tradition dictates that the groom must be the first person to kiss the bride. This symbolizes the couple's faith and love, and seals the confidence that they privately share. For centuries, a kiss has signified respect and obedience to mutual beliefs.

Bridal Party

The roles of various members of the bridal party have origins in ancient customs. Bridesmaids likely developed from the need to have witnesses. Their original purpose for wearing festive attire was to deceive the demons in the identification of the bride. Flower girls originated from a custom that two little girls, identically dressed, walked ahead of the bride carrying garlands of wheat to symbolize the wish for a fruitful union. In the 1600's, it became popular for flower girls to carry baskets.

In the Middle Ages, the groomsmen were known as "Bride Knights" because they served the bride by taking her to the

Notes

church and to the altar, and then relinquishing her to the groom. Today these "duties" are completed by the bridesmaids. The duty of the best man dates back to the era of marriage by capture. Hundreds of years ago, when a man intended to capture a bride, he was accompanied by a strong-armed friend, thus simplifying the capture.

Bridal Shower

It is believed that "bridal showers" originated in Holland. A Dutch father did not approve of the poor miller whom his daughter wished to marry. Her friends "showered" her with gifts so that she would have the necessary dowry to gain her father's permission to marry the man of her choice. Years later, an English woman heard of a good friend who was to be married and wanted to give her a gift to express her congratulations, but the gift seemed too small. She remembered the story of the Dutch girl and the miller and began calling the bride's friends suggesting they present their gifts at the same time. The party was successful, others tried it, and "bridal showers" became popular!

Bridal Wear

Bridal gowns are traditionally white because the ancient Greeks and Romans believed white was a symbol of purity, innocence, and joy. Recently, the white or ivory bridal dress has evolved as a symbol of the celebration of the ceremony itself. Lace, considered a work of art in Europe, was often used for festive celebrations and important occasions and has remained a popular gown ornamentation.

Wearing a veil is another tradition from hundreds of years ago. It originally symbolized youth and virginity. Additionally, women from Far Eastern countries wore veils to protect themselves from evil spirits. In eleventh and twelfth century Europe, the bride stood covered by a veil while her father bargained her away. The bride never revealed her face until the wedding ceremony was over.

Carried over the Threshold

Centuries ago the bride was not always willing to leave her family home; therefore, the groom needed to forcibly carry her over the threshold into her new home. It was also thought that demons dwelled on the newlyweds' doorstep; as a result, the groom carried his bride over the threshold to protect her.

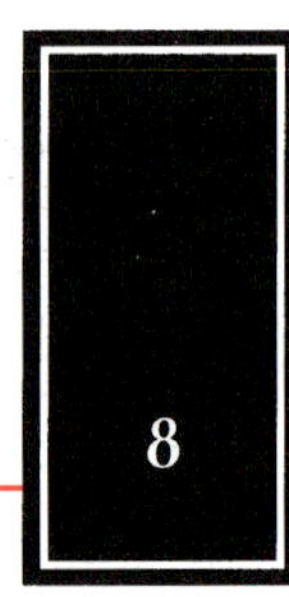

Engagement Ring

Notes

The gift of a ring is a very old tradition which was used to seal any important or sacred agreement. Engagement rings were given in the days of "marriage by purchase," both as a partial payment and as a symbol of the groom's good intentions. Diamonds have been the most popular gems for engagement rings because they are the most durable stones. The first diamond engagement rings were worn in medieval Italy. Superstition maintains that a diamond's sparkle comes from the fires of love.

Flowers

Flowers have been a part of wedding celebrations for centuries. In ancient Rome, the bride would carry herbs under her veil. This custom evolved into the carrying of orange blossoms as a symbol of fertility. Also, it was a Roman custom to light the first fire of the couple's house with a torch, which was then tossed out to be caught by one of the wedding party. In the fourteenth century, the French substituted the bouquet for the torch and thus began the legend that whoever among the bride's attendants caught the blossoms would be the next to marry. Over the years, certain flowers have been selected as "flowers of the month," as shown in Table 1. A bride may wish to have these included in her wedding designs.

TABLE 1

FLOWERS OF THE MONTH

Month	Flower
January	Carnation
February	Violet or Sweetheart Rose
March	Jonquil or Daffodil
April	Daisy or Sweet Pea
May	Lily-of-the-Valley
June	Rose
July	Cornflower
August	Gladiolus
September	Aster
October	Calendula
November	Chrysanthemum
December	Poinsettia or Narcissus

Notes

Flowers have a language of their own. The symbolism associated with many flowers is steeped in two thousand years of tradition and was especially popular in the Victorian period. This romantic language is especially appropriate for love, courtship, and weddings. Sharing this symbolism with brides can help them convey personal sentiments through flowers, creating a lasting memory and making the day more special. Table 2 on page 10 provides traditional meanings for specific flowers.

Honeymoon

Historically, marriage was often brought about by capture and was often not agreed upon by either the bride or the groom. The groom would take his wife to a place where she could not be found. They stayed away approximately 30 days and drank a brew made of honey while the moon went through all of its phases. The term "honeymoon" originated with this practice. Today, newlyweds also go away to celebrate their new lives together.

Something Old, Something New . . .

The popular wedding phrase, "Something old, something new, something borrowed, something blue, and a lucky sixpence for your shoe," has several different meanings. Each of these items is worn or carried by the bride to symbolize something special. "Something old" and "something borrowed" are items which represent security and friendship and are given to the bride by a loved one to bring happiness to the new marriage. "Something new" (often the wedding gown) represents the bride's acceptance of a new life. The origin of something blue can be traced to the rhyme, "Those who dress in blue have lovers true." A "lucky sixpence" (usually a penny today) worn in the shoe or carried by the bride is a very old tradition thought to ensure future wealth and good fortune for the newly wedded couple.

Rice

Showering the wedding couple with rice after the ceremony or reception was originally meant to assure the couple prosperity and express the hope that they would have many children. This "showering" tradition continues as many couples choose birdseed because of the ill effects of uncooked rice on the bird population.

TABLE 2

FLOWERS AND TRADITIONAL MEANINGS

Flower	Meaning
Bachelor's Button	Hope
Bells of Ireland	Good Luck
Camellia	Perfect Loveliness, Gratitude
Carnation	Pure, Deep Love
Chrysanthemum (General)	You are a Wonderful Friend, Cheerfulness, and Rest
Red	I Love You
White	Truth
Daisy	Gentleness, Innocence, Loyalty, and Love
Delphinium	Flights of Fancy, Ardent Attachment
Forget-Me-Not	Faithful Love, Undying Hope, Memory, Do Not Forget
Gardenia	You are Lovely, Sweet Love
Heather	Admiration, Beauty
Iris	Faith, Wisdom, Valor, and Promise
Ivy	Wedded Love, Fidelity, Friendship, and Affection
Jonquil	Affection Returned
Lemon Leaves	Everlasting Love
Lilac	First Emotion of Love
Lily	Purity and Innocence
Lily (Calla)	Beauty
Lily-of-the-Valley	Humility, Sweetness, Return of Happiness, You Have Made My Life
Complete Myrtle	Duty and Affection
Orange Blossoms	Innocence, Eternal Love, Marriage and Fruitfulness
Orchid	Love, Beauty, and Magnificence
Peony	Happy Marriage and Prosperity
Roses (General)	Love, Joy, and Beauty
Basket of Rose Petals	Life of Plenty
White and Colored Roses	Unity
Single Red Rose	I Love You
Yellow	Joy and Gladness
White	Reverence, Humility, Innocence, and Purity
Rosemary	Remembrance
Star of Bethlehem	Purity
Stephanotis	Happiness in Marriage
Stock	Lasting Beauty
Sweet Pea	Blissful Pleasure
Tulips (Red)	Declaration of Love
Violet	Faithfulness

Notes

Notes

Wedding Cake

Cake and bread have always been a vital part of wedding celebrations. In ancient Rome, bread was considered a symbol of fertility. Thus, to ensure fertility, a loaf of bread would be broken over the bride's head and the crumbs shared with all the guests. Also, the couple was not considered married until they ate together.

In contemporary wedding receptions, this practice is continued as the bride and groom cut the first slice of wedding cake together and feed each other. Guests eat from the cake, both as a sign of unity and as a way of wishing luck to the newly wedded couple. The tradition of having a second "groom's" cake at the reception has evolved over the years. Originally, the groom's cake was a dark, rich fruitcake and was said to also provide the couple with the blessings of fertility. Today, the cake may be of any type and is often chocolate or fruit-flavored.

Wedding Ring

Tradition maintains that the wedding ring evolved from the engagement ring. The ancient Egyptians believed an unbroken circular band symbolized unending love and commitment to a permanent relationship. The ring, which replaced the crown of thorns worn in certain cultures, signified the eternal circle which had no beginning and no end and thus should be the love between a husband and a wife.

Levels of Wedding Formality

Weddings are categorized as either formal, semiformal, or informal. Table 3 on page 12 provides a description of each wedding category.

Standard Wedding Procedures

There are standard procedures for a formal wedding as conducted in all major Christian ceremonies. Exceptions to these procedures are noted throughout this chapter. Rules and customs within each faith are changing, and different procedures are permitted in different divisions of the same faith. Also, some clergymen are willing to break tradition within reasonable limits. Others feel that the strict observance of established traditions or

TABLE 3

LEVELS OF WEDDING FORMALITY

	Formal Wedding	Semiformal Wedding	Informal Wedding
Invitations	Engraved invitations and often announcements, at-home cards, and reception cards.	Engraved or informal.	Informal, often hand-written.
Location	Usually in a house of worship, but occasionally in a garden, a club, or a hotel ballroom.	Small church, chapel, or home.	Anywhere including city hall.
Decorations	Lavish decorations, may include pew ribbons, aisle runner(s), candelabras, and an abundance of flowers.	Similar types of decorations as for formal weddings, but less extravagant.	Very simple or none.
Number of Guests	100-500 or more.	50-100.	A few relatives and friends numbering 50-75 people.
Size of Bridal Party	Large bridal party; should have at least one usher for each 50 guests; may have two honor attendants for the bride, along with flower girl(s) and ring bearer.	Smaller wedding party; usually one or two bridal attendants, a best man, two ushers or none, often flower girl or ring bearer.	One attendant for the bride and a best man; guests usually seat themselves.
Bride's Attire	Opulent wedding gown and bridal wear; gown usually floor or waltz length, often with a train; bridal bouquet.	Long or short dress (short veil optional) or even a dressy suit; smaller bridal bouquet or corsage.	Street, afternoon, or dinner dress; flowers vary - usually simple. Bride may wear flowers in her hair, but will not carry a full bouquet.
Groom's Attire	Before six, often a cutaway or dinner coat. After six, white or black tie.	Dark street suit.	Street suit.
Reception	Elaborate decorations; elaborate buffet or a fully served meal; receiving line and customary activities of first dance, toasting, and cake cutting. Often overseen by master of ceremonies.	Less elaborate decorations, simple flower arrangements; champagne may be served, hors d'oeuvres rather than full sit-down meal; may be held at bride's or groom's home.	Sometimes dinner at a restaurant, often at home. May be a sizeable outdoor party or buffet supper for any number of guests.

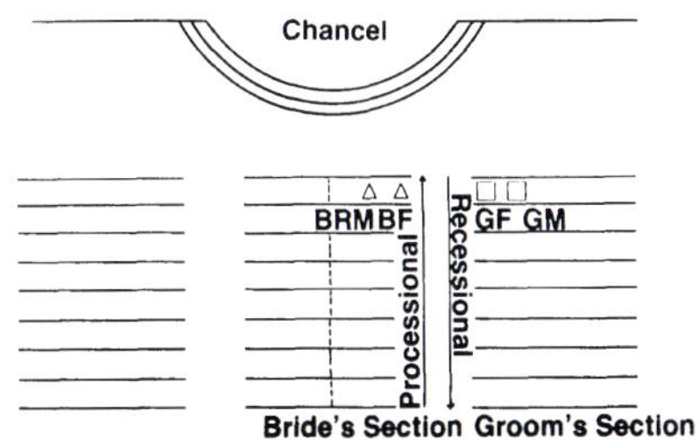

Figure 1.1 Seating in House of Worship with Two Main Aisles for a Small Wedding

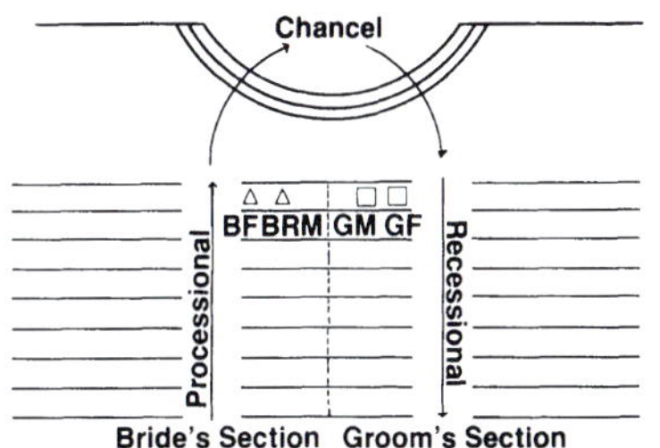

Figure 1.2 Seating in House of Worship with Two Main Aisles for a Medium-Sized Wedding

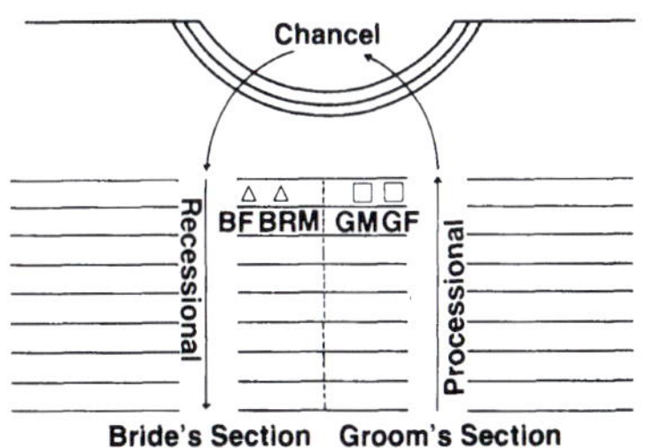

Figure 1.3a Seating in House of Worship with Two Main Aisles for a Large Wedding

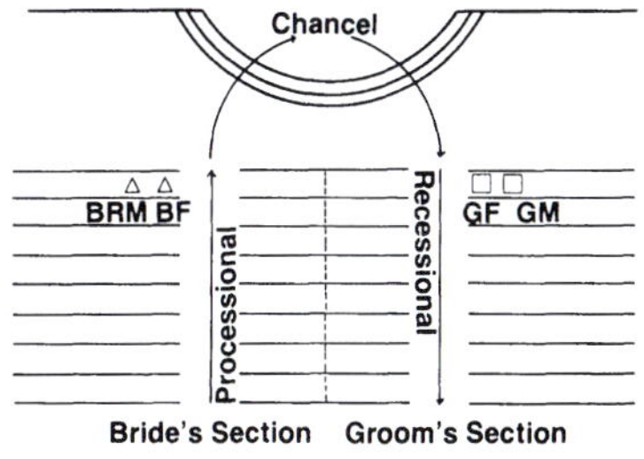

Figure 1.3b Seating in House of Worship with Two Main Aisles for a Large Wedding

BF = Bride's Father
BRM = Bride's Mother
GF = Groom's Father
GM = Groom's Mother

procedures is important. The minister, priest, or rabbi who will officiate at the wedding has the final word on the possibility of changes in established procedures. The following illustrations and tables provide guidelines for ceremonial procedures including the processional, recessional, seating, and altar positions. Chapter 7, "Ceremonial Decorations," describes differences in rituals between various religious denominations.

Seating Procedures

The seating of family and guests at the ceremony is determined by the floor plan of the church and the number of guests attending the wedding. The following guidelines describe the most common seating situations and procedures.

House of Worship with Center Aisle

The bride's section for seating guests of the bride is on the left as one faces the altar; the groom's section is on the right. Parents occupy the first pews; the fathers are seated closest to the aisle. Relatives sit with the parents and in the pews immediately behind them. The processional and the recessional are down the center aisle.

House of Worship with Two Main Aisles and No Center Aisle

If relatively few people will be present, the right aisle can be treated as if it were a center aisle in all details, and the rest of the pews ignored. The marriage is held at the head of the right aisle. ***(Figure 1.1)***

For a medium-sized wedding, all the guests may be seated in the center section. The processional progresses up the left aisle and the recessional down the right aisle. ***(Figure 1.2)***

If the church will be fully seated, two seating options are possible, as illustrated in ***Figures 1.3a and 1.3b***. The processional and the recessional may take place on either the right or the left aisle.

Jewish Weddings

In Orthodox and Conservative synagogues and temples, the bride's section is to the right as one faces the Ark of the Covenant. Reform rabbis endorse the traditional Christian seating arrangement with the bride's section on the left and the groom's section on the right.

Divorced Parents

Notes

Divorced parents do not occupy the same pew. The bride's mother occupies the first pew with her mother and father or her immediate family beside her or in one or two pews immediately behind her. The bride's father takes his place in the pew behind those occupied by his former in-laws after giving his daughter away. His own family sits beside and immediately behind him.

If the bride's parents have remarried, her mother sits in the first pew with her current husband beside her, and the bride's relatives on her mother's side in the next rows. The bride's father, his current wife, and their children, if any, occupy the next pew with the bride's paternal grandparents, aunts, and uncles in the succeeding pews.

Ushers

Large bridal parties typically consist of several groomsmen who are each paired with a bridesmaid, as well as ushers who remain in the back of the church during the ceremony. Smaller bridal parties may have no ushers, but instead assign the ushers' duties to the groomsmen. In either case, the ushers should arrive well in advance of the first guests (1 hour before a large wedding, 45 minutes before a smaller one). Ushers may ask female guests if they are part of the bride's or bridegroom's party, then escort them to the appropriate side of the church. The following is a list of seating procedures for ushers:

- The usher's right arm is offered to arriving female guests.
- If two ladies arrive together and only one usher is available at the moment, he offers his right arm to the elder as the younger follows a few paces behind.
- When a family group arrives, an usher escorts the wife. Her children and husband follow, usually in pairs.
- An usher never offers his left arm to a guest or walks up the aisle between a couple.
- An usher should never offer his arm to a man unless the gentleman is incapacitated and in need of assistance. Instead, they walk side by side, the male guest on the usher's right.

- Guests who arrive early are privileged to take the aisle seats if they are shown to an empty pew. They are not expected to move over when others join them in a row.
- Ushers should be told if the guest list has a disproportionate number of guests from either family so they can distribute the guests evenly.
- Ushers should also be told who the guests of honor are (parents, grandparents, and other close relatives) and if there are any unusual parental situations on either side (parents who are divorced, stepparents, or remarried parents).
- The mother of the bridegroom is seated by the head usher in the front pew or in the row on the right side with the groom's father following a few paces behind.
- The mother of the bride is always the last to be escorted to her place. If she has a son who is acting as an usher, he takes her to her seat. If she has two sons, the older son seats her and the younger son escorts her out after the ceremony. Otherwise, she is seated by the head usher. She is seated on the left side of the sanctuary.

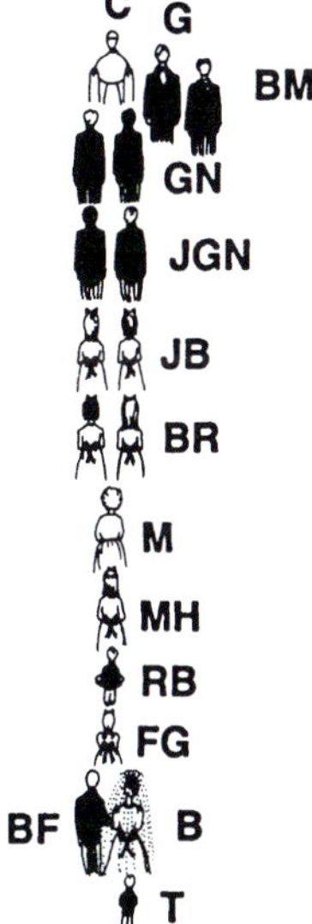

Figure 1.4 Traditional Processional for a Formal Wedding

B = Bride
MH = Maid of Honor
M = Matron of Honor
BR = Bridesmaids
JB = Junior Bridesmaids
BF = Bride's Father
BRM = Bride's Mother
T = Train Bearer
FG = Flower Girl
G = Groom
BM = Best Man
GN = Groomsmen
JGN = Junior Groomsmen
GF = Groom's Father
GM = Groom's Mother
C = Clergyman
R = Rabbi
RB = Ring Bearer

Ceremonial Positions

The positions of the wedding participants while entering and exiting the sanctuary, as well as while standing at the altar and in the receiving line, vary according to the type and size of the wedding. The following guidelines and illustrations describe the most common ceremonial positions for the members of the wedding party.

Traditional Processional

The traditional processional for a formal wedding is shown in ***Figure 1.4***. The entrance of the bridal party may be varied in several ways. The bridesmaids and groomsmen may walk down the aisle singly or as couples. The flower girl and ring bearer may walk together. The bride may be escorted by her mother and father together, or even by children, especially for encore weddings.

Orthodox and Conservative Jewish Processional

The traditional processional for an Orthodox or Conservative Jewish wedding is shown in ***Figure 1.5***. The processional for the Reformed Jewish ceremony usually follows the traditional procedure customary to other faiths. However, the groom often participates in the processional, entering just before the maid of honor.

For Orthodox and Conservative Jewish ceremonies, the entrance of the bridal party may be varied in several ways. The mother of the bride may walk down the aisle on the arm of the best man, while the father accompanies his daughter. Sometimes both fathers walk with the groom, and both mothers with the bride. Another variation is for the groom and the best man to walk side by side. If the grandparents are to participate, the bride's grandparents follow the rabbi, and the groom's grandparents follow those of the bride.

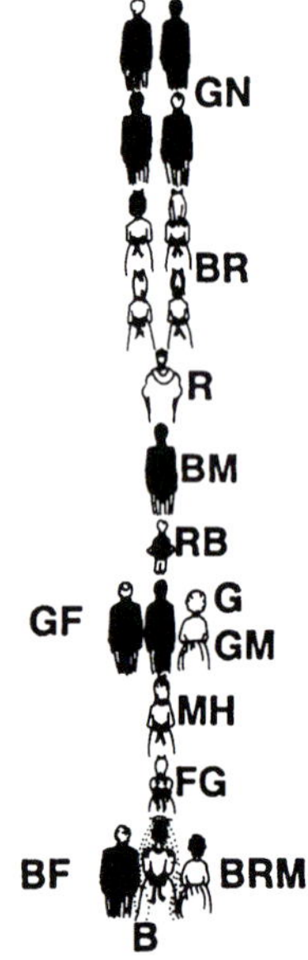

Figure 1.5 Processional for an Orthodox or Conservative Jewish Wedding

Traditional Altar Positions

In traditional weddings, the maid and/or matron of honor stands beside the bride, and the best man stands beside the groom. The remaining attendants stand one step behind and to the sides of this foursome. Usually, all of the bridesmaids stand to the left of the maid/matron of honor and all of the groomsmen stand to the right of the best man. For smaller bridal parties or when there is room on or near a large altar, the bridesmaids and groomsmen may be arranged in a single row. When there is a large number of bridesmaids and groomsmen, they may be divided into two rows. ***(Figure 1.6a)*** A second option is to group half of the bridesmaids and half of the groomsmen on each side of the wedding couple with the women in front of the men. ***(Figure 1.6b on page 17)*** Often the bridal party will move at different parts of the ceremony and may face the congregation for all or part of the wedding.

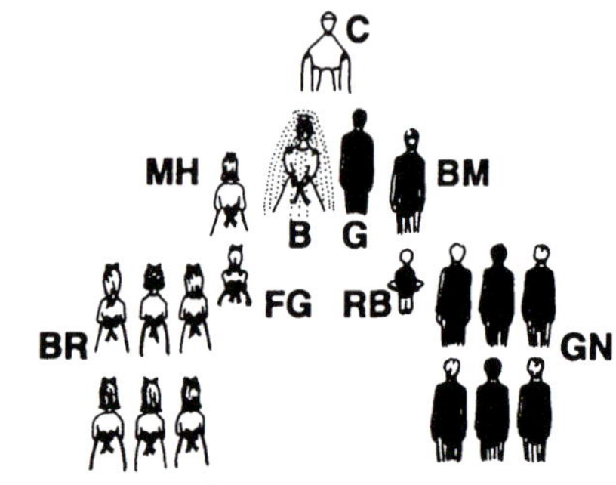

Figure 1.6a Traditional Altar Positions

Orthodox and Conservative Jewish Altar Positions

The Orthodox and Conservative Jewish wedding ceremony takes place under a canopy, called a chuppah (pronounced "hoopa"). The couple's parents are key participants. The bride's father and groom's mother stand next to their respective children. The bride's mother and groom's father stand next to their spouses. The maid or matron of honor and best man stand behind the bridal couple and parents. ***(Figure 1.7 on page 17)***

B = Bride	G = Groom
MH = Maid of Honor	BM = Best Man
M = Matron of Honor	GN = Groomsmen
BR = Bridesmaids	JGN = Junior Groomsmen
JB = Junior Bridesmaids	GF = Groom's Father
BF = Bride's Father	GM = Groom's Mother
BRM = Bride's Mother	C = Clergyman
T = Train Bearer	R = Rabbi
FG = Flower Girl	RB = Ring Bearer

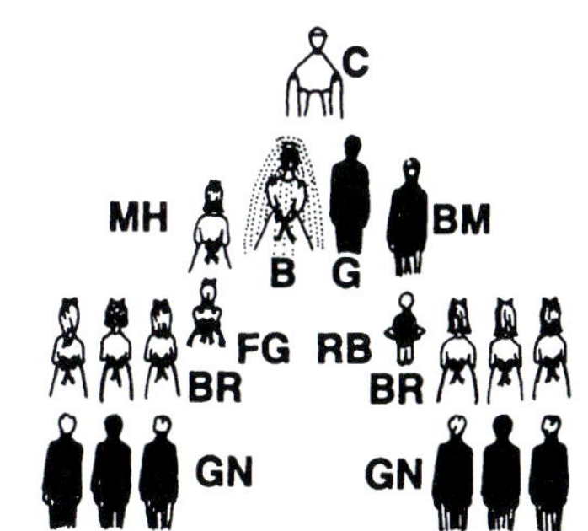

Figure 1.6b Traditional Altar Positions

Figure 1.7 Standard Orthodox and Conservative Jewish Altar Positions

B = Bride
MH = Maid of Honor
M = Matron of Honor
BR = Bridesmaids
JB = Junior Bridesmaids
BF = Bride's Father
BRM = Bride's Mother
T = Train Bearer
FG = Flower Girl
G = Groom
BM = Best Man
GN = Groomsmen
JGN = Junior Groomsmen
GF = Groom's Father
GM = Groom's Mother
C = Clergyman
R = Rabbi
RB = Ring Bearer

Traditional Recessionals

Two different recessional styles for formal weddings are shown in ***Figures 1.8a and 1.8b on page 18***. Following the exit of the entire bridal party, the head ushers typically return to the front of the church and escort the mothers of the bride and groom down the aisle. The fathers follow behind them. Then, the ushers return to the front of the church again and signal guests to exit one row of pews at a time.

The recessional for the Orthodox and Conservative Jewish ceremony is shown in ***Figure 1.9 on page 19***. A flower girl may or may not be a part of this procedure. The rabbi sometimes follows the parents.

Receiving Line

The receiving line may take place in the vestibule of the church if the reception is to be small and informal. If the bride and groom request it, the receiving line may be held at the reception if there is a large number of guests attending the wedding.

The receiving line may be ordered so that the parents stand together as a couple or stand with each other's spouses. The best man, ushers, and child attendants are not traditionally included in the receiving line; however, the bride may choose to have them take part, especially in an informal situation.

The proper position for each member of the receiving line is shown in ***Figure 1.10 on page 19***. As shown, the guests should begin at the left end of the line and proceed to the right.

Wedding Lefts and Rights

Lefts:

- The bride's family and friends sit on the left side of the aisle at the ceremony.
- The men of the wedding party wear their boutonnieres on their left lapels.
- The bride and groom wear their wedding rings on their left hands.

Rights:

- The groom's family and friends sit on the right side of the aisle at the ceremony.
- The ushers offer each female guest their right arm as they escort her to her seat.
- The bride walks down the aisle on her father's right.
- During the wedding ceremony, the bride wears her engagement ring on her right hand.
- In the receiving line, the bride stands to the groom's right.

Division of Wedding Expenses

Traditionally, specific wedding costs have been divided among the bride's family, the groom, and the groom's family. It is becoming increasingly common, however, for wedding costs to be evenly shared by each side. Furthermore, many couples are paying the complete cost of their wedding celebrations themselves.

The following lists show the traditional division of wedding costs. This list is most often used as a guide rather than a rule. However, it is helpful to be familiar with what is customary in order to be of greatest assistance to the bride. If a wedding client requests a complicated division of the wedding flower bill, it may be wise for the florist to send one bill to the bride and allow her to work out the details with the parties involved.

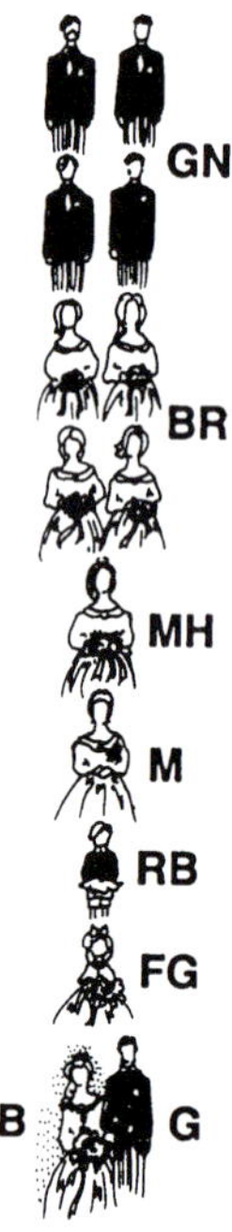

Figure 1.8a Traditional Recessional

Figure 1.8b Traditional Recessional

B = Bride	G = Groom
MH = Maid of Honor	BM = Best Man
M = Matron of Honor	GN = Groomsmen
BR = Bridesmaids	JGN = Junior Groomsmen
JB = Junior Bridesmaids	GF = Groom's Father
BF = Bride's Father	GM = Groom's Mother
BRM = Bride's Mother	C = Clergyman
T = Train Bearer	R = Rabbi
FG = Flower Girl	RB = Ring Bearer

Customary Expenses of the Bride and/or Her Family

- Flowers for the church and reception; bouquets for the honor attendants, bridesmaids, and flower girls.
- Engagement party and photograph.
- Fee for professional wedding consultant.
- Printing - Bride's personal stationery, wedding invitations, announcements, enclosure cards.
- The bride's clothing and accessories.
- Gifts for the attendants.
- Groom's wedding ring and wedding gift.
- Church expenses - Rental fee, aisle carpet, canopy, tent, sexton's fee.
- Music - Organist's and soloist's fees at the ceremony and music at the reception.
- All photography.
- Hotel accommodations, if needed, for the bridesmaids. (They may absorb this expense themselves.)

Figure 1.9 Recessional for the Orthodox or Conservative Jewish Ceremony

Figure 1.10 Positions for the Receiving Line

B = Bride
MH = Maid of Honor
M = Matron of Honor
BR = Bridesmaids
JB = Junior Bridesmaids
BF = Bride's Father
BRM = Bride's Mother
T = Train Bearer
FG = Flower Girl
G = Groom
BM = Best Man
GN = Groomsmen
JGN = Junior Groomsmen
GF = Groom's Father
GM = Groom's Mother
C = Clergyman
R = Rabbi
RB = Ring Bearer

- Transportation to the church and reception for the bride and her attendants.
- Reception - All costs including food, beverages, and room rental.

Customary Expenses of the Groom and/or His Family

- Flowers - Bride's bouquet and going-away corsage, boutonnieres for the men in the wedding party, flowers for the mothers and grandmothers.
- Bride's engagement ring and wedding ring.
- Marriage license fee.
- Fee for clergyman or civil official who conducts the marriage ceremony.
- Tuxedo rental for the groom.
- Gloves, ties or ascots, and accessories for the men in the wedding party.
- Groom's gift to the bride.
- Groom's gifts to the groomsmen.
- Hotel accommodations, if needed, for the groomsmen. (They may absorb this expense themselves.)
- Transportation for the groom and best man to the church and reception.
- Rehearsal dinner.
- All honeymoon expenses.

Optional Expenses

Local customs and personal preference dictate who will pay for these items.

- Flowers - The bride's bouquet may be included in the cost of her ensemble and paid for by her family, but it is traditionally a gift from the groom. The flowers for the bride's mother and grandmother may be paid for by the bride rather than the groom. Often the bride and her family pay for all of the flowers.

- Bridesmaids' dresses are usually paid for by each attendant, but may be paid for by the bride.
- Groomsmen's and ushers' tuxedo rental charges are usually paid for by each individual but may be paid for by the groom.
- Bridesmaid's party or luncheon is usually given by the bride, but may be given by the groom's or bride's mother.
- Rehearsal dinner is usually given by the groom's parents, but may be given by the bride's relatives or friends.

Notes

Wedding References

It is helpful to have a few key reference books on hand to consult for more specific details on wedding customs and etiquette. Also, a professional florist should subscribe to major publications to keep up to date on trends in ceremony, dress, and decorations. A few suggested references are listed below.

Ardman, Harvey and Gisele Nadeau. The Woman's Day Book of Weddings. New York, New York: The Bobbs-Merrill Company, Inc., 1982.

Baldridge, Letitia. The Amy Vanderbilt Complete Book of Weddings. New York, New York: Doubleday, 1978.

Dahl, Stephanie H. and editors of Modern Bride. Modern Bride Guide to Your Wedding and Marriage. New York, New York: Random House, 1984.

McClure, Joan and editors of McCall's. McCall's Engagement and Wedding Guide. New York, New York: The Saturday Review Press, 1972.

Piccione, Nancy. Your Wedding. Englewood Cliffs, New Jersey: Prentice-Hall, Inc., 1982.

Notes

Post, Elizabeth L. Emily Post's Complete Book of Wedding Etiquette. New York, New York: Harper and Row, 1982.

Stewart, Martha. Weddings. New York, New York: Clarkson N. Rotter, Inc., 1987.

A florist must be familiar with proper wedding etiquette. Customs and traditions have evolved which affect every wedding from a simple civil ceremony to a lavish royal wedding. A florist's ideas can be of great help to every bride, particularly when these ideas are presented with the proper knowledge of form and style. A professional florist should help guide the bride through a ceremony which incorporates her individuality with proper etiquette. Armed with the necessary information, courtesy, and common sense, this task will be no more formidable than designing a beautiful arrangement.

Notes, Photographs, Sketches, etc.

Notes, Photographs, Sketches, etc.

Selling Wedding Flowers

Chapter 2

The most important step in the process of becoming a profitable wedding florist is selling the wedding. After all, not one flower can be wired, taped, or designed until the bride has been attracted to the flower shop and convinced to buy her flowers there. This is the complicated art and business of selling. Because wedding flowers are a very specialized product for a special clientele, the selling process is different from that of any other product in the flower shop.

For example, in today's market, flowers to wear are seen as accessories and should be sold as fine pieces of jewelry to complement fashions. Whether worn on the shoulder, at the waist, or in the hair, they should be designed to accessorize fashions with proper proportion, color, texture, and balance to create a total look. Understanding this concept is a key factor in the profitable sale of wedding flowers.

The selling process is simply a matter of finding a need, filling the need, establishing the price, and closing the sale. Selling requires communication and direct feedback with the customer. However, this process is not "cut and dry." Effective communication requires advance preparation. Knowing a product and understanding a customer's need for that product increases one's selling ability. A successful wedding florist has a sales plan. This chapter serves as a guide for developing such a plan.

Attracting the Client

Before a sale can be made, a client must be attracted to the shop. Appropriate advertising and marketing programs geared toward a specific target market can help bring the client to the florist. Advertising and marketing needs vary according to the shop's size, location, and promotional budget. Promotions must

Notes

reach out to the prospective client. This can be achieved through in-store promotions, community presentations, and advertising.

Promotions

In store promotions used to attract the wedding customers may be used in a number of ways. Displays are a simple method of reminding customers that a flower shop provides wedding services. Other special promotional events may be held several months prior to peak wedding season. A combination of year-round and peak season in-store promotions of various types should be used for maximum impact.

Without proper in-store promotions, attracting the client to the store means little. When a client enters a store, he or she expects to see a vibrant and active florist and floral shop. An excellent non-verbal but concrete way of presenting one's knowledge is through in-store displays.

Window Displays

Contact bridal shops, bakeries, and party equipment rental companies for props to create a wedding window display, including dresses, dummy cakes, arches, etc. Remember to keep the emphasis on what is for sale, *flowers.* In return for the loan of props, place an acknowledgement card identifying the company in the window.

In-Store Displays

Create a wedding area within the flower shop to promote wedding products and services. This can be a special room or simply a single table. In this area, show silk bouquet samples, wedding accessories for sale, rental items, and photos of weddings designed by the shop. Color can play a major role here. Use a popular wedding color when creating this area in the store, and change the color scheme as color trends shift. Remember that nothing attracts a bride more than the look of romance. The use or ribbons, lace, and tulle can create this look.

Mini Wedding Shows

Mini wedding shows are typically held within the shop or in a small meeting room in a hotel. The purpose of the show is to educate the bride about the flowers, colors, and new trends in bouquets. Show a variety of flowers and discuss availability, color,

Notes

and longevity, as well as different styles of bouquets. Discuss trends in today's market and how they affect the selection of flowers. Serve refreshments and supply each bride with a promotional packet containing printed materials, such as flower guides and wedding planners. With your business card attached, include a pen, a writing pad, and a keepsake of the event, such as a sachet or wedding favor.

In-Store Giveaways

This kind of promotion is best done between December 25th and February 20th. It is at this time of year that the largest number of engagement rings are bought and given. Run a small ad on the engagement announcement page of the local newspaper. Offer a free single rose to any bride who brings in a copy of her engagement announcement. At that time, if she sets up a consultation appointment, she might receive 10 percent off the church portion of her wedding flower bill.

Community Presentations

In order to capture the attention of the specific audience desired (brides-to-be), many florists participate in various community presentations. This helps the florist become more visible to a larger population of potential wedding clients in a short period of time. A florist may only need to participate in such presentations to realize the benefits of this promotional effort.

Wedding Display Shows

This type of promotion can be one of the most expensive, but can create maximum exposure in a short period of time to the targeted market, the brides-to-be. To acquire information regarding shows in the area, contact hotel catering directors, convention centers, and bridal gown shops. After securing show dates, contact the show manager for information regarding booth prices, availability, rules, and floor plans. Also, find out the number of potential attendees in order to evaluate the overall cost of the project.

Upon securing booth space, establish a budget for the project. The budget should include:

- Booth Space Rental
- Labor (setup, show time, removal)

- Lighting
- Rental Equipment (tables, chairs, etc.)
- Floral Products
- Literature
- Handouts (single flowers, etc.)
- Advertisements
- Carpentry
- Follow-Up Mailings

After the budget has been established, there are several questions which will help determine the booth's potential effectiveness.

- Is the booth in a good position?
- Will there be good traffic flow around the booth?
- Is the space arranged to allow traffic flow into and out of the booth conveniently?
- Does the booth appear cluttered?
- Is the exhibit well lit?
- Does the display reflect the desired image of the shop?
- Does the effort to get attention help sell the product?
- Does every important element in the exhibit function in telling the product story?
- Are the benefits of the featured products spelled out, instead of being left to the imagination?
- Are all statements about product features and benefits believable, immediately acceptable, and truthful?

Notes

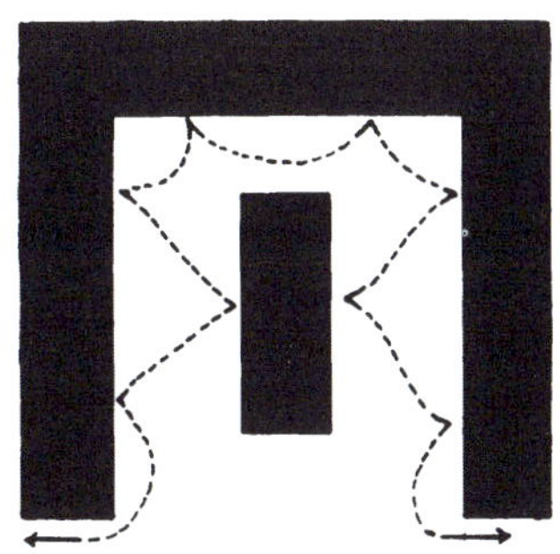

Figure 2.1 Flow Through and Look Display

Display Booth Floor Plans

There are a number of ways to set up a display booth for a trade fair. The amount of space available and the type of products or services to be promoted will influence the number and position of display tables and fixtures used. The floor plans which follow illustrate desirable methods of displaying floral products for a wedding trade fair.

Flow Through and Look. The layout shown in ***Figure 2.1*** provides an effective way for customers to look at a floral display or pick up literature. It would be ideal for handling a heavy traffic flow or to expose the audience to a quick message or presentation of the product. Here, the florist must do the sales work.

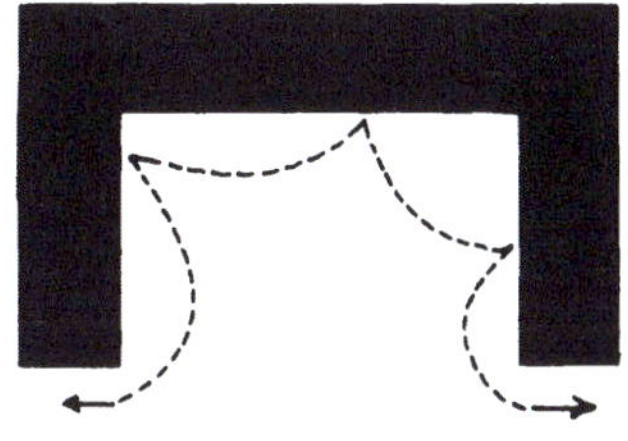

Figure 2.2 Display Center

Display Center. The spaciousness of the display center shown in ***Figure 2.2*** allows sales people to approach customers as they are looking at the displays. The customers can then be moved out of the traffic flow to discuss their weddings, and sales personnel can answer any questions concerning the wedding flowers on display.

Demonstration Center. The demonstration center shown in ***Figure 2.3*** is designed to demonstrate a variety of different products or services. Each table typically has something different displayed on it. For example, bridal bouquets might be displayed on one table, and cake tops and trims on another. This type of exhibit allows sales people to greet customers and identify their needs. The salesperson can then guide each customer to the table or tables that would be most interesting to her.

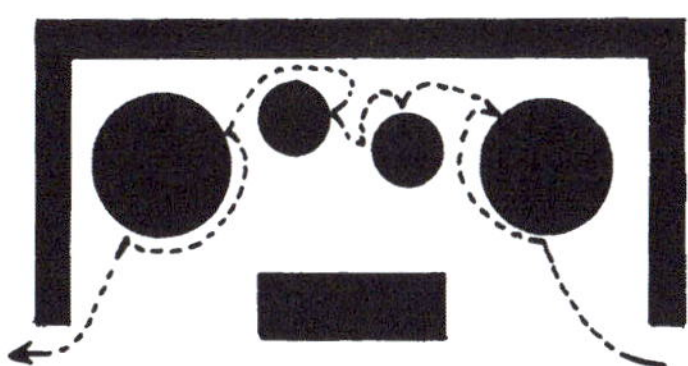

Figure 2.3 Demonstration Center

Store Counter. The display shown in ***Figure 2.4*** is designed to be used like a store counter. It allows the salespeople to meet customers briefly, hand out literature, and answer questions. This type of display can become a traffic flow problem if customers linger to look at photos or flowers on display.

End and Cap. The entire end and cap exhibit is both an entrance and an exit. This random access type of exhibit is often used to display large floral pieces, such as candelabras, arches, and decorated reception tables. ***(Figure 2.5 on page 30)***

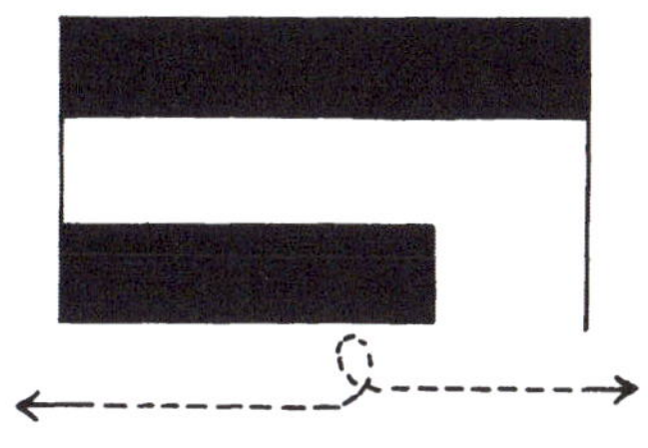

Figure 2.4 Store Counter

Service Club Presentations

How many fathers or mothers know what is expected of them as parents of the bride or groom? A 20-minute to 30-minute program on current trends in weddings could be offered to service clubs in order to inform parents of their roles. Civic or church organizations are good choices to present such a program. This type of program should be short, informative, and entertaining for all. It could include a slide presentation on weddings or a game using customs of the wedding day, both past and present. Gold covered chocolate coins could be handed out to each person in attendance and used to create interest in the topic of budgeting. The florist might discuss creative ways of stretching a wedding budget with particular emphasis on the flowers. Visuals, such as silk bouquets and fresh flower samples, should be provided for the participants to see, smell, and touch.

Selecting the right individual to present this type of program is the key to its success. Criteria for selecting presenters should include the following:

- Product Knowledge - Are they well informed about the product and services to be offered?
- Sales Ability - Are they capable of selling the product?
- Communication Skills - Do they present themselves well to large groups?
- Overall Appearance - Are they neat and well groomed?
- Personality - Are they businesslike, yet friendly?

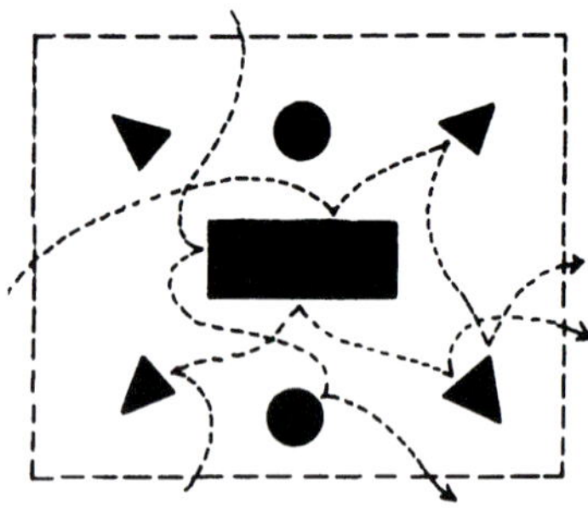

Figure 2.5 End and Cap

Wholesale Involvement

Often wholesalers will provide a location and products needed to produce a small wedding show. Contact wholesalers in the area and suggest a mutually beneficial wedding show to be held in their location.

Self-Promotion

Word-of-mouth can be the easiest or hardest form of advertisement to generate. It depends solely on the product, the service of the shop, and the memory of the client. A satisfied bride will remain a client and refer friends for future business. Photographs can be acquired by contacting the bride's photographer. Request copies of any photos showing bridal flowers. Also, suggest that the photographer prepare a portfolio of

Notes

his work to keep on display in the flower shop. This will create a working relationship with the photographer and may lead to additional sales in the future.

Advertising

Brochures, flyers, circulars, and direct mail are common forms of printed advertising. Content can be created by a professional copywriter or someone with knowledge of the product and service to be offered.

Brochures

Brochures usually consist of four or more pages created by folding one piece of paper in half. It is best to fill at least three of these pages. Additional cost may be incurred when printing on more than one side of the paper. A brochure should grab the consumer's attention and provide descriptive content.

Flyers and Circulars

Flyers and circulars consist of a single page, printed on either one or both sides. This type of literature can be handed out, mailed, or placed on a counter with a sign reading "take one" for general distribution in the shop or at shows. When creating content for flyers or circulars, keep the information simple. Provide important information, including the company name, address, and phone number, as well as a shop logo. Describe the services offered and products sold to create visual images of the items. Include art work to attract attention and further describe the products.

Direct Mail

Direct mail can provide inexpensive advertising for florists who have already generated mailing lists from bridal shows, guest books, engagement announcements, and the like. A handwritten letter or note to the bride congratulating her on her engagement and extending an invitation to visit the flower shop is an effective form of direct mail advertising. The letter should include a brief summary of the wedding services offered, wedding consultation hours, the shop phone number, and the name of the person to contact for a consultation appointment. The closing of the letter should extend congratulations to the bride and offer to help her create the wedding of her dreams.

Print Advertising

Notes

Print advertising includes newspaper, magazine, or Yellow Pages ads. Often, these types of advertisers can provide in-house graphic artists to assist in illustrating and laying out the ads.

Newspapers

Multiple runs are required to generate sales from this type of advertising. On an average, an ad must be placed six to eleven times in a newspaper before it generates sufficient turnaround to cover the cost of the ad. Most newspapers run a special section exclusively for brides once or twice a year. The florist might offer to supply the newspaper with bouquets to be photographed and included with articles on wedding flowers in this section of the newspaper. In return, the florist should receive flower credits, acknowledging the name of the shop that supplied the flowers as a caption beneath the photograph.

Magazines

This type of advertising is beneficial only if the store is located in a metropolitan area. Many national magazines publish regional editions. When doing so, they sell advertising space to regional advertisers. A florist may purchase this advertising space for the regional edition of the magazine. City or state magazines may also be a wise advertising option.

Yellow Pages

Yellow Pages advertising can be arranged by contacting the local telephone company. A sales representative can offer advice about ad sizes and layouts, but it should be noted that these salespeople are paid a commission on each sale. Obviously, they will encourage florists to print the largest size ad possible. The florist should notice ads run by competing florists. The alphabetical position of the shop's ad among the others should also be considered.

Yellow Pages ads on the right hand page are generally most effective. However, a well designed ad will be effective on either page. Large ads attract more attention than small ones. Colored ink (usually red) also helps draw potential clients to an ad. The ad itself should be clean and informative. Major services offered should be listed along with credit cards accepted and the shop's

Notes

address and phone number. Placing the ad in additional areas of the book (party, wedding, consultants) can generate additional sales.

Radio and Television Advertising

In radio and television advertising, the florist can appeal to multiple senses by using sound and pictures. Text, voice, music, and sound effects used to punctuate and enhance the message, work to grab the listener's attention. This type of advertising should not be created without the help of professionals. Radio and television costs can be reduced by employing students majoring in communications to produce ads or by running ads on television community access channels or minor radio stations in the area.

Co-op advertising can also be arranged. This involves participation of more than one business in a single ad. For example, a bridal salon and a florist might share an ad describing both of their services. The key advantage to this type of advertising is the shared cost of the ad, but the florist must be careful about joining with one business to the displeasure of others.

Networking with Other Professionals

Networking can be the most inexpensive method of advertising wedding products and services. The florist has more control over the cost of this advertising than any other. The first step in networking is establishing contact with fellow wedding suppliers. This should be a friendly exchange of information about products and services supplied by each business. Once information has been collected, networks should be established with trustworthy professionals offering quality goods.

The networking process is most effective when all parties involved benefit in some way. The following is an example of effective low-cost networking.

> After designing the flowers for an elegant wedding, the florist contacts the wedding photographer and arranges to receive two pictures of the wedding cake. The florist asks the photographer to display a third picture of the cake in his studio with the florist's business card. The florist, in turn, displays a photo of the cake in her shop with recognition of both the photographer and baker. The florist takes the other picture to the baker and asks that the florist and photographer receive proper credit for their

work. In this way, the work of all three is displayed in three different wedding related businesses, providing "free" advertising for all.

Notes

Professionals who might be contacted for networking include:

- Bakeries
- Balloon Stores
- Bridal Salons
- Calligraphers
- Caterers
- Church Wedding Consultants
- Department Store Bridal Registries
- Hotel Catering Directors
- Ice Sculptors
- Jewelry Stores
- Limousine Services
- Music Contractors
- Nurseries (Plant Rental Suppliers)
- Party Rental Equipment Suppliers
- Photographers
- Professional Wedding Consultants
- Travel Agents
- Tuxedo Rental Stores
- Valet Parking Companies
- Yardage Fabric Stores (Bridal Departments)

Notes

The Consultation

The wedding consultation is an extended order-taking session during which the florist has an opportunity to use a variety of sales techniques in order to increase the total order. The ability to conduct wedding consultations effectively comes with experience in both sales and design. The proper environment also contributes to the creation of a positive selling atmosphere. The florist should give much consideration to the personnel and shop space devoted to wedding business, as well as the procedures used to conduct the consultation.

Consultation Areas

Once a client has been attracted to a business, the client's needs must be determined and fulfilled. The need starts the minute the phone rings or when the client steps through the front door. Creating the proper setting to generate wedding sales requires setting aside a designated area in which the florist and the bride may meet undisturbed. The area should be located away from traffic flow and telephones. If space allows, a table should be used with seating accommodations for two or three people. This area could be placed adjacent to the in-store wedding display area. Good lighting is essential. The following is a list of suggested items to keep in this area:

- Teleflora Floral Selection Guide
- Current copies of bridal magazines
- Wedding forms
- Pens and pencils
- Calculator
- Photograph albums of wedding work designed by the shop
- Ribbon selections in current colors used in the wedding industry
- Wedding etiquette books
- Current publications on wedding trends or styles

Notes

A file containing rules and regulations governing churches, reception halls, hotels, and restaurants in the area should be created to assist in the consultation process. This file should be kept current and up to date with fire codes and facility regulations. Pictures of the interiors of the facilities might also be included in the file. These are helpful when making suggestions to the bride during the consultation. If possible, a mirror should be located close to the consultation area so that the bride may view the appearance of different bouquets when held in position.

Scheduling the Consultation

Once the proper environment has been established, the selling process can begin. The wedding consultation should be conducted by appointment only, to ensure that the florist will be able to devote full attention to the client. When setting up the consultation appointment, basic information about the wedding should be collected, including dates, times, and locations of the ceremony and reception.

Generally, the consultation should be conducted no sooner than 3 months before the wedding date. By this time, the bride has usually confirmed most of the details which will influence the choice of wedding flowers. At least 1 hour should be allowed for the consultation. If the appointment takes more than 1 1/2 hours, cost effectiveness is reduced.

Qualifying the Customer

The first 10 minutes spent with the bride will help determine her wants, needs, and ability to pay for what she desires. This process of qualifying the customer is vital to any wedding consultation. Before discussing details for the wedding flowers, the florist must have an idea of what the bride will be able to afford, but care should be taken not to prejudge a client based on appearances or personal biases. The following questions (asked in a subtle manner) will help qualify a wedding client.

- Where was the gown purchased?

- Who was the manufacturer of the gown?

- What type of wedding is the bride planning?

Notes

- Will it be formal or informal?
- Will it be a subdued or party atmosphere?
- Is there an overall theme which will dictate the look and feel of the wedding?
- Where will the service take place and at what time of day?
- Will the ceremony follow religious customs?
- Where will the reception be held?
- How many guests are expected?
- Will it be a sit-down dinner, buffet, or simple cake and punch reception?
- Who will be paying for the flowers?

Answers to these questions help establish the size and budget of the wedding. By determining the location and religious influence of the ceremony, special flower needs are established. For example, if the ceremony will take place in a hotel ballroom, the florist will need to create an altar and aisle within the room. The number of guests and type of reception help determine the extent of decorations needed. The question regarding payment for the wedding often determines the florist's ability to seal the wedding contract the same day as the consultation. For example, if the bride's parents will be paying for the wedding, additional time is often required for the bride to get her parents' approval.

Wedding Planner

Whether using the wedding planner in Appendix B of this book or one specifically created for the shop, the order in which the information is gathered should remain the same. Some of the information on the form may have already been discussed in the process of qualifying the client. This information should be entered on the form while the customer is present to ensure accuracy.

The florist should always be in control of the consultation. Gentle suggestions will help keep the bride from straying to subjects out of sequence. For instance, when the bride's attention moves form the bridesmaids' bouquets to the reception flowers, a gentle suggestion to follow the form in order to avoid overlooking details will draw her attention back to the subject at hand. The bride should be assured that her other concerns will be discussed shortly.

Notes

Items for Discussion

A friendly and casual approach is effective when conducting a wedding consultation. Forceful sales techniques will often lose prospective customers. A few moments alone with a floral selection guide will help the bride gather her thoughts and ideas before the formal consultation begins. The bride should be encouraged to order everything she desires and make reductions as needed at the end. The following information provides the key topics and most effective sequence for discussion at a wedding consultation.

Bride's Bouquet

Following the discussion of general wedding information, the consultation should begin with the bride's bouquet. Typically, the bride has given much thought to what she will carry and is eager to discuss her ideas. A brief description of the gown will help determine the most appropriate bouquet choices. Generally, a gown with a full skirt and train will look best with a large, lush bouquet, such as a cascade or a crescent. Slim, sheath style gowns are more suited to bouquets with less fullness. Presentation or hand-tied bouquets are a good choice. Very traditional gowns are complemented by the classical colonial bouquet, while gowns with modern styling are most suited to more unique bouquets, such as European contemporary style.

The bouquet style and color should be determined before discussing specific flowers, because certain flowers lend themselves well to certain bouquet styles. Flower availability at a particular time of year may also influence the bride's selection. In order to avoid having leftovers, the florist should advise the bride of any expected difficulties in obtaining specific flowers selected for the bride's bouquet. For example, if the bride's bouquet is to include four gardenias, and gardenias are sold in boxes of three, the florist might later suggest using the additional two gardenias in the mother's corsages.

Notes

Bridesmaids' Bouquets

Typically, the bouquets for all of the bridesmaids are designed in the same style and color scheme. Sometimes the maid of honor is given a slightly different bouquet with either more flowers or a change in color. The bridesmaids' bouquets may be designed as a modified version of the bride's bouquet or in a style which complements their gowns. In either case, the bouquets should not compete with the bride's flowers. Hair flowers are an additional item the florist might suggest for the bridesmaids. A reluctant bride can be persuaded to add this to her order by explaining that these flowers will be visible to the congregation as the bridesmaids stand at the altar and that they will remain with the bridesmaids during the reception even after the bouquets have been laid aside.

Flower Girl

When discussing flowers for the flower girl, it is helpful to know the age and size (height, weight) of the child. This helps the florist select and design an appropriately sized arrangement for her. If the flower girl will be carrying a basket, the florist should clarify whether she will be dropping petals from it. For situations where fresh petal dropping is not allowed, potpourri or metallic confetti may be possible. Another alternative might be to use silk petals, either in white or in colors coordinating with the wedding's color scheme. A miniature version of the bridesmaids' bouquets is another option for the flower girl. Also popular is the addition of a personal item, such as a small toy or teddy bear. This gives the child a sense of security during the ceremony, as well as providing a lasting keepsake or remembrance of the event.

Boutonnieres

The groom's boutonniere should be discussed first to ensure that his design is distinctive. Often, the color and flowers for his design will be selected to match those in the bride's bouquet. Boutonnieres for the groomsmen may be designed to match the bouquets of the bridesmaids. It is desirable to encourage the same type of boutonniere for the rest of the men in the wedding including ushers, fathers and grandfathers. This helps create a uniform look and eases the distribution of flowers. The exception to this is the boutonniere for the ring bearer. His design may need to be made smaller depending on his age and size. A decorative floral accent for the ring pillow might also be suggested.

Corsages

Notes

Corsages for the mothers should coordinate with their gowns. The style, color, and fabric of the gown will influence the choice of corsage and location where it is worn. For example, delicate fabrics which are difficult to pin into might restrict the ability to use a shoulder corsage. A wristlet or purse decoration might be chosen instead. Corsages for the mothers may be designed independently to go with each gown, or they may be designed to be identical. Typically, the mothers' corsages are more elaborate than the rest. Stepmothers might receive a slightly smaller version of the mother's corsage. The remaining corsages for grandmothers, soloists, servers, and other female members of the wedding party can all be the same to simplify distribution of the flowers.

Ceremony

Typically, the bride will want to discuss flowers for the altar area first. If possible, the discussion should begin with the entry to the church or ceremony site and continue up the aisle with a discussion of the altar area last. Decorations should be described from the perspective of the guests as they enter the facility. The florist should emphasize the need for impact at the key locations the guests will view as they enter and are seated. These key locations include the guest book table, the entry to the sanctuary, the aisle(s), and the altar/chancel area. For a bride with a tight budget, transition flowers might also be suggested. These designs may be used for the ceremony and then transported to the reception site.

Reception

The wedding cake is a key focal item at the reception. Decorations for the cake and cake table are the logical point from which to begin discussing this portion of the wedding. Other major areas within the reception area, such as the buffet table, bandstand, and receiving line, should be considered next. Guest tables may then be discussed, followed by the head table, which often receives the most elaborate decoration of all. If the bride's budget will not accommodate extensive floral decorations for all of these areas, the florist might suggest using the entire remaining budget to create two or three large showy designs in featured locations for optimum impact.

Notes

Theme Weddings

Theme weddings can be fun or formal. They may run the gamut from "old world" to "out of this world." By establishing a definite theme, the bride has made the job of decorating and accessorizing the wedding much easier. Although it may require a bit more time to plan or research the project, the end result can be extremely effective. The following list offers examples of wedding themes.

- A Black-and-White Art Deco Wedding
- A Country and Western Wedding
- A French Country Wedding
- A "Gone with the Wind" Wedding
- A "Great Gatsby" Wedding
- A Nature Lover's Wedding
- A Renaissance Wedding
- A Royal Wedding
- A Tropical Wedding
- A Victorian Wedding
- A Winter Wonderland Wedding

Rehearsal Dinner

Although the rehearsal dinner is usually hosted and paid for by the groom's parents, the florist should take advantage of the opportunity to mention possible decorations for this function, as well. The bride might be encouraged to discuss her flower style and color scheme with the groom so that he might pass along the idea of having coordinating flowers at the rehearsal dinner. The florist might also provide an extra business card to the bride for her to give to the groom's mother.

Add-On Wedding Sales

Notes

Add-on wedding sales refer to merchandise not normally considered the florist's responsibility. Many of these items can be suggested to the bride throughout the consultation. Others can simply sell themselves through appealing displays in the consultation area. The following list of merchandise and hard goods are excellent sources of add-on sales in the flower shop.

- Bridal Bouquet Preservation Service
- Bridal Veils
- Cake Knives and Servers
- Cake Tops
- Garters
- Gift Favor Baskets
- Guest Books
- Headpieces
- Photograph Albums
- Picture Frames
- Toasting Glasses
- Tuxedo Rentals
- Wedding Favors
- Wedding Invitations
- Wedding Music Cassettes

Bridal Fashion Terminology

To select appropriate bouquet styles and flowers for a particular gown, a florist needs a basic knowledge of fashion terminology. The shape of a sleeve and the length of a train can

Notes

strongly influence the style or shape of the bouquet to be designed. A heavy bridal satin may be best complemented by gardenias or cattleya orchids which repeat the texture of the fabric. With the knowledge of current bridal fashions, fabrics, and trends, the florist can better guide the bride in her selection of the perfect bouquet to accessorize her look. Bridal fashion illustrations and complete descriptions are provided in Appendix A.

Fabrics

The following information provides the names and descriptions of fabrics and laces commonly used in bridal fashions.

Crystal Organza

Organza with a high sheen and a slightly frosted, crystal-like finish with a grainy texture.

Crystalline

A fine, semi-transparent fabric, made from rayon woven with silk threads. This fabric is similar to crystal organza, but has a higher sheen and smoother texture.

Faille

A medium to heavyweight fabric constructed of nylon, silk, and a very fine cotton thread. A very tailored fabric, not recommended for use in designs where draping is required or fluid movement of the fabric is needed. This fabric is very low in sheen, is densely woven, and the overall texture has a slightly ridged appearance.

Organdy

A thin, fine, stiff, semitransparent muslin fabric. It is woven from cotton and nylon threads and has no sheen.

Organza

A fabric similar to organdy, made of pure silk. Organza has a smooth finish and is a lightweight, flowing fabric.

Satin

Notes

A fabric usually made from silk threads with a very smooth and shiny surface, similar in texture to a rose petal. This texture is only found on one side of the fabric. Satin is classified into three categories according to weight:

- Summer Satin - lightweight
- Slipper Satin - medium weight
- Bridal Satin - heavyweight

Taffeta

A thin, stiff fabric, semi-glossy in appearance and often made of natural or artificial silk threads. It creates a rustling sound when it moves. Special taffetas are classified in the following categories:

- Midnight Taffeta - Iridescent taffeta with a black thread cross-woven into it to create a dark undertone.
- Summer Taffeta - Iridescent taffeta with a white thread cross-woven into it to create a light overtone or frosted effect.
- Moiré Taffeta - Taffeta woven with a thread pattern to create a wood grained or water-washed look.

Laces

Laces most commonly used in bridal fashions and accessories are described in the following section.

Alencon Lace

Cotton and silk based threads are used in the construction of alencon lace. It usually has an overall rose or flower pattern, leaving little space between the patterns. This lace has a very detailed, three-dimensional look created by heavy thread that is placed and re-embroidered over the top of the outside edge of the lace pattern.

Notes

Battenburg Lace

Battenburg lace is created on cotton fabric. A stencil is used to create a design on the fabric. Heavy embroidery is then placed on the edge of the stenciled pattern on the face of the cotton fabric. The stencils are then cut out of the fabric by hand, leaving only the embroidered edge on the cotton fabric. This creates an openwork (cutout) lace.

Chantilly Lace

Cotton and nylon-based threads are used in the construction of chantilly lace. It usually has an overall rose pattern. This lace is always a lightweight to medium weight fabric. It is very seldom used for appliqué work because the pattern runs so close together. This lace is used in the overall construction work of the garment (skirt, sleeves, etc.).

Cluny Lace

This lace is constructed with linen or silk thread. Lower grade cluny lace may also be constructed of cotton. It has the look of chantilly lace with a distinctive Quaker pattern. This lace is typically used for appliqués or edge trims on heavy linen dresses.

Lace Appliqués (also called motifs)

Lace appliqués are individual pieces of elaborately embroidered lace (alencon, Venetian, etc.) which have finished edges on all sides, versus a roll of a continuous lace pattern. These appliqués are applied to a fabric (usually a gown or veil) which serves as a background. Lace appliqués are often used with a background of netting on the train of a gown to provide cut-outs or windows in the fabric.

Schiffli Lace

Nylon, silk, and cotton threads are used in the construction of schiffli lace. This lace has a very broad-based pattern, leaving large areas of a net-like (tulle) texture between the patterns. This lace is always re-embroidered and has a heavy, expensive appearance.

Venetian Lace (also called Venice Lace)

Notes

Cotton threads are used in the construction of Venetian lace. The pattern is almost always used as appliqués in border work. This lace is usually used in a floral pattern and is typically used for trimming the skirt, sleeve, or neckline. It is sometimes given a slight sheen by incorporating a nylon thread in its production.

Closing the Sale

Once all of a customer's floral needs have been discussed, the florist must begin the process of closing the sale. This final step involves discussing prices, rental options, and terms of payment. It is important for the florist to be thorough in explaining these details; however, this step should not be too lengthy or complicated. The customer should receive the same friendly, yet business-like, treatment as established at the beginning of the consultation. Most of all, after closing the sale, the bride should leave the flower shop feeling pleased with her flower selections and confident in the florist's ability.

Equipment and/or Plant Rentals

Near the end of the wedding consultation, the florist will discuss the procedures involved in renting and/or subcontracting items for the wedding. It is important to handle these arrangements in a professional manner to avoid later misunderstandings.

Renting plants, props, or other items to a client can be a profitable venture or a costly disaster. To avoid the latter, the florist should draft a rental contract before renting anything. This contract should clearly state the client's responsibility for rented items and for their return to the florist. Consequences of damage to, or loss of, items should be stated, as well. A sample rental contract is provided in Appendix C.

It is a good practice to require a refundable deposit on all rental items. The deposit should be at least 90 percent of the total replacement cost of the equipment. Taking a deposit on a major credit card makes it easier to collect the full value of the rental item if an item disappears. A price must be established for all items the florist intends to rent. Within the first year, the fee for the

Notes

rental item should cover its original cost and all storage costs, and furnish a reasonable profit.

Any props or non-perishable goods can be rented. Fresh flower arrangements should be sold outright rather than rented in most situations. It is best to stock only the items that can be rented profitably. An inventory should be kept for each rental item in the shop. The inventory should include the following:

- Type of item
- Manufacturer or source
- Original cost
- Rental price
- Quantity available for rental
- Date used
- Quantity used

This inventory helps the florist determine prop availability, level of use, and relative profitability.

Plant rentals for weddings require special considerations. Keeping rental plants full and lush takes time and effort. Some plants should only be rented once, while others may be rented for several different occasions. For example, a blooming azalea might be rented once at the peak of bloom and then be put on the sales floor before blooming declines. In contrast, a pair of large palms might be rented repeatedly for as long as a year or more before being sold. A good way to price blooming plants is to charge half the retail price for rental. For example, a $20.00 mum would rent for $10.00, or a $30.00 azalea for $15.00. Green plants rent for one-third their retail price. Additional trims, such as bows or pot covers, may be included in the rental price or sold separately and included in the overall wedding setup fee.

Subcontracting Products and/or Services

Weddings frequently offer opportunities for florists to subcontract various types of work to other professionals. Subcontracting involves hiring a company to provide products or services the florist does not typically offer. It allows the florist to make the best use of employees' time and talents, while allowing other professionals to carry out portions of the wedding order for which the florist may not be qualified. Examples of subcontracting for weddings might include hiring a balloon specialist to create balloon arches or a production company to install lighting and sound systems in a reception hall.

Notes

The first step in subcontracting is to find companies with upstanding reputations. The florist should become familiar with the products, prices, and procedures of these companies. To protect all parties involved, a simple contract form should be drawn up, checked by an attorney, and signed by both the florist and the contracted company. This contract should contain a list of everything being sold, along with prices, delivery dates, and times. The florist should take responsibility for the proper completion of all phases of installation. A sample subcontracting agreement is provided in Appendix C.

It is best to meet at least twice with the contracted company. The first meeting should involve planning all necessary items and scheduling installations. The second meeting should occur a few days before the event. At this time, the florist should check to see that all items are available and ready, and confirm all delivery times and places. The florist should submit a final floor plan to all subcontracted companies. This ensures that everyone involved clearly understands where individual items will be located and allows for a smooth and speedy installation.

When determining a price for subcontracted items, several factors should be considered. The total cost to the client should include the following:

- The price the florist will pay for the item.
- The time a florist will spend planning and arranging for the items' setup and installation.
- Any charge for additional materials or labor the florist must provide to complete the installation of the item.
- The florist's profit margin.

A simple way to price an item for a client is to charge the cost of the item plus a service charge at a set hourly rate. For example, a balloon arch which costs a florist $125.00 to have built and installed might require 2 hours of the florist's time to arrange all of the details. If the florist uses a $25.00 per hour rate for

Notes

making subcontracting plans, the price to the client would be $175.00 ($125.00 arch cost plus 2 hours planning multiplied by $25.00 per hour).

The labor charge for overseeing all installations at the site is covered in the florist's overall delivery and setup fee. Items which are commonly subcontracted for weddings along with typical sources for each item are given in Table 4.

TABLE 4

ITEMS COMMONLY SUBCONTRACTED FOR WEDDINGS

Item	Source
Table settings	Party rental companies
Candelabras, arches and other wedding props	Party rental companies
Tents, tables and chairs	Awning companies, party rental companies
Lighting - indoor	Theatrical agencies, lighting companies
Lighting - outdoor	Party rental companies, construction firms dealing with night work
Music	Talent agencies, musicians' unions
Calligraphy	Printers, individual hobbyists
Balloon arches, drops and decorations	Balloon stores and specialists

Discussing Flower Prices

Once the wedding planner is complete and rental/subcontracting procedures have been covered, prices must be discussed. It is best to offer the client three choices in price for each item, along with a brief explanation of the differences in products for the various prices. For example, the florist might offer the prices of $27.50, $37.50, and $45.00 for a table centerpiece. The florist would then explain that at the $37.50 price level, the design would be large and showy and at the $45.00 price level the design would be large and showy with more unique individual

Notes

flower placements. This encourages the bride to choose at least the mid-level price, if not the highest one. This example should offer a bench mark for a dollar range the bride is looking for, and the process should be used consistently throughout the planning of the wedding.

As prices are discussed, if the bride consistently selects prices in the mid-to-upper level price range and then suddenly chooses the lowest price for an item, the florist should explain that the look of this piece will probably not have as great an impact in comparison to the decoration in the higher price range. If the price range selected is consistent, the overall look of the wedding flowers will be more uniform.

After the entire order has been priced and totaled with sales tax, the total price should be presented to the bride. She will usually make it clear if the total is too high for her budget. If so, it is best to eliminate one or two decorations of lesser importance rather than recalculating the entire order at lower prices.

Collecting Deposits

Once the total price is agreed upon for the wedding, the shop's policies for deposits, checks, credit cards, and payment schedules should be explained to the bride. Deposits of 10 to 20 percent of the total are required by most florists. Some require the payment of the remaining balance as much as 10 days prior to the wedding. Others do not collect the remaining balance until after the wedding date. Generally, advance collection provides more security and a better cash flow to the florist. This ensures working capital from which to purchase necessary flowers and supplies. It also provides sufficient time for checks to clear the bank. In either case, if additional costs are incurred, such as a sudden increase in the cost of gardenias, a bill can be sent after the wedding date. Occasionally, if a bride cancels an item on the wedding order after the balance has been paid, a small refund may be necessary. The creative florist can suggest to the bride that she use that credit to upgrade some other portion of the order. For example, if the bride cancels a three-rose corsage, the florist might suggest the roses be incorporated into her bouquet instead.

Some florists charge a consultation fee for the time spent with the bride. This fee might be deducted from the required deposit if the bride chooses to hire the florist for her wedding. If the bride agrees to the florist's terms, the deposit should be collected and a wedding agreement signed. A copy of the completed wedding order should be given to the bride as a reminder of the types,

Notes

quantities, and colors of flowers and arrangements ordered. Finally, the bride should be given a business card with the name of her personal wedding consultant so that she has a specific person whom she may contact with any questions or additions to her order. A sample wedding agreement is given in Appendix C.

One of the most challenging aspects of wedding work is the sales process. The florist must meet the needs of the bride, the groom, and both of their families. It is also during this time that the florist must ensure that the wedding is a financial, as well as a creative success for his or her shop. By following the guidelines outlined in this chapter, selling the wedding should be an enjoyable and rewarding experience.

Notes, Photographs, Sketches, etc.

Notes, Photographs, Sketches, etc.

Purchasing and Handling Floral Products

Chapter 3

The total success of a wedding depends not only on creative talent but profitability and flower quality, as well. This involves the careful planning of product purchasing, preparation, and protection. Purchasing is much more than asking for flowers or ribbon of a certain color. It is a well planned, organized process of buying a product at the right price, at the right stage, and at the right time of year. Preparing and protecting flowers are also steps which require organization along with thorough product knowledge. These steps, often referred to as "care and handling" or the "Chain of Life" procedures, are the key to long lasting flowers. Creative design work will not be a beautiful part of the bride's special day if the flowers fail to last. These key steps are just as critical to wedding success as selling and designing a wedding.

Purchasing and Inventory Control

There are many pitfalls to be aware of when ordering flowers and hardgoods for a wedding. Picking up additional flowers or accessories because they would look attractive with a gown or because they are on special can reduce profits. In fact, over-ordering reduces profit more than any other single mistake a florist can make. On the other hand, under-ordering means that the designs can not be completed as specified during the consultation.

Every florist has a different markup factor based on operating expenses and profit margin requirements. The information in this section can serve as a general aid in buying and successfully controlling costs. The following are several factors to consider in order to plan buying and control inventory.

Availability and Seasonality

Notes

Availability and seasonality refer to the time of year when flowers are available in quantity on the market. With the expansion of worldwide production, more flowers are available on a year-round basis. However, there is still a "season" or time of peak supply for most flowers. The availability and seasonality affect not only quantity, but quality and price of flowers, as well. These factors should be considered in the buying plan. Information regarding availability and seasonality is provided in the Care and Handling Chart packaged with this book.

Timing Flower Purchases

Wedding flowers should be purchased at the ideal stage recommended for longest vase life and then conditioned and allowed to develop to the stage needed by the florist. If flowers are purchased at a more open or developed stage, they are probably older and will not hold up as well in the cooler or in arrangements (especially if they are purchased several days in advance). The florist should keep in mind the following important factors when deciding how far in advance to purchase flowers.

- Storage Potential - Flowers with minimal storage potential should be purchased 24 to 48 hours before the wedding. Those with good or excellent potential can be purchased earlier in the week.

- Source of Flowers - Both country of origin and grower should be known if possible. This can affect harvest stage, packaging, special treatments, and overall quality. Certain growers tend to harvest flowers at a tighter stage than others. Extra time is needed to allow tight buds to open.

- Previous Treatment - It is common for flowers to move through the distribution system dry (out of water). This is especially true for whole or half boxes of the same flower. Extra time must be allowed to condition these flowers before designing. Flowers that have been in water, on the other hand, are sometimes more developed and may be too open to be useful. Orchids, which must be shipped in water, are the exception to

Notes

this rule. It is also helpful to find out if flowers have received special treatments to prevent problems, such as wilting, leaf yellowing, or ethylene damage.

Pre-Booking and Standing Orders

Pre-booking and standing orders are becoming increasingly popular practices in the floral industry, particularly for fresh flowers. More wholesalers are pre-booking orders with retailers 1, 3, and even 6 months in advance, especially for major holidays. Advance planning can help a florist take advantage of pre-bookings, which often means a discount off the regular price. Standing orders, such as two cases of certain flowers every week, can also mean a substantial savings. The florist should once again be careful and pay close attention to quantities offered and make sure the product will be used.

Packaging

A knowledge of how flowers and hardgoods are packaged is a critical element of successful buying. Some flowers, stephanotis for example, can only be purchased by the box. Other flowers, such as the tropical anthurium, are often sold by the individual stem. The number of stems in a bunch or box may also vary according to the source of the product. For example, roses might be packaged in bunches of twelve from one source and in bunches of ten from another.

If buying from multiple sources on a regular basis, it is helpful to devise a chart listing suppliers' names and quantities in which supplies are packaged. The care and handling charts packaged with this book provide information on how fresh flowers and foliage are packaged. If a box or large bunch must be purchased to complete a wedding order, the number of excess flowers should be calculated and used to decrease the regular shop flower order for the week.

Bruise-sensitive and shatter-sensitive flowers (such as orchids, gardenias, anthuriums, gerbera daisies, roses, fuji chrysanthemums, delphinium, and snapdragons) must have protective packaging to minimize flaws and mechanical damage. If a bruise-sensitive or shatter-sensitive flower is purchased without protective packaging, an extra day or two should be allowed to give time for any damage to show physical symptoms.

Discounts

Notes

There are several types of discounts that may be offered by suppliers of fresh flowers and hard goods. If used properly, discounts can often generate as much net return to the retail florist as the sale of the merchandise itself. Examples of buying discounts include trade discounts (discounts offered at a cost below the suggested price), quantity discounts, and cash discounts. There may also be special "sales" offered by suppliers. It is helpful to keep suppliers' sale flyers on hand in order to make planning easier and buying more efficient.

When ordering hard goods on discount, the florist should keep two things in mind - product turnover and the true value of the discount. The florist must strive to maximize product turnover and not be tempted to order more of an item than can be used within a few months. Specifically, utility hard goods inventory should be turned over at least every 2 months. (A monthly turnover is even more profitable.) Gift items and silks should be turned over three or four times per year. When overbuying results in items being held for long periods of time, potential profit of the merchandise is lost and the true value of the discount is actually not realized. This is particularly critical when the florist is basing the price of the item on the discounted cost. An example illustrates this point:

> A $1.00 vase is purchased at a 10 percent discount for $.90, and a 2.0 markup multiple is applied at the store for a selling price of $1.80. The vase then sits in the store for 3 months. Due to the cost of holding inventory, however, it costs the store 2 percent per month to keep the vase. Therefore, at the end of 3 months, the true value of the discount is only 4 percent. If the selling price is not adjusted, some potential profit is lost.

Budget Calculation

When ordering wedding flowers, it is important to establish a wholesale budget. There are various ways to develop a budget including the following two methods.

Method A

The total retail price of the wedding (not including labor or delivery charges) is divided by the shop's established markup multiple. This provides the wholesale budget for all flowers and materials needed to fill the order.

Notes

Example:

There is a $300 wedding (fresh flowers and hardgoods).
The shop has a 5 times markup.
300 ÷ 5 = 60
The wholesale budget is $60.00.

Some shops have different markup multiples for different items, such as a two to three times markup for hardgoods and three and one half to six times markup for fresh flowers. Too many markup multiples, however, can make this method of buying confusing and inefficient.

Method B

This is a more specific and disciplined method that simplifies the selling and buying processes. It is based on the concept of selling from pre-priced illustrations or photographs. Each item then has a formula for the exact number of flowers and greenery required. This process involves:

1. Determining the specific number of flowers and greenery needed for each arrangement.

2. Totaling the flowers and foliage needed.

3. Adding 5 to 10 percent to the total quantity needed to compensate for damage or improper opening.

The goal of this method is to order only what is needed.

Checklists and Charts

Checklists and charts help the florist to be more efficient, organized, and profitable. These can be used to plan the overall buying for a single wedding, a group of weddings in 1 week, or an upcoming wedding season. A wedding supply checklist and a fresh flower market and inventory control list are included in Appendix D for use in maintaining inventory and planning the purchase of fresh items and hardgoods. The checklists are especially helpful if taken along on wholesale buying trips.

Care and Handling

Notes

A good florist understands the art and science of floristry. Floral science involves the understanding of flower needs to retain their beauty for as long as possible. A thorough knowledge of flower seasonality and quality is essential in extending flower life.

Care and handling is an integral part of wedding flower preparation. Behind the design talents should lie buying, conditioning, and packaging skills. Wedding flowers must hold up throughout an important and busy day and for several days afterwards, whether they are enjoyed in the church or in the family's home. Wedding designs can be a great source of a florist's pride, achievement, and public relations, but only if they epitomize lasting flower beauty.

This section highlights key care and handling procedures, with special notes for wedding flowers and foliage. An extensive reference chart with tips for specific popular wedding floral items was also provided with this book. This information applies to flowers and foliage used in arrangements, bouquet holders, wired and taped bouquets, and body flowers.

Conditioning (Hardening Off)

Conditioning is essential for ensuring beautiful, long lasting flowers. It is especially critical for flowers that will be wired and taped or arranged in foam. The goal of flower conditioning is to encourage and maximize the uptake of food and water which have been lost in transit and which are needed to prolong the flower's vase life. Key steps to the conditioning process are the following:

1. Remove lower leaves that will be under water to prevent bacteria build-up.

2. Recut stems to remove blockage from air, bacteria, and debris. Recutting with stems held underwater ensures that the stems initially take up water, rather than air. This helps prevent air bubbles and greatly facilitates water uptake. Underwater cutting is especially beneficial for tight bud flowers, flowers that have been shipped dry, and wilt-sensitive flowers.

3. Place flowers into a fresh solution of floral preservative and warm water that has been mixed in a clean

Notes

bucket. Commercial floral preservatives are special mixtures that have been developed and perfected to prolong flower life. They contain a sugar base which provides food for the flowers, as well as ingredients to inhibit bacteria and microorganisms. They also contain ingredients which lower the water's pH and greatly enhance water uptake. Plain sugar, chlorine bleach, or other mixtures do not contain the ideal combination of ingredients to serve all of these functions.

4. Mix floral preservative according to package directions. Using different amounts, especially lesser amounts, does not help and can actually harm the flowers. To promote bud opening, however, twice the recommended rate can be used for 24 to 48 hours with flowers placed in a warm location. (See package directions for different brands.)

5. Keep flowers out of the cooler for at least 2 hours to maximize uptake of the preservative solution. Place flowers into the cooler for another few hours to finish "hardening off." It is best to allow the flowers to harden off for 6 hours to overnight before designing with them. Conditioning times will be longer for flowers in the bud stage. Flowers that have been shipped dry, especially from other countries, should be conditioned for 24 to 48 hours before being used.

The practice of soaking entire flowers and branches is common for some foliage, orchids, and tropical flowers. This may help, especially in warm, dry conditions or if the product feels soft and limp, but should be used in combination with the regular conditioning procedures.

Flowers that are purchased early in the week may be kept dry in the cooler and conditioned later, or they may be put in a preservative solution and then placed directly into the cooler so they do not open quickly. Tulips may be put in cool preservative water and placed directly into the cooler. Roses that are starting to open should be kept out for an hour and then put in the cooler.

For stems that will be separated later, such as spray chrysanthemums or miniature carnations, the stems should be conditioned and stored whole and cut apart at design time. Conditioning times in and out of the cooler are dependent upon how long flowers have been dry, how developed they are, and when they will be used. Proper conditioning requires close observation and practice to perfect the procedure.

Special Problems and Treatments

Notes

Special treatments are available that can help to prevent certain flower problems and greatly extend vase life. They are used in addition to floral preservatives. Those to check for include:

Ethylene Reduction Treatments

Ethylene reduction treatments help reduce ethylene gas action and minimize damage to sensitive flowers. A popular treatment is STS or silver thiosulfate. It is best used by the grower or wholesaler, but should be used by the retailer if flowers arrive untreated. If uncertain whether a flower has been treated, a second treatment by the florist should not be harmful. Commercial solutions are available and treatment time usually takes an hour; then flowers are put into a preservative.

These solutions should be used with environmental awareness in mind. Manufacturers' directions for safe mixing, use, and disposal must be carefully followed. Special disposal kits are available from some manufacturers to ensure maximum disposal safety. For quick reference, flowers that are ethylene-sensitive and respond to ethylene reduction treatments (such as STS) are noted on the care and handling charts.

Growth Regulator Treatments

Growth regulator treatments are special solutions used by growers to prevent problems, such as leaf yellowing on alstroemeria, lilies, and chrysanthemums. Growers who use these treatments are often known for producing an excellent product. It is important to find out who these growers are so their products can be requested.

Citric Acid

Citric acid can be used by the grower, wholesaler, and retailer as needed to help prevent water stress problems, such as "bent neck" in roses. A florist would consider using citric acid if large quantities of roses are shipped dry from long distances or if wilting and "bent neck" are consistent problems. Commercial solutions are available, and treatment takes only 30 minutes to 1 hour. After treatment, flowers are put into a floral preservative solution.

Notes

Stem Sanitizing Solutions

Stem sanitizing solutions can be used by the grower, wholesaler, and retailer, as needed, to prevent stem clogging problems associated with field grown flowers, such as gypsophila, which may have dirty stems. These solutions may also be used on flowers prone to stem blockage from bacteria and dirt, such as gerbera daisies. Commercial solutions are available, and treatment may take anywhere from a few seconds to an hour, depending on the product. After treatment, flowers are put into a floral preservative solution.

There are unique mixtures or "home remedy" type solutions recommended by some florists. Some work and some do not. Those that do work are probably successful because they are serving functions similar to floral preservatives. For example, chlorine bleach, cleanser, or tobacco may be mixed in the flower water as a miracle cure for flower problems, when in reality these substances are simply helping to control bacteria and sanitize stems. It is best to use commercial solutions to take care of these needs. If one of these unique mixtures does work for a florist, then it should be used with caution, for if overdone there will almost certainly be damage to the product.

Refrigeration and Storage

Proper refrigeration and storage procedures are an integral part of keeping wedding flowers and designs at their peak. The key is to have at least one floral cooler that maintains a temperature of 34 to 36 degrees Fahrenheit and 85 percent relative humidity.

The storage potential of specific flowers is given on the care and handling charts. These numbers are based on ideal refrigeration conditions. If temperatures are warm (higher than 40 degrees Fahrenheit) and/or there is low humidity, flowers will not store successfully. The following storage tips should be followed for maximum flower life.

- Flowers that have good storage potential can be purchased a few days in advance and stored. If storage is planned for a long period of time (such as when flowers are purchased a week or more in advance to get a good price), they can be kept dry. It is best to keep the flowers in their plastic sleeves and shipping boxes in the cooler. Never lay bare flowers and foliage on the floor or cooler shelf for storage.

Notes

Check the flowers periodically for molding and limpness.

- Short term storage is usually in buckets with preservative solution. (Tulips may be placed in cold water to prevent opening.)

- Some flowers, such as snapdragons and gladioli, respond to gravity by bending upwards if they are kept in a horizontal position.

- Wilt-sensitive flowers and others with poor or minimal storage potential should never be stored dry or held for more than 24 to 48 hours.

The storage potential of floral arrangements is a common question among florists. Many florists design wedding flowers 2 or 3 days in advance. This is workable if flowers are properly conditioned and packaged. However, these designs must be kept in a floral cooler. Arrangements containing wilt-sensitive flowers should not be designed until the day of the wedding. If necessary, wilt-sensitive flowers can be inserted into previously arranged designs on the wedding day.

Proper packaging is essential to minimize water loss and prevent damage during storage. The general practice for bouquets and body flowers is to put the finished design in a plastic or cellophane bag, spray it with water, seal the bag, and place it in the cooler. This is absolutely essential if the design is made a few days in advance. Designs can be put in a box for added protection. The bags should be opened daily (in the cooler) to allow for some ventilation and to spray with additional water. This practice should be followed until the day of the wedding, at which time excessive misting should cease in order to avoid the flowers wetting clothing, tablecloths, etc.

Design Tips for Increased Floral Life

Proper conditioning of flowers before designing is essential. Additional practices used while designing can help further extend flower life. The following tips should be routine practices for all designers.

- Remove only the number of flowers from the cooler that will be needed for a short period of time.

- Keep flowers in a bucket of preservative water.

Notes

- When wiring and taping flowers for corsages or bouquets, keep the wired flowers on a moist layer of paper towels and mist them occasionally.

- Soak floral foam bricks and bouquet holders in water with floral preservative prior to designing. Allow the foam to float freely rather than forcing it underwater or pouring water on top.

- Water tubes (aqua picks) can be used in some types of designs to extend flower life, particularly for wilt-sensitive flowers. Designs created without floral foam, such as garlands or arches featuring an abundance of greens, may be enhanced with simple floral accents in water tubes. Key tips for using water tubes are listed here.

    1. Use the proper size tube for the specific flower type. The tube should be big enough to provide an adequate water supply to the flower. However, the opening in the tube cap must be small enough to grip the flower stem tightly.

    2. Avoid forceful insertions of flower stems into the water tubes. To prevent stem breakage, first remove the rubber cap, push the cap into the end of the flower stem, then place the cap holding the stem back onto the tube.

- Finishing sprays and dips are useful for wedding designs created in advance. They are also appropriate for treating wilt-sensitive flowers and foliage designed on the wedding day. Certain general steps should be followed for use, along with product-specific instructions, including:

    1. Remove flowers and foliage from the cooler in time for them to dry completely.

    2. Items with moisture-free surfaces can be dipped once or misted lightly several times.

    3. Items should be allowed to dry completely before they are packaged and returned to the cooler or prepared for delivery. They should not be saturated with water.

Notes

Examples of several sprays and dips are given below. The florist should also realize the importance of simple water misting; water can actually be as effective or even more effective in prolonging life than some special products. When using on designs created in advance, the designer can forego the above instructions and simply mist with plain water, package, and return the item to the cooler. Packaging can be opened daily to allow ventilation and more misting until the day of the event, at which time excessive misting should cease to prevent the flowers from wetting clothing, etc.

Finishing sprays and dips include:

- Aerosols that are sprayed on flowers to seal pores and minimize water loss (such as Design Master Clear Life or Floralife® Clear Set).

- Light glues used to prevent petal shattering, for flowers, such as chrysanthemums (including Floralife® Mum-Tite and OASIS® Mum Mist).

- Liquid anti-transpirants, such as Crowning Glory®, are used as sprays or dips that coat the flower or foliage and minimize transpirations (water loss). In order to be effective, cover all surfaces completely, rather than simply spritzing the item.

- Self-made glue dips made by mixing one part white glue, such as Elmer's Glue-All™, to three parts water. Flowers are dipped into this mixture to seal and prevent shattering of flowers, such as chrysanthemums, and prevent browning on flowers, such as gardenias.

- Self-made gelatin sealer made by dissolving one envelope of flavorless gelatin in one cup of boiling water. This mixture is allowed to cool to room temperature (but is not chilled) and is then painted onto the backs of delicate flowers (such as orchids or pansies) and then set in the cooler to stiffen them.

Notes

Reference Chart

Complete care and handling charts, packaged with this book, summarize information to be used in the purchasing, conditioning, and storage of popular wedding flowers. The following list explains how the information in the charts might be used:

- Availability/Seasonality - This can be used not only to determine whether the product is available, but also as a possible indicator of price and quality. "Out-of-season" may mean higher prices and a smaller quantity or a lesser quality product.

- Purchasing Tips - This highlights "hallmarks of quality" to look for when purchasing flowers to ensure the longest vase life possible.

- Storage Potential - This shows whether a product has minimal, good, or excellent storage potential, thus indicating whether it can be purchased and stored in advance of the wedding. Products with minimal potential should be received 24 to 48 hours prior to the wedding, while products with 5 to 7 day potential can be received at the beginning of the week.

- Vase Life Potential - This shows the potential maximum vase life in days. Long lasting products with good storage potential may be purchased and arranged in advance of the ceremony.

- Conditioning - This highlights key conditioning steps, including whether a product should be recut underwater (indicated by UW) and whether it should be treated with silver thiosulfate (STS). Flowers should be treated by the retailer only if they have not been treated by the supplier or if previous treatment is unknown.

- Special Problems and Tips - This includes unique helpful pointers for each particular flower. Wilt-sensitive flowers are indicated so that they can be unpacked immediately and given special attention to allow sufficient water uptake and prevent drying out.

- Packaging - This indicates how flowers are typically packaged. Often, the number of stems in a bunch varies according to the source. These exceptions are noted.

Notes

To ensure maximum profits, proper purchasing and handling methods of all products are essential. Special attention should be paid to the individual needs of each type of flower used in the shop. Some flowers are available only during a particular season or from a unique country or producer. Some flowers can be stored for weeks with minimal care while others must be used within hours of arrival. Good conditioning and handling procedures can prolong the life of any flower. Planned ordering procedures and rapid turnover of inventory can dramatically increase profits.

Notes, Photographs, Sketches, etc.

Notes, Photographs, Sketches, etc.

Notes, Photographs, Sketches, etc.

Design Mechanics and Specialty Bouquet Techniques

The key to a well styled and well constructed wedding bouquet, corsage, or boutonniere is good mechanics. The proper use of wire, tape, and other special supports can greatly improve the appearance of flowers in a design and help ensure that flowers will stay in position despite much handling throughout the wedding day.

There are multiple mechanical methods used to secure, support, extend, and bend floral materials for design. Key techniques specifically related to wedding work are described in this chapter. In some cases, more than one method is given for the same mechanical need. The florist need not master each of these methods. Instead, he should find one method that is most comfortable and use it consistently.

Basics of Wiring

Flowers for corsages and bouquets are wired in order to eliminate bulky stems and to provide flexibility in flower positioning. The wire gauge used is determined by the weight of the flower and the distance it will be from the binding point of the design. Heavy flowers close to the binding point require heavier wires than small flowers at the perimeter of the design.

The most common wire gauges used in wedding work are #24, #26, and #28. A wiring chart is provided in the back of the book, listing flowers and foliage used in wedding designs, the proper wire gauge, and the wiring technique for that flower. The chart might be detached from the book and hung in the flower shop as a reference for design assistants to ensure that flowers and foliage are wired correctly.

Chenille stems may also be used to wire some types of flowers. Moistened chenille stems may be inserted into flower stems providing a wicking action which brings water to the flower. The chenille fibers along the chenille stem help grip the stem and prevent the flower from coming off. Short-stemmed flowers, such as stephanotis or cymbidium orchids, may be wired with chenille stems for use in foam bouquet holders, as well.

A simple rule of thumb to help decide when and how to wire flowers is to use wire in order to lengthen, strengthen, or control stems.

Extending Flower Life with Cotton

When working with special flowers, it is helpful to apply a piece of wet cotton at the end of the stem after wiring and just before taping. This provides the flower with needed moisture and helps extend flower life. Flowers that respond particularly well to this treatment are:

Roses
Orchids
Alstroemeria
Gardenias
Lilies

Basic Wiring Techniques

Following are the seven basic techniques for wiring flowers and foliage. Some materials may be wired with more than one of these methods. Other flowers have their own special wiring techniques that differ from any of these. Refer to the wiring chart provided with this book to determine the proper technique for each flower being wired.

An understanding of basic flower morphology is helpful in following the steps in many of the wiring techniques described. The flower diagram in ***Figure 4.1*** shows the basic parts of the flower.

Pierce Method

Flowers with a thick calyx beneath the flower head, such as roses and carnations, are wired by piercing.

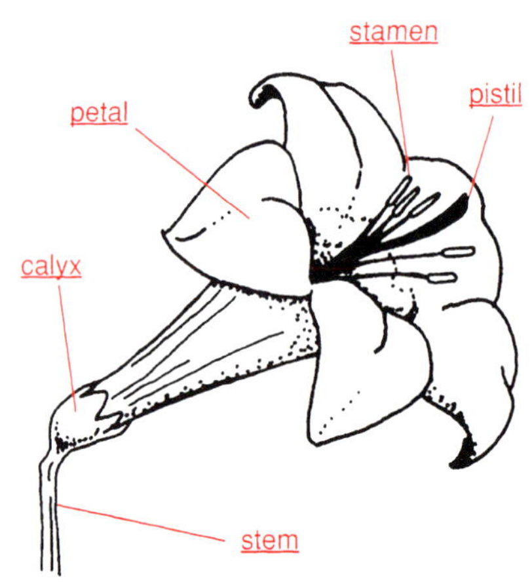

Figure 4.1 Basic Parts of the Flower

Figure 4.2a Pierce Wiring Method Step 2

1. Trim the flower stem to a length of 1/2 to 1 inch.

2. Push one end of a wire horizontally through the calyx using half the length of the wire. ***(Figure 4.2a)***

3. Bend both ends down parallel with the stem. ***(Figure 4.2b)***

4. Tape, starting just above the pierce. ***(Figure 4.2b)***

5. For heavy flowers in need of additional support, a second wire may be inserted through the flower so that the two wires are crisscrossed. This method is called cross-piercing.

Figure 4.2b Pierce Wiring Method Steps 3 and 4

Insertion Method

This method can be used for flowers with the heads firmly fastened to the stem, such as asters. Use wire 6 to 9 inches long and strong enough to hold the flower head erect.

1. Cut the flower stem to about 1 inch in length.

2. Push the wire inside the stem and up into the flower head until it is firm. The wire should not be visible from the top of the flower. ***(Figure 4.3)***

3. Tape the stem and the wire tightly together.

Figure 4.3 Insertion Wiring Method

Hook Method

This method can be used with any flower that has a hard disc-like center, such as daisies and mums. It may also be used with a light gauge wire on individual florets, such as those of delphinium or hyacinths.

1. Cut the flower stem to about 1 inch in length.

2. Push a wire along or through the stem until the wire has emerged through the center of the flower to a height of about 1 1/2 inches. ***(Figure 4.4a)***

Figure 4.4a Hook Method Steps 2 and 3

3. Form a hook 1/2 to 3/4 inch long and pull the wire gently back down into the flower, making sure that the hook is concealed in the blossom. The end of the hook should emerge back through the base of the flower. ***(Figure 4.4a on page 75)***

4. Tape the stem, beginning at the base of the flower and making sure to catch the end of the hook within the tape. ***(Figure 4.4b)***

Figure 4.4b Hook Method Step 4

Wrap-Around Method

Almost any flower can be wired with this method, but it is especially effective for small flowers in clusters, such as baby's breath and statice.

1. Cut the flower stem or stems to 1 to 1 1/2 inches.

2. Wrap a light wire around the stem or cluster tightly to create a "bunch" appearance. ***(Figure 4.5)***

3. Bend the two wire ends parallel to the stem and tape.

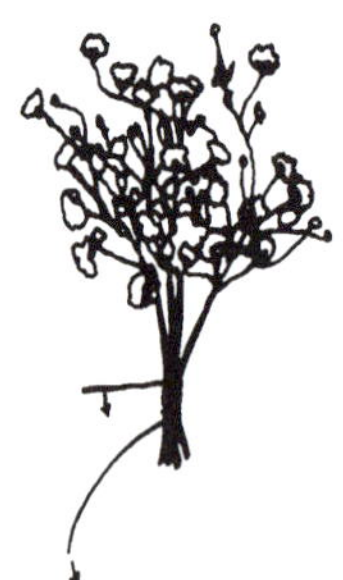

Figure 4.5 Wrap-Around Wiring Method

Stitch Method

This method is used almost entirely for broad-leaved foliage, such as camellia, ivy, or salal.

1. Cut the stem of the leaf to about 1/2 inch.

2. Pierce a wire through the back of the leaf near the center rib. Pierce the wire high enough on the leaf to again complete control of the leaf, but not so high that the wire will show in the bouquet (about half the length of the leaf). ***(Figure 4.6a)***

Figure 4.6a Stitch Wiring Method Step 2

3. Push the wire halfway through the leaf and bend the wire ends down.

4. Wrap one wire around the leaf stem and around the second wire for extra security. ***(Figure 4.6b)***

5. Tape the stem.

Figure 4.6b Stitch Wiring Method Step 4

Hairpin Method

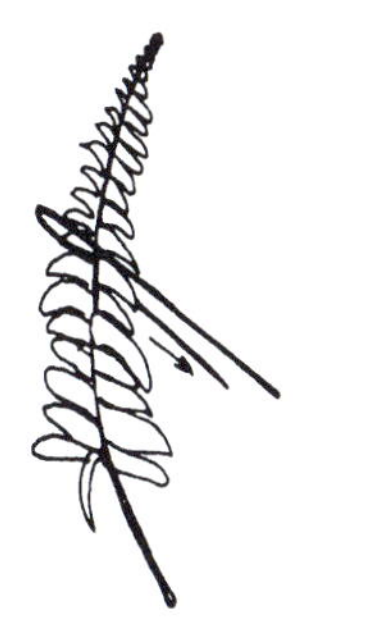

Figure 4.7a Hairpin Wiring Method Step 2

This method is used to wire multi-flowered stems or fern-like foliage when support is needed high on the stem.

1. Bend a wire in half to form a hairpin.
2. Straddle the hairpin over the stem near the center or top, depending on the amount of control desired. ***(Figure 4.7a)***
3. Pull the wire down until the bend of the hairpin rests on the stem.
4. Wrap one wire around the stem and the second wire. ***(Figure 4.7b)***
5. Tape the stem.

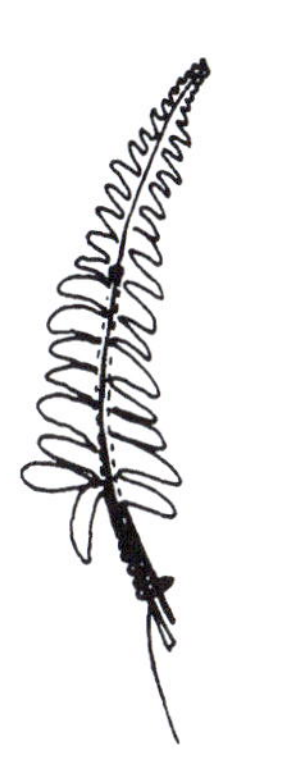

Figure 4.7b Hairpin Wiring Method Step 4

Splinting Method

This method is used primarily when designing a bouquet that uses the flower's natural stems, such as a hand-tied bouquet or a design in a foam bouquet holder. The splinting method adds strength to the stem and allows the stem to be slightly bent for design purposes. ***(Figure 4.8)***

1. Insert a full-length wire vertically into the base of the calyx.
2. Loosely wrap the wire around the full length of the stem in a gentle spiral. ***(Figure 4.8)***
3. Trim any excess wire from the end of the stem.
4. If desired, tape the stem to cover the wire. (Do not tape over the end of the flower stem.)

Figure 4.8 Splinting Wiring Method

Wiring Techniques for Special Flowers

Certain flowers are either too delicate or unusually shaped to be wired using any of the standard methods. The following are proven techniques for wiring commonly used wedding flowers.

Camellias

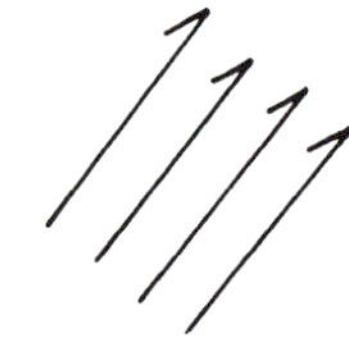
Figure 4.9a Wiring Camellias Step 1

Traditionally, camellia flowers are cross-pierced through the flower petals about 1/4 inch above the calyx. The following method is also effective for these delicate blossoms.

1. Bend the top 1/2 inch of four #24 gauge wires down toward the wire at a 45 degree angle to create a hook. ***(Figure 4.9a)***

2. Gently insert the hooks of the wires, one at a time, into the base of the flower petals on four sides of the flower. ***(Figure 4.9b)***

3. Pull the wires together under the flower and tape.

Figure 4.9b Wiring Camellias Step 2

Gardenias

Gardenias are easily wired, but are very fragile and easily bruised. Bruising can be lessened by keeping one's hands wet while working with the flowers. Avoid touching the petals of a gardenia if at all possible. Gardenias may be wired using the cross-pierce method previously described or with a chenille stem in the following way.

1. Turn the flower upside down and cut the stem about 1 inch below the collar and remove the calyx.

2. Place a chenille stem up into the stem until secure. ***(Figure 4.10a)***

Figure 4.10a Wiring Gardenias Step 2

3. Use a #24 gauge wire to pierce-wire the stem directly under the collar. ***(Figure 4.10b)***

4. Bend the wire parallel to the stem and tape. ***(Figure 4.10c on page 79)***

5. After the gardenia has been prepared, a wet tissue may be placed over the flower to help maintain freshness and reduce bruising.

Figure 4.10b Wiring Gardenias Step 3

Note: If the gardenia is not already tailored, wire as directed and edge the gardenia blossom with wired camellia leaves

Figure 4.10c Wiring Gardenias Step 4

or create a collar as outlined below. If the gardenia is collared with plastic leaves, clip them off and staple fresh galax or other broad-leaved foliage in their place. Be sure the ends of the staples face the flower to prevent scratching.

Creating a Gardenia Collar

1. Cut a circle about 1 1/2 inches in diameter out of thin green or white cardboard.

2. Bend the cardboard slightly and clip crisscrossed slits through the center to provide an opening for the flower stem. ***(Figure 4.11a)***

Figure 4.11a Creating a Gardenia Collar Step 2

3. Staple flat, broad-leaved foliage, such as camellia or salal, around the edge of the cardboard circle with the backside of the leaf against the cardboard. The base of each leaf should overlap the cardboard about 1/3 inch. ***(Figures 4.11b and 4.11c)***

Figure 4.11b Creating a Gardenia Collar Step 3

4. Slide the flower stem through the center opening of the cardboard. Gently position the collar underneath the gardenia so that it supports the petals.

5. Wire and tape as directed.

Lily-of-the-Valley

Lily-of-the-valley can be wired in clusters with two or three stems using a #28 gauge wire in a wrap-around method. A single stem is wired in the following manner.

Figure 4.11c Creating a Gardenia Collar Step 3

1. Wrap a #28 gauge wire with light green floral tape leaving about a 1/2 inch piece of unused tape extended beyond the end of the wire. ***(Figure 4.12a)***

2. Place a single stem of lily-of-the-valley against the wired stem so that the extra, unused portion of tape is about two-thirds of the way up the stem. ***(Figure 4.12b on page 80)***

Figure 4.12a Wiring Lily-of-the-Valley Step 1

3. Carefully wrap the unused portion of tape around the stem between the florets, and pinch the tape so that it will stick together. ***(Figure 4.12c on page 80)***

4. Tape the stem and wire together starting directly under the bottom floret down to the base. ***(Figure 4.12d)***

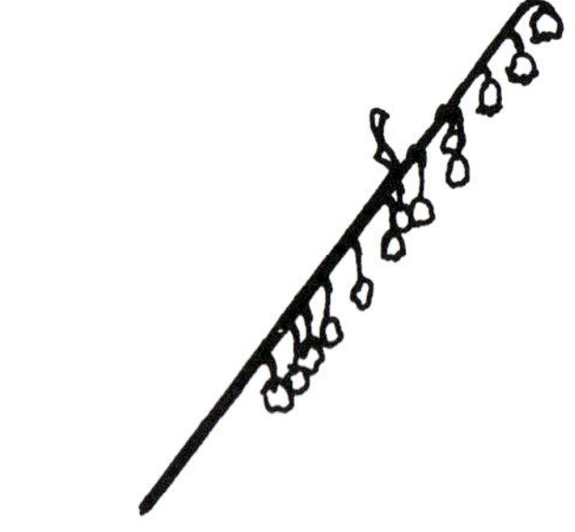

Figure 4.12b Wiring Lily-of-the-Valley Step 2

Cattleya, Cymbidium, and Japhet Orchids

Although these flowers are traditionally wired using the pierce method, the following method may be used when additional support is needed.

1. Cut the orchid stem to a length of 1 to 1 1/2 inches.

2. Insert a chenille stem up through the orchid stem as far as possible without entering the throat of the orchid. ***(Figure 4.13a)***

3. Pierce-wire the orchid stem at the base of the flower with a #24 gauge wire. ***(Figure 4.13b on page 81)***

4. Begin taping at the base of the flower and tape all the way down, binding the stem, wire, and chenille into one unit.

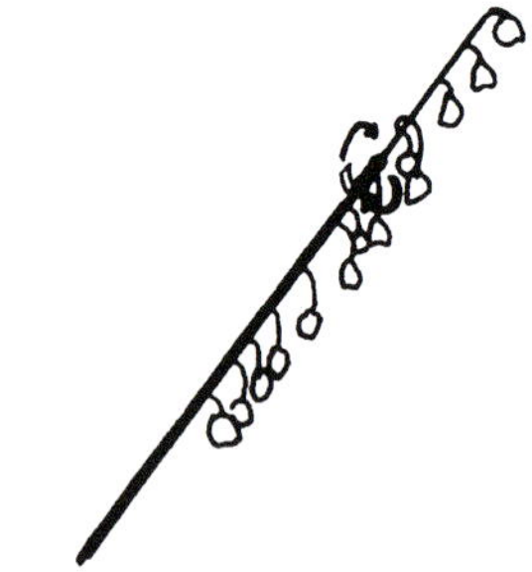

Figure 4.12c Wiring Lily-of-the-Valley Step 3

Dendrobium and Cypripedium (Lady Slipper) Orchids

These flowers may be wired in more than one way depending on how they will be used in design. The following steps are for wiring individual blossoms for bouquets or body flowers.

1. Pierce a #24 or 26 gauge wire vertically into the orchid where the stem and the flower meet. ***(Figure 4.14a on page 81)***

2. Push the wire out through the throat of the flower, and bend the end into a small hook. ***(Figure 4.14a on page 81)***

3. Pull the wire hook back into the orchid until it reaches the flower base. The end of the hook should protrude through the back of the flower. ***(Figure 4.14b on page 81)***

4. Tape the end of the hook to the flower stem, and continue taping to the end of the wire.

Figure 4.12d Wiring Lily-of-the-Valley Step 4

Figure 4.13a Wiring Cattleya, Cymbidium, and Japhet Orchids Step 2

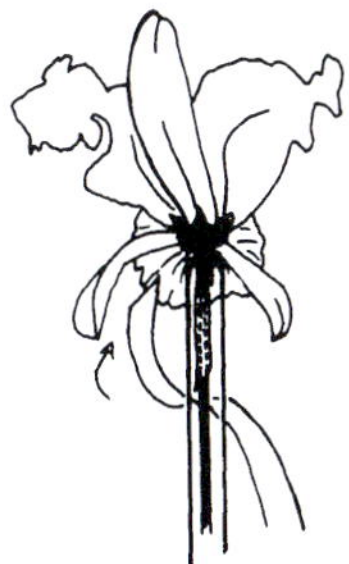

Figure 4.13b Wiring Cattleya, Cymbidium, and Japhet Orchids Step 3

Figure 4.14a Wiring Dendrobium and Cypripedium Orchids Step 3

Figure 4.14b Wiring Dendrobium and Cypripedium Orchids Step 6

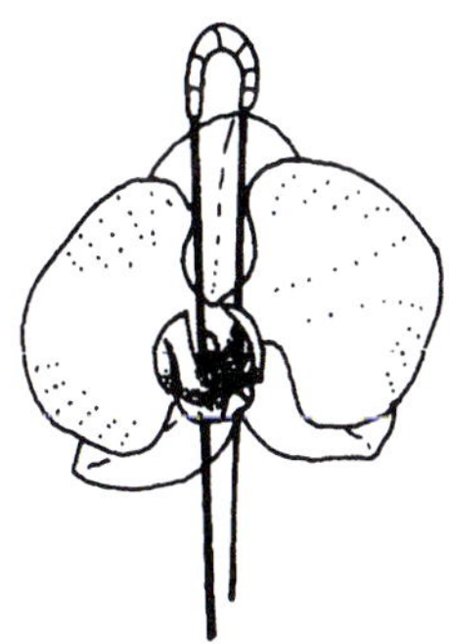

Figure 4.15a Wiring Phalaenopsis Orchids Step 3

Note: The pierce method may also be used to wire individual dendrobium blossoms by inserting a wire through the thick chin at the base of the flower. Full-length dendrobium orchid sprays with multiple flowers on a stem may be wired using the wrap-around method with a #22 gauge wire.

Phalaenopsis Orchids

Phalaenopsis orchids are extremely delicate and must be handled carefully when designing. The following wiring technique is used to provide support without damaging the flowers.

1. Tape the center 1 inch of a #26 or #28 gauge wire with white tape.
2. Bend the wire in half, forming a *U* in the middle of the white-taped section.
3. The lip of the orchid is connected to the rest of the flower by a delicate, narrow membrane. Place one end of the bent wire on each side of the narrow membrane. ***(Figure 4.15a)***
4. Gently pull the wire down until the taped center rests against the membrane. The wire should not be inserted through any part of the flower.
5. Align the wires with the stem on the underside of the orchid. It may be necessary to bend the wire slightly where it meets the narrow membrane.
6. Wrap one wire around the flower stem and around the second wire a few times to secure the wire in place. ***(Figure 4.15b on page 82)***
7. Tape the wire from top to bottom.

Stephanotis

Stephanotis, a very popular flower for weddings, may be wired using any one of the following methods.

<u>Wiring Stephanotis with Cotton</u>

1. Dampen a piece of cotton and twirl it with the fingers onto the middle of a #28 gauge wire.

2. Bend the wire in the middle to form a very straight, long hairpin. The cotton should be in the fold of the hairpin.

3. Push the ends of the hairpin down the tube of the flower through the bottom of the blossom, making sure that one wire end comes out on each side of the stem. ***(Figure 4.16a)***

4. Pull the wire through the flower until the cotton is inside the flower tube and rests at the base. The cotton keeps the wire from tearing through the flower and also provides moisture. ***(Figure 4.16b)***

5. Tape the stem.

6. To harden blossoms, submerge the wired heads loosely in ice water for several hours.

<u>Wiring Commercial "Stephanotis Stems"</u>

1. Moisten the wick of a stephanotis stem in a bowl of water. ***(Figure 4.17a)***

2. Remove the green calyx and stem from the base of the flower. ***(Figure 4.17b)***

3. Insert the moistened wick through the base of the flower. ***(Figure 4.17c on page 83)***

4. The moistened wick will expand inside the throat of the flower and hold the stem in place. However, the flower may be taped to the stephanotis stem for added security. ***(Figure 4.17d on page 83)***

<u>Wiring Stephanotis with Chenille Stems</u>

1. Moisten the end of a white chenille stem in about an inch of water.

Figure 4.15b Wiring Phalaenopsis Orchids Step 6

Figure 4.16a Wiring Stephanotis with Cotton Step 3

Figure 4.16b Wiring Stephanotis with Cotton Step 4

Figure 4.17a Wiring Commercial "Stephanotis Stems" Step 1

Figure 4.17b Wiring Commercial "Stephanotis Stems" Step 2

Figure 4.17c Wiring Commercial "Stephanotis Stems" Step 3

Figure 4.17d Wiring Stephanotis with Commercial "Stephanotis Stems" Step 4

Figure 4.18a Wiring Stephanotis with Chenille Stems Step 2

Figure 4.18b Wiring Stephanotis with Chenille Stems Step 3

Figure 4.19a Creating Stephanotis Strands Step 3

2. Insert the moistened end of the chenille stem up through the base of the flower next to the flower's stem. The chenille stem is inserted far enough when the tip is barely visible from the top of the flower. ***(Figure 4.18a)***

3. Once in position, tape the chenille and stephanotis stems together. The tape will need to be overlapped a little more than usual, due to the rough texture of the chenille stem. ***(Figure 4.18b)***

Creating Stephanotis Strands

Strands of stephanotis may be created to cascade from corsages, hairpieces, or bouquets. The length of the strand is determined by the desired use. Other small flowers with long, open throats, such as hyacinth florets, may also be used to create such strands.

1. Use a heavy white thread and needle or a #26 or #28 gauge wire.

2. Tie a knot in the thread or bend the wire into a hook.

3. Thread the flowers onto the needle, or wire one after another, all in the same direction. The opening of the flowers should face the knot or hook. ***(Figure 4.19a)***

4. Pull the flowers to the end of the thread or wire until reaching the knot or hook. ***(Figure 4.19b page 84)***

5. Continue adding flowers until reaching the desired length. Flowers should overlap each other so that there is no interruption in the strand. ***(Figure 4.19c page 84)***

6. Finish the strand by taping the remaining portion of the wire or by tying the thread onto a chenille stem. ***(Figure 4.19d page 84)***

Delicate Blossoms

Small, delicate flowers, such as pansies, violets, and begonias, are often requested for wedding bouquets. Many of these blossoms are quite fragile and difficult to work with. The following techniques may be used to simplify designing with these flowers.

Gluing Delicate Blossoms

Floral adhesive glue (not hot glue) may be used to add delicate flowers directly into a bouquet. For more precise placement of these flowers, the following technique may be used.

1. Select a fresh broad-leaved foliage, such as salal. The leaf should be approximately the same size as the flower. Wire it using the stitch method and tape. Make sure the wire is heavy enough to support the weight of the leaf and flower.
2. Apply a generous amount of floral adhesive glue to the back of the flower. ***(Figure 4.20a)***
3. Lay the flower on the leaf and set it aside for about 30 minutes to allow the glue to dry. ***(Figure 4.20b page 85)***
4. Use the wired leaf to incorporate the flower into the design.

Using Gelatin with Delicate Blossoms

A diluted gelatin mixture may be used to coat delicate blossoms and make them more firm. The flowers may be wired and taped before or after the coating is applied. The gluing method described above may also be used to secure them into a design.

1. Mix one envelope of clear gelatin with one cup of boiling water until dissolved.
2. Allow the mixture to cool to room temperature.
3. Dip the flowers into the gelatin and put them in the cooler to stiffen.

Basics of Taping

Floral tape is a lightweight, waxed crepe paper. The adhesive is activated when the tape is stretched and wrapped tightly around wire or other design elements. A certain amount of adhesiveness remains after the tape is wrapped around an item. When designing a bouquet or corsage, this adhesiveness helps

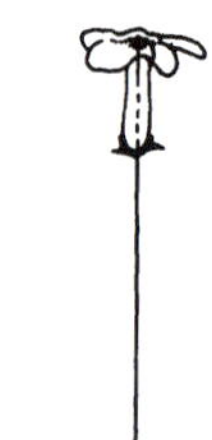

Figure 4.19b Creating Stephanotis Strands Step 4

Figure 4.19c Creating Stephanotis Strands Step 5

Figure 4.19d Creating Stephanotis Strands Step 6

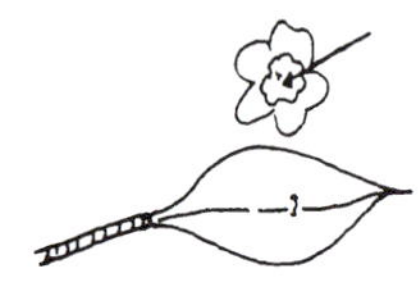

Figure 4.20a Gluing Delicate Blossoms Step 2

Figure 4.20b Gluing Delicate Blossoms Step 3

individual, taped wires stick together until the group can be bound by a separate piece of floral tape.

Floral tape comes in a wide variety of colors including several shades of green, the most widely used color. Two widths of floral tape are also available. One-half inch tape is typically used to tape the wires of individual flowers. One-inch tape is most often used to bind wired stems together in bouquets. Floral tape is a staple item in wedding design, and it is imperative that designers learn to use it well.

Figure 4.21a Taping a Wired Stem Step 1

Taping a Wired Stem

1. With the wired flower in hand, start at the calyx of the flower and wrap a piece of tape around the top of the wire, pressing it securely into place. ***(Figure 4.21a)***

2. Begin twirling the flower stem with one hand while stretching and pulling the tape on a downward angle with the other. The tape should be tightly wrapped around the wire with no buckles or gaps along the stem. ***(Figure 4.21b)***

3. When the end of the wire is reached, tear the tape off the roll and wrap the remaining piece around the wire. ***(Figure 4.21c)***

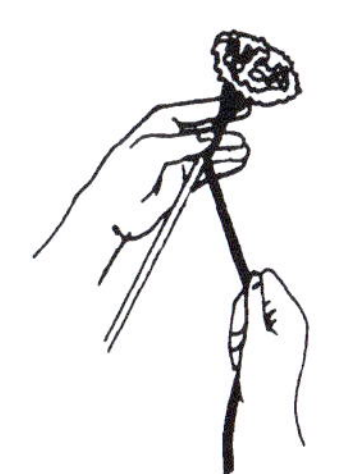

Figure 4.21b Taping a Wired Stem Step 2

Wireless Taping

This method of taping is used primarily for small flowers or accessories. It is used to create free-flowing pieces from a corsage or bouquet. Only lightweight materials should be used with this technique since there is no wire to support the item.

1. Cut the stem of the item to be taped to about 1 inch in length.

2. Wrap a piece of floral tape around the top of the stem the same way one would if the flower were wired.

3. Twirl the flower in one hand and twist the tape tightly around itself. The resulting "stem" will be soft and pliable.

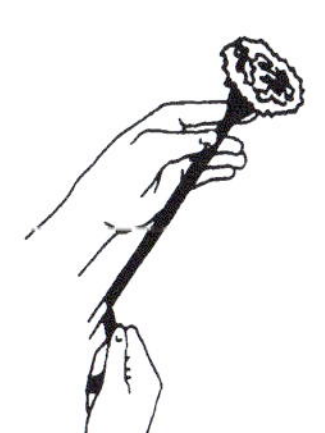

Figure 4.21c Taping a Wired Stem Step 3

4. Continue taping until the "stem" reaches the desired length.

5. For added support and control, the "stem" may be taped a second time.

Bouquet Holder Techniques

Foam bouquet holders offer two primary advantages in the construction of wedding bouquets. First, the bouquet holder contains a wettable foam which provides a water source for the flowers. This prolongs the life of the bouquet and allows it to be designed further in advance. The second advantage in using foam bouquet holders is the reduced amount of labor involved in comparison to designing a wired and taped bouquet.

The key disadvantage to designing with foam bouquet holders is the risk of flowers falling out of the design. Several techniques have been developed to prevent this problem from occurring.

Securing Stems in Bouquet Holders with Chenille Stems

Use of chenille stems is one method of securing stems in foam bouquet holders. For large-stemmed flowers, such as gerbera daisies or roses, the chenille is inserted into the stem and then cut off, leaving about 1/2 inch beyond the end of the flower stem. Thinner-stemmed flowers can be secured by taping a piece of chenille next to the stem. The flower stem is inserted into the foam as usual. The fibers of the chenille stem give an additional gripping action to help hold the flowers in the foam. ***(Figure 4.22)***

Figure 4.22 Stems Secured in Bouquet Holders with Chenille Stems

Securing Stems in Bouquet Holders with Glue

Another method of securing the stems is with floral glues, such as Oasis® Floral Adhesive. (Glue guns and pan-melt glues should not be used for this purpose.) Large-stemmed flowers are inserted into the foam, touching a piece of the plastic cage. Glue is then placed at the point where the stem and cage meet, as shown in ***Figure 4.23***. When using the wooden pick method, glue can be placed on the pick to add greater security.

Figure 4.23 Stems Secured in Bouquet Holders with Glue

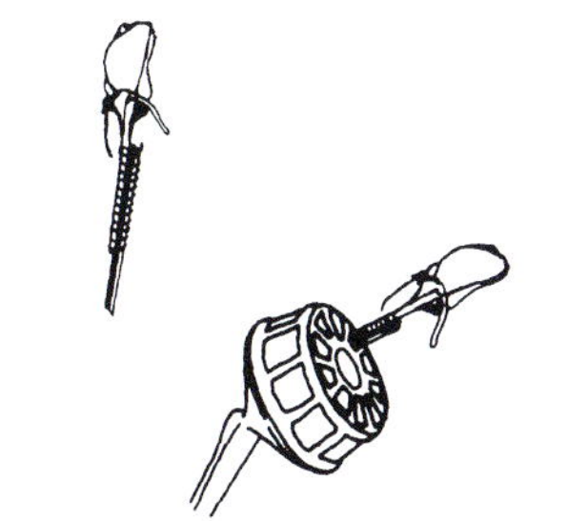

Figure 4.24 Stems Secured in Bouquet Holders with Wooden Picks

Securing Stems in Bouquet Holders Using Wooden Picks

One method of holding the stems in saturated foam is by using wooden picks. As shown in ***Figure 4.24***, the thin wire from the pick is wrapped around the flower stem and inserted into the foam. The insertion must be deep enough so that the flower stem reaches the foam along with the pick. The moisture from the foam will cause the wooden pick to swell and hold the flower more securely. This technique is best used for large-stemmed flowers. It also works well for securing ribbon and streamers into the bouquet.

Securing Stems in Bouquet Holders with Pins

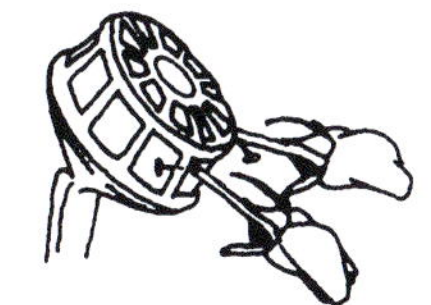

Figure 4.25 Stems Secured in Bouquet Holders with Pins

Large-stemmed flowers are often difficult to keep in place. The pinning method can be used to secure these heavy stems by inserting a straight pin or a section of #20 gauge wire over a rib of the cage and then through the portion of the flower stem that is in the foam. ***(Figure 4.25)*** When using this method, it is easiest to begin the bouquet with the largest flowers.

Securing Cascades in Bouquet Holders

Figure 4.26 Cascades Secured in Bouquet Holders

Cascades may be designed directly into foam bouquet holders. However, for large cascades or added security it is sometimes necessary to wire and tape a cascade and add it to the bouquet holder. To secure a wired and taped cascade into a bouquet holder, construct the cascade with as thin a stem as possible. This can be accomplished by continually trimming excess wires from the cascade as it gets longer. Tape the cascade all the way to the end.

Starting at the bottom of the bouquet holder, insert the cascade into the back of the foam until it comes out the other end. Push the cascade up through the foam and into the desired position. Bend the end of the cascade over a rib of the plastic cage and insert it into the foam. For additional security, the stem of the cascade can be wired to the rib of the cage. ***(Figure 4.26)***

Backing Techniques for Bouquet Holders

Bouquet holders may be finished using the following backing techniques.

Lace Backing for Bouquet Holders

Lace backings are often used to finish the back of a foam bouquet holder. This type of backing is simply a collar of lace surrounding a plastic cup which slides up over the handle and fits around the holder. The base of the cup has several broad plastic threads attached which are taped onto the bouquet handle to secure the backing, in place. These threads are easily trimmed from the backing if desired. A small bow in the wedding colors may be placed at the top of the handle to give a finished look to the design.

Foliage Backing for Bouquet Holders

Another method of backing the bouquet holder is with foliage. Broad-leaved foliage, such as salal or galax leaves, can be glued directly to a plastic backing in an overlapping pattern. Floral adhesive glues are the best adhesives for this, because they will withstand moisture and temperature change. ***(Figure 4.27)***

Figure 4.27 Foliage Backing for Bouquet Holders

Using Bouquet Holders Horizontally

Foam bouquet holders are most often designed with the handle in a vertical position, pointing toward the floor. When a large bouquet is designed with the holder in this position, the bouquet can become top-heavy and tip forward in the hands.

The horizontal bouquet holder is constructed with the handle taped flat across the design table. This helps distribute the weight of a bouquet more evenly and makes it more comfortable to carry. Bouquet styles designed with a strong vertical line or an abundant cascade work well with this method. ***(Figure 4.28)***

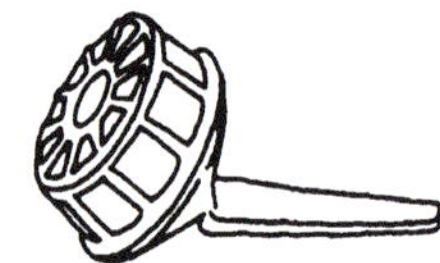

Figure 4.28 Bouquet Holder Used Horizontally

Specialty Bouquet Techniques

Brides sometimes request special touches in their bouquets which require specialized mechanics. Often these mechanics must be custom designed to coordinate with the flower or accessory being used. The following are specialized mechanical techniques for unique bouquet additions.

Removable Corsages for Bouquets

Several years ago it became popular to design the bridal bouquet so that a portion could be taken out after the wedding

Figure 4.29a Creating a Wire Holder for a Removable Corsage Step 1

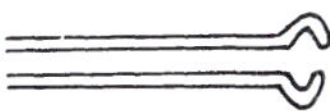

Figure 4.29b Creating a Wire Holder for a Removable Corsage Step 4

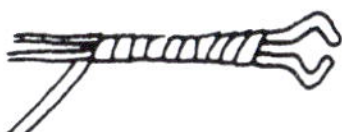

Figure 4.29c Creating a Wire Holder for a Removable Corsage Step 5

Figure 4.29d Creating a Wire Holder for a Removable Corsage Step 6

Figure 4.29e Creating a Wire Holder for a Removable Corsage Step 7

Figure 4.29f Creating a Wire Holder for a Removable Corsage Step 8

and worn as a going-away corsage. This trend started before the days of foam bouquet holders; thus, the mechanism used to hold the corsage was wired right into the bouquet. With a foam bouquet holder, the removable corsage may also be incorporated. The corsage holder is simply inserted into the foam and wired to a portion of the cage for added security.

Creating a Wire Holder for a Removable Corsage

1. Wrap two pieces of #18 gauge wire with green tape. ***(Figure 4.29a)***
2. Bend both wires in half.
3. About 2 inches below the bend in each wire, make a 45 degree angle.
4. Bend the top inch of the wire back so the wire appears to have a small hill at the end. ***(Figure 4.29b)***
5. Place the two wires next to each other so the peaks of the hills are facing away from each other. Tape the wires together just below the bends. ***(Figure 4.29c)***
6. Maneuver the bent ends so one fits into another. This forms an opening for the corsage stem. ***(Figure 4.29d)***
7. Place the corsage stem into the opening and insert a corsage pin below the wire holder and into the corsage stem. ***(Figure 4.29e)***
8. Treat the corsage holder as a flower and tape it into the bouquet. For a foam bouquet holder, attach the corsage holder to a wooden pick before inserting it into the foam. It is better if the corsage holder is positioned in the lower part of the bouquet so the corsage will blend into the bouquet. ***(Figure 4.29f)***

Creating a Tulle Holder for a Removable Corsage

An alternative method for incorporating a corsage into a bouquet is to make a tight ball of tulle (about the size of a golf ball) and wire it with #24 gauge wire. Tape a #18 gauge wire to the #24 gauge wire for added support. The ball is then placed into the bouquet, and the corsage is pinned securely into the mesh of the tulle.

Creating a Bouquet Blusher

Notes

A unique way of finishing off a bridal bouquet is to encase the entire design in a blusher of illusion similar to the blusher veil a bride wears over her face during the ceremony. The illusion used should be very light so that the flowers are softened, but still clearly visible. This technique may be used for any bouquet style except those with lengthy cascades. It may also be used on a smaller scale to create a softened effect for a corsage.

1. Secure a broad piece of tulle or illusion to the back of a finished bouquet, with the tulle extending downward in the direction of the handle. Use a taped wire or chenille stem wrapped around the top of the handle.

2. Flip the tulle or illusion up and over the top of the bouquet.

3. Secure it loosely on the other side of the handle with a second wire or chenille stem.

4. Excess tulle or illusion may be allowed to cascade from the bouquet as streamers.

5. The blusher may be lightly dotted with pearls or glitter for a special touch.

Uses of Glue In Wedding Design

Florists use many different types of glue. Several can be used on fresh flowers for various purposes. Floral adhesives are particularly useful for weddings, as in the construction of a glamellia or as a quick way to add foliage to a corsage.

Floral adhesive is a rubber base glue that has been especially developed for use on fresh flowers. Commercial rubber cement is harmful to flowers, but the harmful chemicals have been removed from floral adhesive. This glue is not affected by moisture or temperature changes, therefore, it will hold when put into the cooler and then taken back out.

Standard household white glues, such as Elmer's Glue-All™, are effective sealers that help retain moisture within flowers, such as gardenias and stephanotis. The glue is mixed with water at a ratio of three parts water to one part white glue. The flowers are then dipped into the solution and allowed to dry before designing

Notes

with them. The glue turns clear when it dries and the coating on the flowers becomes unnoticeable.

Large or heavy accessories may be attached to a bouquet with pan melt glue. This glue may also be used to assemble certain church and reception decorations. Other non-floral glues are effective for many of these uses. Table 5 provides the names of floral and non-floral glues with a variety of uses in wedding design.

TABLE 5

RECOMMENDED GLUE TYPES AND MOST EFFECTIVE USAGE

Types of Glue	**Objects**
Linoleum Glue	Heavy Objects
Aleene's "Tacky" All-Purpose Glue	Dried Materials
Elmer's Glue-All™	Fresh Flowers and Dried Materials
Pan Melt Glue Chips	Fabric, Dried Materials, and Heavy Objects
Hot Melt Glue Sticks	Fabric and Dried Materials
Design Master Good Glue	Fresh Flowers
Low Temperature Glue Sticks (Cold Melt Glue Sticks)	Fresh Flowers
3-M 77 Spray Adhesive	Fresh Flowers
Glitter Glue	Fresh Flowers
Oasis® Floral Adhesive	Fresh Flowers and Fabric

Just as a sturdy house cannot be built without a good foundation, a well styled bouquet cannot be constructed without good mechanics. Wire and tape provide the basic frame around which the flowers can create a beautiful design. However, this frame must be solid without being obtrusive. The correct gauge of wire and the correct technique of wiring should be used to maximize the effectiveness of every corsage or bouquet. And, just as details, such as landscaping, can alter the appearance of a house, details, such as lace or foliage backings, can greatly enhance any arrangement. Likewise, too much attention cannot be paid to the gluing or pinning of fragile or exotic flowers required to elevate a bouquet above the ordinary.

Notes, Photographs, Sketches, etc.

Notes, Photographs, Sketches, etc.

Chapter 5

Wedding Bouquets

Wedding bouquet styles have changed over the years in conjunction with changes in ceremony styles and fashion trends. In the Middle Ages, chaplets of roses were worn around the head. Swiss brides wore wreaths of orange blossoms while Greek brides favored Hawthorn blossoms and English brides wore Rosemary bridal wreaths. In 1585, "tuzzy-muzzy" bouquets, derived from the English word meaning cluster or knob, were carried by women. A real "tuzzy" always contained fragrant flowers, such as roses, dianthus, tuberoses, or lemon verbena. The holders were silver filigree, but in later years were replaced by fern, lace, or paper frill holders.

In America, the colonial bouquet was the favorite bouquet style for decades and remains a favorite. By 1860, the hand-held bouquet had replaced the fan as the finishing touch to a lady's ensemble. From the beginning of the century until World War I, roses were the flower of the day. Brides carried white rose nosegay bouquets with showers of ribbons. In 1912, wedding bouquets became more spray-like, and cascades of flowers were added. During the 1920's, bouquets became larger with an abundance of ferns, greenery, and showers of ribbons. In 1929, bouquets became more simple and streamlined. In the 1930's, a softness in bouquet styling was added. Feathers and delicate flowers were used in abundance. In 1934, the cascade design returned and has since remained a favorite.

Many of these historical bouquet styles are still in use. However, traditional styles are often given a modern look with the use of specialty flowers or personalized embellishments. Bright flowers may be used to accent or replace the traditional white or pastel color schemes. Thus, florists must be able to design a wide variety of bouquet styles. Table 6 on page 96 classifies the major bridal bouquet styles into three categories.

Notes

TABLE 6

BRIDAL BOUQUET STYLES BY CATEGORY

Traditional Classic Styles	Novelty Styles	Advanced Styles
Cascade	Bible	Biedermeier
Colonial	Basket	Clutch
Crescent	Basquette	European Contemporary
Presentation (Arm)	Fan	Hand-Tied
Wreath	Muff	
	Parasol	
	Posey Drop	

Bouquet Construction

Construction techniques for many of the different wedding bouquet styles are similar. Generally, bouquets are constructed in three different ways. They may be assembled with individually wired and taped flowers, constructed in a foam bouquet holder, or tied together with waxed string or wire. Some styles may be designed in more than one way. For each bouquet style, the florist should choose the method which is the most comfortable, quickest, and produces the best quality design.

Cascade Bouquet

The cascade bouquet is a formal bouquet style created by extending the colonial bouquet into a flowing garland. The cascade may be of any length from less than a foot, to the floor, or beyond. Of key importance, however, is the maintenance of proper proportion between the top of the bouquet and the cascade. Small cascade bouquets may be designed in foam bouquet holders, while larger cascades should be wired and taped. As an alternative, a long cascade may be wired, taped, and added to a foam bouquet holder in which the rest of the bouquet is designed.

Creating a Cascade

1. Wire and tape flowers, foliage, and filler materials in varying sizes.

2. Start with the smallest flowers to create the tip of the cascade.

Figure 5.1a Creating a Cascade Step 3

Figure 5.1b Creating a Cascade Step 6

Figure 5.2a Constructing a Cascade Bouquet Step 2

Figure 5.2b Constructing a Cascade Bouquet Step 3

3. Begin with two flowers, placing one flower to the left and about 2 inches below the other. ***(Figure 5.1a)***

4. Add one flower in each of the four quadrants, as illustrated.

5. Add the next filler flower to the right of the stem and slightly below the left-most flower. Tape this flower on in the same manner, as in Step 4.

6. Continue adding flowers, as well as foliage and filler materials, left to right until the cascade reaches the desired length. As the cascade increases in length, flower size should increase and flower spacing should get closer together. As excess wire accumulates, trim out pieces while designing. This will make the cascade appear more natural and flowing. ***(Figure 5.1b)***

7. Adjust the flowers along the cascade into more natural curves and angles to eliminate a rigid appearance.

<u>Constructing a Cascade Bouquet</u>

1. Hold the finished cascade by the stem with the tip pointing upward and the flowers facing the designer.

2. Bend the stem of the cascade over backwards, about 3 inches below the last flower, creating a sharp angle. ***(Figure 5.2a)***

3. Begin designing a colonial bouquet by taping flowers onto the stem of the cascade at the bending point. ***(Figure 5.2b)*** The initial taping at this point must be especially tight to prevent the cascade from "rocking" in the bouquet.

4. When creating the lower portion of the colonial bouquet, the flowers should be positioned to blend with the garland rather than following the circular pattern.

5. Add foliage to the back of the design to disguise the mechanics. ***(Figure 5.2c on page 98)***

6. Finish off the bouquet handle, as described on pages 115 and 116.

<u>Cascade Bouquet in a Foam Holder</u>

Cascade bouquets can sometimes be difficult to design in bouquet holders because motion and gravity cause the cascading flowers to fall out of the foam. Lightweight materials can be used to some extent to create a cascade. Other materials can be given added security with the addition of floral adhesive glue to the stem before insertion. An even greater amount of security can be ensured if the cascading portion of the bouquet is constructed with wire and tape and inserted into the bouquet holder, as described in Chapter 4.

Once the cascade is in place, the top of the bouquet can be designed in the same manner, as described for a colonial bouquet in a foam holder. Special care must be taken to blend the cascade with the rest of the design. The diameter of the top should be proportioned to the length and width of the cascade. Matching flowers and colors should be used in order to unify the parts. By wiring and taping only a portion of the flowers in the bouquet, design time can be reduced dramatically.

Figure 5.2c Constructing a Cascade Bouquet Step 5

Colonial Bouquet

The colonial bouquet is a circular design, with strong radiation from a central point, like a daisy. A side view reveals a round sphere. Three methods for designing the colonial bouquet with wire and tape are listed here. Once the style has been mastered with wire and tape, it can easily be created in a foam bouquet holder, as well.

Figure 5.3a Constructing a Colonial Bouquet - Individual Flower Placements Step 2

<u>Individual Flower Placements</u>

1. Wire and tape all flowers and foliage.

2. Tape three wired flowers together in a cluster, making sure that they extend at least 4 inches above the taping point. This creates depth in the center of the bouquet. ***(Figure 5.3a)***

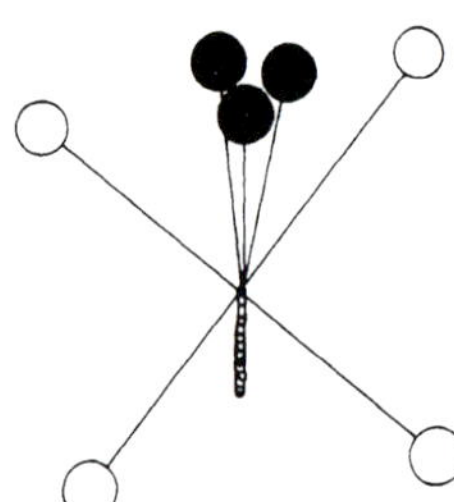

Figure 5.3b Constructing a Colonial Bouquet - Individual Flower Placements Step 3

3. To complete the circular pattern, place four flowers, 4 inches long, to the top, bottom (bent over the thumb and downward), left, and right of the three center flowers. ***(Figure 5.3b)***

4. Add one flower in each of the four quadrants, as illustrated. ***(Figure 5.3c)***

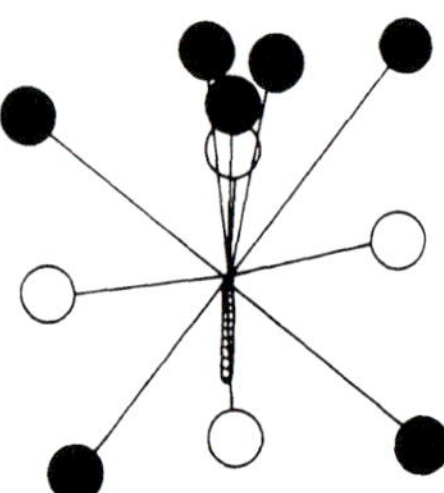

Figure 5.3c Constructing a Colonial Bouquet - Individual Flower Placements Step 4

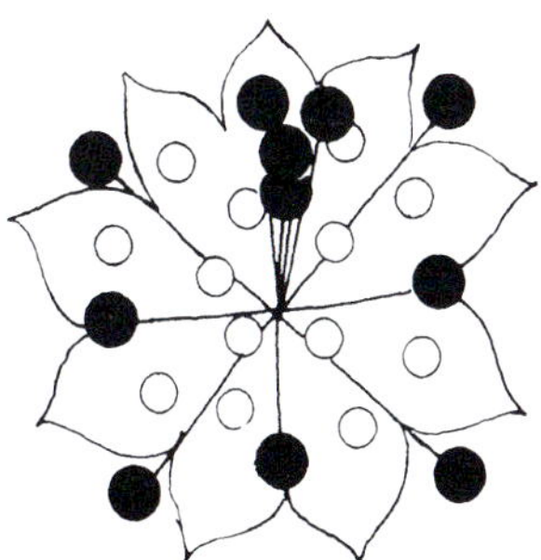

Figure 5.3d Constructing a Colonial Bouquet - Individual Flower Placements Step 5

5. Add foliage and filler flowers between the major flower placements, maintaining a circular shape. ***(Figure 5.3d)***

6. Add foliage around the back of the bouquet to disguise the mechanics.

7. Add ribbon or tulle on taped wires, as desired.

8. Finish the bouquet handle, as described on pages 115 and 116.

Clustering Flower Placements

1. Wire and tape all flowers and foliage.

2. Place all flowers 4 inches from the taping point in a cluster with heads close together.

3. Tape the stems together. ***(Figure 5.4a)***

4. Radiate all flowers out from the cluster to form a circular pattern. ***(Figure 5.4b)***

5. Complete the bouquet following Steps 5 through 8 (above) for individual flower placement for colonial bouquet construction.

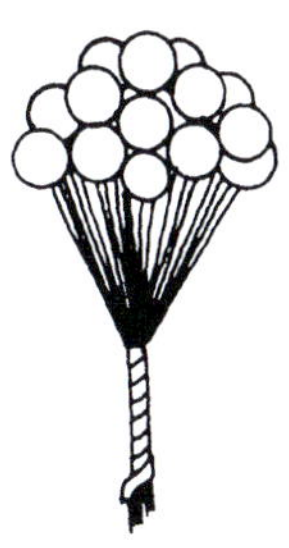

Figure 5.4a Constructing a Colonial Bouquet - Clustering Flower Placements Step 3

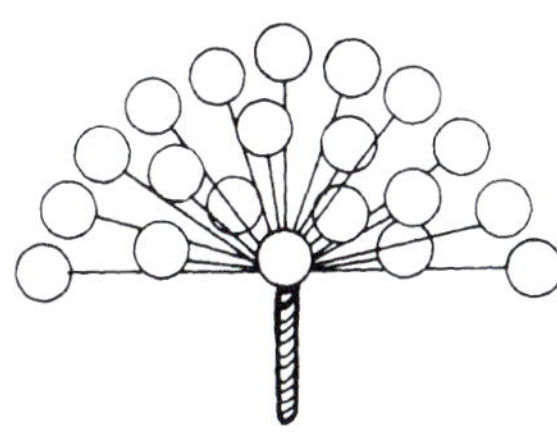

Figure 5.4b Constructing a Colonial Bouquet - Clustering Flower Placements Step 4

Circular Flower Placements

1. Wire and tape all flowers and foliage.

2. Gather three to five flowers together and tape 4 inches below the flower head. This will be the center of the bouquet. ***(Figure 5.5a)***

3. Start adding flowers in circles around the center.

4. Tape at the binding point after the addition of every three or four flowers. ***(Figure 5.5b on page 100)***

5. Continue adding circles until reaching the desired size. ***(Figure 5.5c on page 100)***

6. Add foliage and filler flowers between the major flower placements to soften the ring-like pattern.

Figure 5.5a Constructing a Colonial Bouquet - Circular Flower Placements Step 2

7. Add foliage around the back of the bouquet to disguise the mechanics.

8. Add ribbon or tulle on taped wires, as desired.

9. Finish the bouquet handle, as described on pages 115 and 116.

Figure 5.5b Constructing a Colonial Bouquet - Circular Flower Placements Step 4

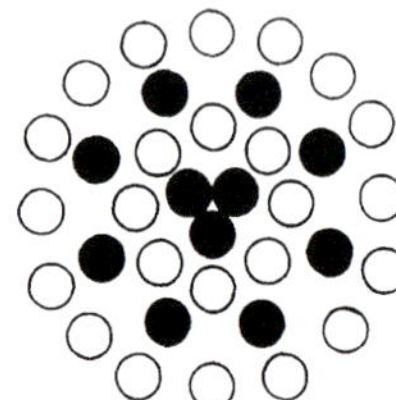
Figure 5.5c Constructing a Colonial Bouquet - Circular Flower Placements Step 5

Colonial Bouquet in a Bouquet Holder

Colonial bouquets and other styles without significant cascades are good choices for designing in foam bouquet holders. They can be constructed quickly and easily with little concern about flowers falling out of the foam. Because the flowers have a water source, they may be designed further in advance.

1. Soak a foam bouquet holder in preservative water and place it in a bouquet stand. (Commercial stands are available, or one can be constructed by securing a 22-inch piece of 1-inch diameter PVC pipe to an 8-inch x 8-inch square wooden base.)

2. Begin by greening the bouquet holder. Place pieces of foliage, such as leatherleaf, all the way around the edge of the holder in a circular pattern. ***(Figure 5.6a)***

3. Insert two or three pieces of foliage into the center of the holder at a length of about 3 inches. ***(Figure 5.6b)***

4. Add foliage between the center and outer placements to cover the mechanics and create a rounded shape. Be sure each stem is placed so that it appears to radiate from a central point. ***(Figure 5.6c)***

5. Add four flowers to the holder to create a plus sign at the perimeter. Each flower should extend slightly beyond the tips of the foliage. ***(Figure 5.6d on page 101)***

6. Insert additional flowers between the four flowers at the perimeter to create a circular outline with the flowers. ***(Figure 5.6e on page 101)***

7. Group three of the largest flowers together in the center of the foam to create a focal point. Vary the

Figure 5.6a Constructing a Colonial Bouquet in a Bouquet Holder Step 2

Figure 5.6b Constructing a Colonial Bouquet in a Bouquet Holder Step 3

Figure 5.6c Constructing a Colonial Bouquet in a Bouquet Holder Step 4

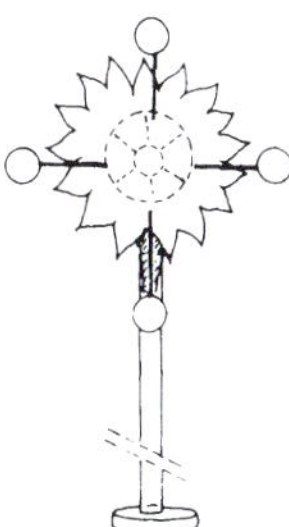

Figure 5.6d Constructing a Colonial Bouquet in a Bouquet Holder Step 5

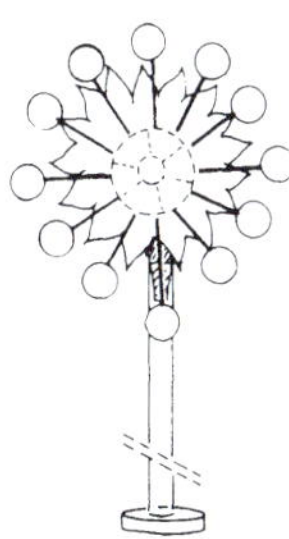

Figure 5.6e Constructing a Colonial Bouquet in a Bouquet Holder Step 6

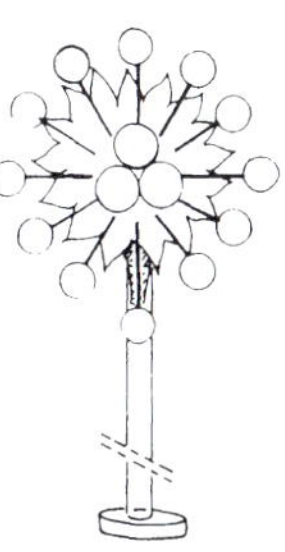

Figure 5.6f Constructing a Colonial Bouquet in a Bouquet Holder Step 7

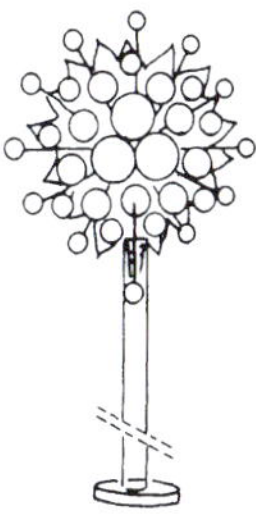

Figure 5.6g Constructing a Colonial Bouquet in a Bouquet Holder Step 9

heights of these flowers to give the design depth. ***(Figure 5.6f)***

8. Add flowers between the center and the side placements to create a rounded form from one side, over the top, and to the other side.

9. Add filler flowers or foliage to soften the overall outline. ***(Figure 5.6g)***

10. If desired, attach a bow and streamers to a wooden pick and insert it into the base of the holder.

Crescent Bouquet

The crescent bouquet is designed with a curved line for a classic, flattering look with a beautiful flow. The design combines elements of the colonial and cascade bouquet styles for fairly simple construction.

1. Design a colonial bouquet.

2. Create two cascades in proportion to the size of the colonial bouquet, as described on page 98. Use materials matching those used in the colonial bouquet. One cascade should be 8 to 10 inches long and will be used as the upper portion of the crescent line. The second cascade may be of any length greater than 10 inches and will form the lower, cascading portion of the crescent.

3. Position the stems of the two cascades on each side of the colonial bouquet handle and tape the three handles together. The tape must be very tight in order to prevent rocking or slipping of the cascades. ***(Figure 5.7a on page 102)***

4. Bend the cascades into position to form the desired crescent line. It is important to make sure the two cascades visually connect into a smooth curved line before proceeding further. ***(Figure 5.7b on page 102)***

5. Add flowers and foliage, as needed, to blend the cascades into the colonial bouquet and unify the design. ***(Figure 5.7c on page 102)***

6. Add foliage to the back of the bouquet to disguise the mechanics.

7. Finish off the bouquet handle, as described on pages 115 and 116.

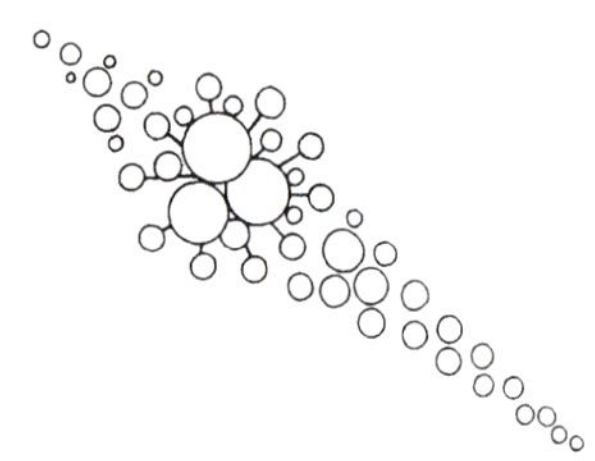

Figure 5.7a Creating a Crescent Bouquet Step 3

Presentation (Arm) Bouquet

The presentation bouquet has grown in popularity. The bouquet looks like a sheath of flowers that is carried over the arm. It is comparable to the type of bouquet presented to the prima ballerina at the end of a ballet. The bouquet is designed with the natural stems remaining on the flowers and offers the advantage of being able to be kept fresh in a vase of water until the wedding.

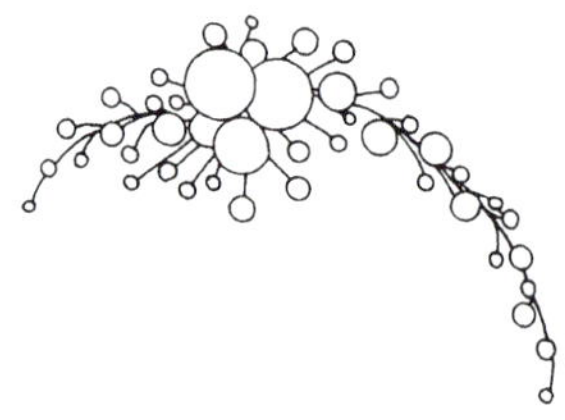

Figure 5.7b Creating a Crescent Bouquet Step 4

1. Select and prepare all flowers and foliage by removing the leaves from the lower two-thirds of the stem. Wire the flowers for control, if necessary.

2. Place the flowers on the design table grouped according to size.

3. Start with three pieces of strong greenery. Lay the three pieces in a fan-like pattern so the foliage overlaps about halfway.

4. Bind the stems at the cross point by wrapping waxed string or #24 gauge paddle wire around the stems three to four times. ***(Figure 5.8a)***

Figure 5.7c Creating a Crescent Bouquet Step 5

5. Add three flowers at different heights of the bouquet and bind them with the same continuous piece of wire or string. ***(Figure 5.8b on page 103)***

6. Continue adding flowers, two or three at a time, to form an elongated triangular shape. After each addition, wrap the binding wire or string around the stems two or three times. It is important to bind the stems continuously at the same point rather than slipping the string or wire gradually down the stems.

Figure 5.8a Creating a Presentation Bouquet Step 4

7. Add foliage to the bouquet after every six or seven flower placements.

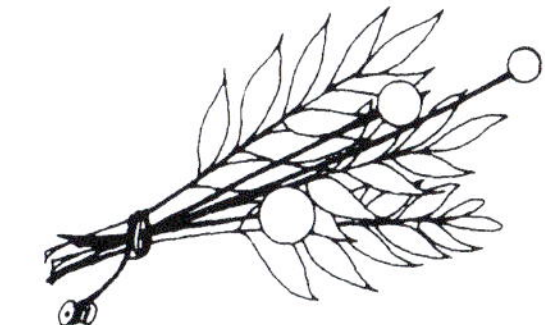

Figure 5.8b Creating a Presentation Bouquet Step 5

Figure 5.8c Creating a Presentation Bouquet Step 8

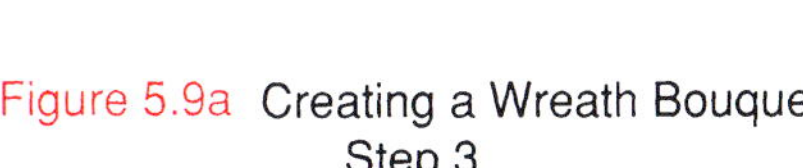

Figure 5.9a Creating a Wreath Bouquet Step 3

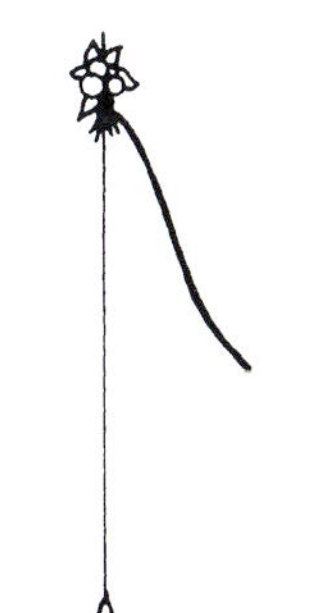

Figure 5.9b Creating a Wreath Bouquet Step 8

8. When the bouquet has reached the desired size and shape, bind the stems three or four more times and tie off the end of the string or wire. ***(Figure 5.8c)***

9. Use 1-inch floral tape to tape over the binding point and disguise the string or wire.

10. Trim the stem ends to varying lengths. The longest stems should be about half the length of the bouquet.

11. Finish the bouquet with a bow and streamers at the binding point, if desired.

Wreath Bouquet

The wreath bouquet is a classic style which traditionally symbolizes the wedding rings. It is usually 10 inches in diameter. A double wreath bouquet is sometimes used for a more dramatic effect by connecting two wreaths of different sizes with the smaller wreath below the larger one. The wreath bouquet can be carried by placing the hand through the wreath and resting the ring on the wrist. Alternatively, it may be carried by grasping the top of the wreath or by grasping an attached ribbon handle.

1. Tape two #20 gauge wires from top to bottom.

2. Tape the two wires together, end to end, with 4 inches of wire overlapped. The resulting wire should be 28 inches long.

3. Bend the top 1 inch of the wire down to form a hook. Tape the end of the hook to the wire to create a small loop. ***(Figure 5.9a)***

4. Gather flowers and foliage into twenty-two small clusters, 3 to 4 inches long.

5. Tape the lower 1 1/2 inches of stems together to secure each cluster.

6. Tape two #28 gauge wires from top to bottom.

7. Tape the two wires together, end to end, with 6 inches of wire overlapped. The resulting wire should be 24 inches long.

8. Starting at the end of the #20 gauge wire opposite the loop, lay clusters of flowers along the wire with stems facing the loop. Bind each cluster to the #20 gauge wire by wrapping the #28 gauge wire around the stems in a spiral motion. ***(Figure 5.9b on page 103)***

9. Continue adding clusters, overlapping the stems of the previous cluster with each addition. ***(Figure 5.9c)***

10. When the clusters reach the end of the wire, add one more cluster in the opposite direction to the rest, bind it into place, and disguise the stems under the foliage. ***(Figure 5.9d)***

11. Bend the decorated wire into a circle and thread the straight end of the wire through the looped end. Bend 1 inch of the straight wire over the loop to secure the ring. ***(Figures 5.9e & 5.9f)***

12. Decorate the wreath with ribbon, bows, and streamers, as desired.

Note: For a different look, the wreath can be designed completely with foliage and accented with a few specialty flowers glued into position.

Figure 5.9c Creating a Wreath Bouquet Step 9

Figure 5.9d Creating a Wreath Bouquet Step 10

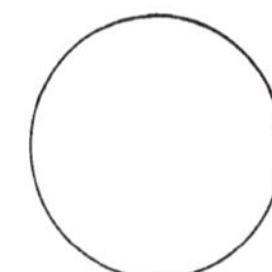

Figure 5.9e Creating a Wreath Bouquet Step 11

Figure 5.9f Creating a Wreath Bouquet Step 11

Bible Bouquet

The Bible has a personal and sacred meaning to the bride who elects to carry one in her wedding. Flowers can be incorporated as a beautiful accent to the Bible. The florist must be careful, however, to attach the flowers securely without harming the book. The following technique for creating a Bible bouquet is recommended.

1. Cut five or six pieces of #3 ribbon and one piece of #9 ribbon into 3-foot lengths.

2. Wire the ribbon together with a #28 gauge wire about two-thirds from the top of the ribbon, creating long and short streamers. ***(Figure 5.10a)***

3. Open the Bible near the center and lay the ribbon in the crease of the book with the wire at the top of the page and the shorter streamers extending over the top of the book. ***(Figure 5.10b on page 105)***

Figure 5.10a Creating a Bible Bouquet Step 2

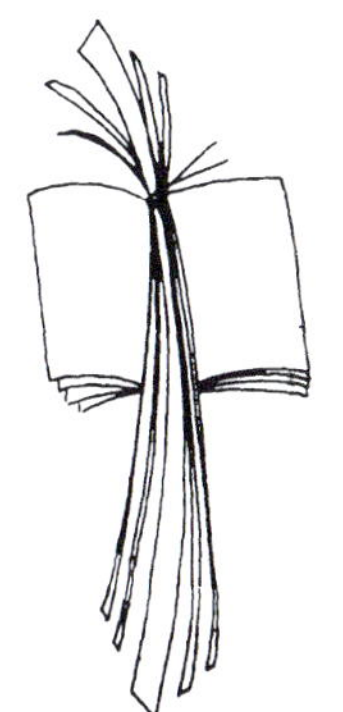

Figure 5.10b Creating a Bible Bouquet Step 3

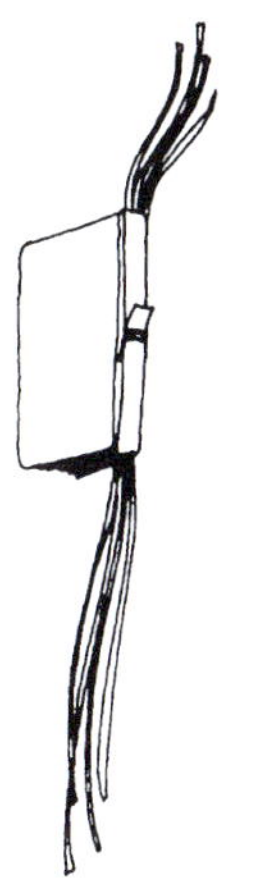

Figure 5.10c Creating a Bible Bouquet Step 4

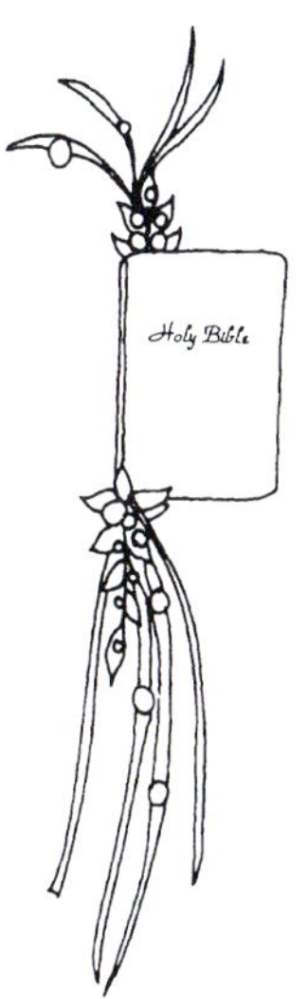

Figure 5.10d Creating a Bible Bouquet Step 8

4. Close the Bible and wrap the #9 ribbon from the bottom of the book around the back and to the top. Tie the long and short #9 ribbons together to secure the streamers to the book. ***(Figure 5.10c)***

5. Design a small and medium corsage-like cluster with wire and tape. Keep the stems as thin and flat as possible.

6. Tie the medium-sized corsage into the Bible with a long #3 streamer. Position the corsage so that its stem is inside the lower edge of the book.

7. Tie the small corsage into the top edge of the Bible in the same way.

8. Tie additional flowers, foliage, and love knots in the streamers to create the illusion of a cascade. ***(Figure 5.10d)***

Note: For small Bibles, a modified version of this bouquet can be styled into an exaggerated wristlet and secured around the book with an elasticized wrist band or chenille stems looped into a figure *8*.

Basket Bouquet

Basket bouquets are most often used as designs for flower girls. However, baskets of various types may be carried by the bride and bridesmaids, as well. They are especially charming when filled with a mixture of old fashioned garden flowers for an informal outdoor wedding.

The basket bouquet may be designed in two different ways. A hand-held basket is designed to be carried with two hands in front of the body. The arm basket is a gathering of flowers laid in a basket that is carried on the forearm to the side of the body.

Hand-Held Basket

1. If the basket does not have a liner, use heavy plastic or green poly-foil to line the bottom and sides.

2. Attach a soaked OASIS® IGLU®, foam cage, or piece of foam wrapped in foil to the basket with pan melt glue or chenille stems crossed over the foam and wired to the basket.

3. Design the basket in an all-around arrangement, but keep the flowers at least 2 inches below the basket handle so it is easy to carry.

4. Add trailing foliage over the edges of the basket on three sides. The fourth side will be the back of the design.

5. Add ribbon loops, bows, and streamers, as desired.

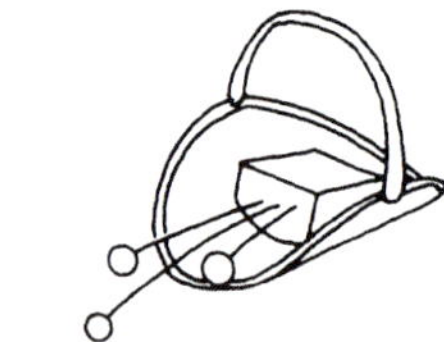

Figure 5.11a Creating an Arm Basket Bouquet Step 3

Arm Baskets

1. Select a shallow or open-ended basket.

2. Secure the mechanics in the basket, as described for the hand-held basket.

Figure 5.11b Creating an Arm Basket Bouquet Step 4

3. Begin designing the basket by inserting flowers horizontally in one end of the floral foam so that they appear to lie in the basket. ***(Figure 5.11a)***

4. Continue adding flowers of different lengths at horizontal to slightly vertical angles, working in toward the center of the foam. The flowers must be kept quite low (about 6 to 7 inches below the handle) in order to leave room for the arm holding the basket. ***(Figure 5.11b)***

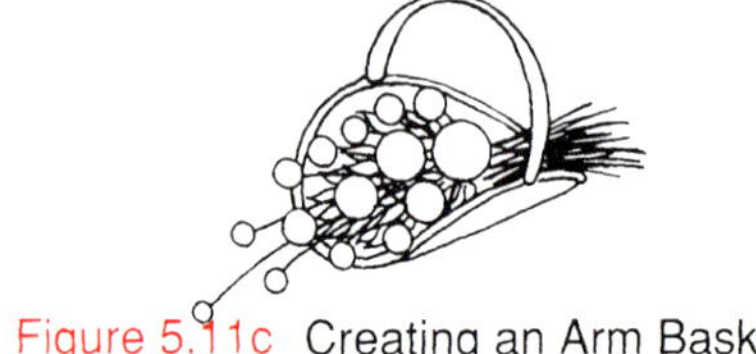

Figure 5.11c Creating an Arm Basket Bouquet Step 6

5. Add foliage between the flowers to cover the mechanics and unify the design. Allow some foliage to trail over the edge of the basket for a cascading effect.

6. Use the pieces of stems cut off the flowers as placements in the opposite end of the foam. Position these stems so that they appear to connect to the flowers right through the foam. ***(Figure 5.11c)***

7. Add small pieces of foliage between the stem placements to cover the mechanics.

8. Add a bow at the point where the flowers and stems meet, giving the appearance of a tied bunch of flowers in the basket. ***(Figure 5.11d)***

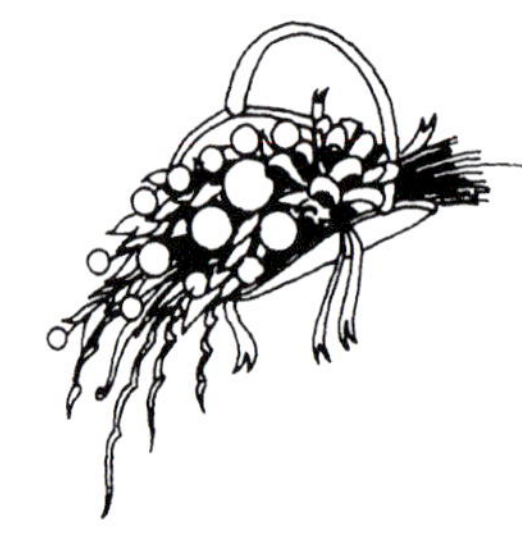

Figure 5.11d Creating an Arm Basket Bouquet Step 8

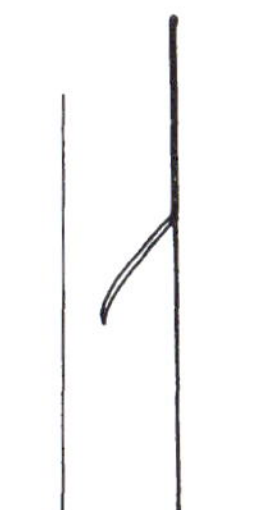

Figure 5.12a Creating a Basquette Bouquet Step 2

Figure 5.12b Creating a Basquette Bouquet Step 3

Figure 5.12c Creating a Basquette Bouquet Step 4

Figure 5.12d Creating a Basquette Bouquet Step 5

Basquette Bouquet

The basquette bouquet appears to be a petite basket of delicate flowers; however, no basket is used in its construction. Although this style may be created with wired and taped materials, construction is made less complicated and time consuming by using a foam bouquet holder. This style may be carried by any member of the bridal party, but it is most appropriate for the flower girl.

1. Tape three #18 gauge wires from top to bottom with floral tape.

2. Wrap each wire with #3 ribbon by taping the ribbon to one end, wrapping the ribbon around the wire in the same way as if taping (making sure to overlap the ribbon and cover the wire), and taping the end of the ribbon to the bottom of the wire. ***(Figure 5.12a)***

   Note: The three wires may be wrapped all in the same color ribbon or with three different colors.

3. Tape the three wires together at one end. Tape about 1 inch down. ***(Figure 5.12b)***

4. Weave the three wires into a loose braid. Tape the last 1 inch of the ends together. ***(Figure 5.12c)***

5. Bend the braid into a loop and tape the ends together. ***(Figure 5.12d)***

   Note: A pearl band, intended for use as a headpiece, can be used in place of the braided wires.

6. Clip the handle from a foam bouquet holder.

7. Dip the taped end of the braided loop into hot melt glue and insert it into the top side of the foam bouquet holder. Allow the glue to dry several hours or overnight. ***(Figure 5.12e on page 108)***

8. Soak the bouquet holder in preservative water without wetting the braided handle.

9. Lightly green the bouquet holder to cover the mechanics.

10. Use a trailing foliage, such as ivy, to create the cascading lines of the bouquet. Extend two or three pieces of varying lengths from each side in a downward arch. Then add four or five stems at the lower front edge of the holder in a "waterfall" angle. ***(Figure 5.12f)***

Figure 5.12e Creating a Basquette Bouquet Step 7

11. Follow the cascading foliage placements with shorter placements of petite flowers at similar angles.

12. Continue adding flowers to the holder to develop the bouquet shape. Remember the overall design is that of a basket brimming with flowers. ***(Figure 5.12g)***

13. Add filler and additional foliage, as needed, to complete the design.

Figure 5.12f Creating a Basquette Bouquet Step 10

Fan Bouquet

Fans may be decorated simply or lavishly for use as a bouquet. Generally, fans which are heavily embellished or intricately detailed require only a simple floral accent. Unadorned fans may be enhanced more extensively with flowers. In either case, it is important not to cover the shape or the design of the fan. A crescent-shaped design is often the most effective style with which to decorate a fan. Two different construction methods are used to create a fan bouquet depending on the type of fan used. ***(Figure 5.13 on page 109)***

Keepsake Fan Bouquet

This method is used when the bride provides her own fan for the design. It allows the flowers to be removed and the fan to be saved after the wedding.

1. Construct an exaggerated crescent corsage in proportion to the size of the fan. The lower portion of the crescent may be lengthened to create a cascade, if desired.

2. Keep the stem thin and flat as the corsage is constructed. Trim the stem of the completed corsage to 1 inch in length.

Figure 5.12g Creating a Basquette Bouquet Step 12

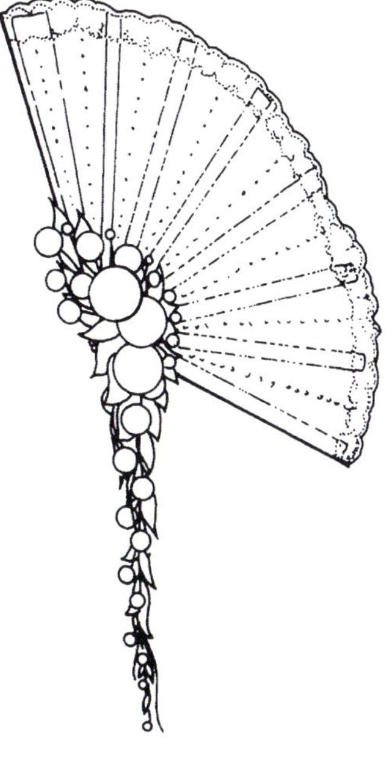

Figure 5.13 Fan Bouquet

3. Position the corsage at the base of the fan and align the center of the corsage with the center point of the fan.

4. Use corsage pins to attach the corsage to the fan, starting at the outermost corners, and working in to the center. Weave each pin through the fan, over a corsage stem and throughout the fan again. The point of the pin should be end up on the front side of the fan.

5. Cover the point of each corsage pin with a small (pea size) ball of floral tape to prevent scratching. ***(Figure 5.13)***

Fan with Foam Bouquet Holder

Several types of specially designed lace fans are available with attachable foam bouquet holders. These allow for a more elaborate use of flowers and also provide handles with which to hold the bouquets.

1. Soak the foam bouquet holder in preservative water.

2. Dry the plastic cage and attach the bouquet holder to the fan. (Follow assembly directions on the package.)

3. Lightly green the bouquet holder to cover the mechanics.

4. Establish the crescent lines of the bouquet using a naturally arching foliage, such as sprengeri. If an extended cascade is desired on the lower portion of the crescent, the cascade should be wired, taped, and attached to the bouquet holder, as explained in Chapter 4.

5. Group three focal flowers, such as cymbidium orchids, in the center of the bouquet holder.

6. Add a flower at the top and the bottom edges of the bouquet holder to establish the width of the crescent. These placements will typically extend only 1 to 2 inches beyond the holder.

7. Follow the crescent lines of the foliage with flower placements. Flowers should decrease in size and be spaced further apart as they extend from the focal point.

8. Fill in the crescent outline with flowers.

9. Add filler and additional foliage, as needed.

Muffs

Muffs are usually carried in the winter. They can be carried in formal or informal weddings. The muff may be purchased or made of velvet, tapestry, or satin.

The muff is best suited to a crescent-style decoration. This bouquet is constructed in the same manner as the fan decoration. An exaggerated crescent corsage is designed and pinned or sewn to the muff. The crescent may be placed either in the front, center position, or allowed to curve up over the top of the muff. A decorated muff is shown in ***Figure 5.14***.

Figure 5.14 Decorated Muff

Parasols

Decorated parasols are sometimes carried instead of a traditional bouquet. They may be carried either open or closed and are most often used for garden weddings. Construction of these designs is relatively simple. Most often, decorations are styled in cluster-like corsages and attached to the parasol in one of the following ways.

- Secure the decorations to the parasol with corsage pins.
- Tie the decorations onto a lace parasol with narrow ribbon woven through the openings in the lace.
- Tape the decorations to the inner spokes of the parasol with floral tape.
- Sew the decorations onto the parasol.

An alternative to the corsage-style construction of parasol decorations is the use of floral adhesive glue. Flowers and foliage may be glued to ribbon in small clusters. The ribbon is then tied to the parasol in the desired position. The following list suggests a variety of ways in which decorations might be designed on a parasol.

Figure 5.15 Decorated Parasol

Decorating on the Outside of an Open Parasol

- Floral clusters at the end of each spoke with a matching ring of flowers at the center point.
- Floral crescents connecting the end of one spoke to the next.
- A floral cluster in the center of the parasol with a shower of foliage and ribbons down the back. ***(Figure 5.15)***

Decorating on the Inside of an Open Parasol

- Ribbons or garlands of foliage spiralled around the inner spokes.
- Floral clusters at the end of each spoke with a larger, matching cluster in the center.
- A floral cluster at the center with a foliage garland spiralled down the handle.

Decorating on the Outside of a Closed Parasol

- An *S*-curved floral piece along one side of the parasol.
- A garland of flowers and foliage spiralled around the parasol from the tip to handle.
- A cluster of flowers at the top of the parasol with ribbons and foliage spiralled up the handle.

Posey Drop Bouquet

The posey drop bouquet is a unique design consisting of three connected nosegays. This bouquet has a dramatic effect when carried with the proper dress style, such as a ball gown. It is generally considered a youthful style most appropriate for young brides or bridesmaids.

1. Construct three colonial bouquets - small, medium, and large. When taping the stems into each bouquet, tape only at the top of the stem so the individual stems are free. Trim the ends of the stems in proportion to the size of the bouquet.

2. Tape three #18 gauge wires from top to bottom with green floral tape.

3. Bend the top inch of two of the wires down to form a hook. ***(Figure 5.16a)***

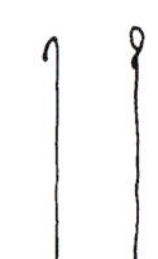

Figure 5.16a Creating a Posey Drop Bouquet Step 3

4. Tape the end of the hook to the wire to form a small loop.

5. Insert the one remaining straight wire into the center of the large colonial bouquet until the end is deeply enough within the flowers that it cannot be seen. ***(Figure 5.16b)***

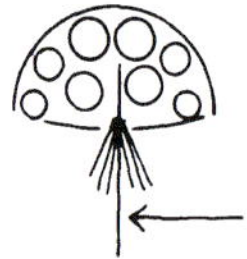

Figure 5.16b Creating a Posey Drop Bouquet Step 5

6. Tape the wire tightly to the bouquet stem.

7. Insert the two prepared wires into the small and medium bouquets so that the loops are just below the flowers. ***(Figure 5.16c)***

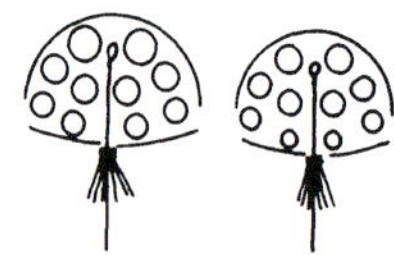

Figure 5.16c Creating a Posey Drop Bouquet Step 7

8. Tape the wires tightly to the bouquet stems.

9. The end of each #18 gauge wire should extend a few inches beyond the rest of the bouquet stems. Hold the large bouquet above the medium one and slip the end of the #18 gauge wire through the loop of the #18 gauge wire in the medium bouquet.

10. Pull the wire through the loop until the medium bouquet hangs 4 to 5 inches below the large bouquet. ***(Figure 5.16d)***

11. Twist the end of the #18 gauge wire around itself to secure the attachment and trim any excess wire.

12. Repeat Steps 9 through 11 to connect the small bouquet below the medium one. ***(Figure 5.16d)***

13. Ribbon streamers may be attached at the binding point of each bouquet to help disguise the connecting wires and give the appearance that the bouquets are hanging by the ribbons. ***(Figure 5.16e on page 113)***

Figure 5.16d Creating a Posey Drop Bouquet Steps 10 and 12

Biedermeier Bouquet

The Biedermeier is a round bouquet style designed with flowers tightly patterned into concentric rings of color and/or flower type. The shape is very similar to the colonial bouquet, but

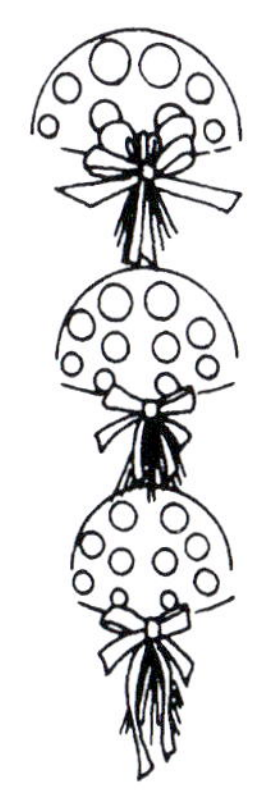

Figure 5.16e Creating a Posey Drop Bouquet Step 13

it is more dome-shaped with the center flowers a bit longer for greater depth. The bouquet is also carried in a more upright position than a colonial bouquet.

The Biedermeier may be constructed with wire and tape or in a foam bouquet holder. In contrast to some methods of constructing a colonial bouquet, the Biedermeier style is constructed by clustering a group of flowers in the center first. Then an outline of flowers is created to form the perimeter of the bouquet. Flowers are placed one directly against another, eliminating space, in order to create a solid rounded outline. Once the height and width of the bouquet have been established, the rest of the design is created one ring at a time, working from the center cluster to the outer perimeter.

Each ring should be clearly defined. The use of foliage or filler flowers between the rings helps differentiate the pattern. Individual rings may be created with one type of flower or with a patterned placement of two to three different flowers. Distinction between rings is most easily achieved by a contrast in color. Combining textures, by adding berries, seed pods, or other unique materials, also helps create visual separation, as well as providing more interest to the bouquet.

Figure 5.17 Clutch Bouquet

Clutch Bouquet

The clutch bouquet is a casual gathering of flowers tied with ribbon or string for a "garden-picked" appearance. It is similar to the hand-tied presentation bouquet styles but has a looser, less formal shape. Although the bouquet is typically designed with flowers on natural stems, wired and taped materials may also be used. The key is to create a bouquet with a light, open appearance and a feeling of motion. In contrast to hand-tied or presentation bouquets, the clutch bouquet is usually carried casually to the side of the body. ***(Figure 5.17)***

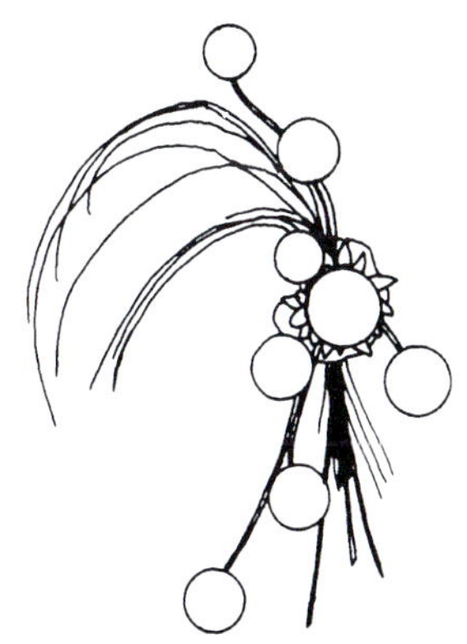

Figure 5.18 European Contemporary Bouquet

European Contemporary Bouquet

The European contemporary bouquet is a modern style with an upright thrust and an emphasis on strong lines and minimal flower placements. Unique botanical specimens are typically used at the focal area of the design. Exotic foliage often replaces massed flowers at the perimeter. Open space and a less obvious geometric outline are key ingredients of this style. It may be designed with natural-stemmed flowers, wired and taped blossoms, or a foam bouquet holder. The dramatic, contemporary styling of this bouquet makes it best suited for use with sheath or mermaid style gowns. ***(Figure 5.18)***

Hand-Tied Bouquet

Notes

The hand-tied bouquet style is created by utilizing flowers and foliage on their natural stems. The fresh materials are tied together with waxed string or another binding material to create a rounded shape. The finished bouquet has a flared appearance. Like the presentation bouquet, this style may be designed well in advance and kept fresh in a vase of water.

Two common methods are used to create the hand-tied bouquet. Both require practice in order to achieve the desired shape and appearance.

Dutch Spiral Technique

1. Assemble a collection of mixed, long-stemmed flowers and foliage and remove the leaves from the lower half of the stems.

2. Begin by holding the flowers 6 to 8 inches down the stems in a crisscrossed manner.

3. Tie a piece of waxed string to the flowers and wrap it around the stems two or three times.

4. Add the next flowers around the first placements so that the stems follow the same direction. Bind them into place with the waxed string after the addition of every two or three stems. The stems should begin to create a spiral pattern with each flower positioned at an angle.

5. Add flowers and foliage working from the center to the perimeter of the bouquet until reaching the desired size.

6. Tie the ends of the waxed string tightly together.

7. Finish the design with a bow and ribbon wrapped around the binding point, if desired.

German Nesting Technique

1. Assemble a collection of mixed long-stemmed flowers and foliage and remove the leaves from the lower half of the stems.

Notes

2. Begin with a base foliage, such as leatherleaf. Form a circle with the fingers and thumb of one hand and insert three or four stems of the fern at angles into the circle, as if it were a vase.

3. Add flowers in the same manner, as if designing a vase arrangement.

4. Add foliage as needed for support around the flowers. Moss may also be inserted deep into the bouquet to form a supporting nest which helps separate and hold stems in the desired positions.

5. Continue adding flowers and foliage until the bouquet reaches the desired size.

6. Use waxed string to tie the flowers together where they are joined in the hand.

7. Finish the bouquet with ribbon, as desired.

Finishing a Wired and Taped Bouquet Handle

Bouquets constructed with wired and taped materials will have a wire handle created by the excess wires extending below the binding point of the bouquet. Depending on the size of the bouquet, this handle may be too thick or too thin to be held comfortably. As a general rule, a bouquet handle should be approximately 1 inch in diameter at the top (about the size of a quarter) and gently taper to a rounded end.

A handle which is too thick may have wires clipped from it to reduce bulk. This may also be done during the construction process as stems are added to the bouquet. A bouquet handle which is too thin may be thickened by wrapping narrow strips of tissue paper around it and then taping the tissue into place with a covering of floral tape. This technique may also be used to soften a handle with awkward wire ends poking through the tape.

When the wire handle is ready to be finished, the wires should be smoothed into a straight line and trimmed. In order to trim the handle to the proper length, grip the handle in a fist-like manner with one hand and trim the wires 1 to 2 inches below the fist. (A designer with hands smaller or larger than an average woman's hand should make appropriate adjustments.) Use wire cutters to trim the handle, clipping only two or three wires at a time to avoid a difficult, uneven cut. The finished handle should be 5 to 6 inches in length.

Tape the trimmed handle from top to bottom, making sure to cover the wire ends thoroughly. Satin ribbon is then used to cover the tape in the following manner ***(Figure 5.19)***.

1. Use the ribbon with the finished side outward.

2. Begin about 2 inches from the end of the handle.

3. Align the ribbon with the handle at a 45-degree angle toward the handle's end. Begin wrapping the ribbon tightly around the handle downward toward the end. Overlap the ribbon about halfway as it is wrapped. ***(Figure 5.19a)***

4. Continue wrapping the ribbon about 1 inch beyond the end of the handle, creating a small tube. ***(Figure 5.19b)***

5. Bend the tube up over the handle's end and begin wrapping the ribbon around the handle in the reverse direction toward the top. Make sure to catch the folded tube in the wrapping to ensure a finished handle end.

6. Continue wrapping to the top of the handle. ***(Figure 5.19c)***

7. Make a loose loop around the top and feed the end of the ribbon through the loop. Pull the end of the ribbon tight to create a knot. ***(Figure 5.19d)***

8. Insert a small corsage pin at an angle into the center of the knot and up into the bouquet to secure the knot in place. Make sure the pin does not go through the handle. ***(Figure 5.19e)***

9. Trim the ribbon end.

10. A bow may be tied around the top of the handle for an added touch.

Figure 5.19a Ribbon Wrapping a Bouquet Holder Step 3

Figure 5.19b Ribbon Wrapping a Bouquet Holder Step 4

Figure 5.19c Ribbon Wrapping a Bouquet Holder Step 6

Figure 5.19d Ribbon Wrapping a Bouquet Holder Step 7

Figure 5.19e Ribbon Wrapping a Bouquet Holder Step 8

Bouquet Accessories

Some brides choose to incorporate non-floral accessories into bouquets, either for themselves or for their bridesmaids. Often

Notes

these items become wedding keepsakes which are cherished for years to come. Some suggestions are:

- Potpourri sachets wired into the center of a bouquet or tied to ribbon streamers.
- Pearl strands, loops, and sprays inserted throughout a bouquet or in the center of focal flowers, such as gladiola florets or cymbidium orchids.
- Fruit, such as grape clusters or lemon slices picked, glued, or wired into the bouquet.
- Bridal purse or money pouch tied to the bouquet handle.
- Candles with hurricanes incorporated into bouquets using specially designed candle bouquet holders.
- Beaded wires formed into heart shapes extending above and framing the bouquet.
- Tulle loops and puffs of various sizes inserted throughout the bouquet.
- Feathers, shells, nuts, floating butterflies, or millimeter balls picked, wired, or glued into the bouquet.
- Handkerchief incorporated as a decoration in the bouquet or inserted into the back of the bouquet to be used by the bride.

Carrying Wedding Bouquets

Traditional wedding bouquet styles, such as colonials, cascades, and crescents, are designed to be carried in front of the body. These bouquet styles should be carried with two hands slightly below waist level to avoid covering intricate gown detailing. The arms should hang comfortably with a slight bend at the elbows. A simple way to explain this positioning to the bridal party is to tell them to keep their thumbs just below the navel.

A well balanced bouquet should naturally remain upright in the hands; however, the bridal party may need to be reminded not to let the bouquet tip forward. Bouquets designed in foam

Notes

bouquet holders are sometimes heavier than wired and taped bouquets due to the water held in the foam. This can make holding them in the proper position more awkward. (If necessary, the bridal party can be instructed to hold the handle of the foam bouquet holder with the thumb, pinkie, and ring finger on the back side of the handle and the index and middle fingers on the front side of the handle.) An alternative way to make the foam bouquet holder more comfortable to carry is to design the bouquet with the bouquet holder in an inverted position. When designed in this way, the bouquet handle is grasped in a fist-like manner.

Presentation bouquets are designed to be carried to the side of the body in the crook of the arm. Large, full presentation bouquets may lie directly on the arm in a cradled manner, while smaller, less formal presentation bouquets might be carried along the arm in a more upright position. The bouquet should be grasped at the binding point, and a second hand may rest comfortably along the stems.

If the attendants are escorted down the aisle during the wedding ceremony, the presentation bouquet is carried on the left arm. If the attendants enter alone, the presentation bouquet should be carried on the right arm so that the flowers are visible while the attendants stand at the altar.

Hand-tied or clutch bouquets may be carried in one of three ways. The bouquet may be held in front of the body in the traditionally formal style. More informally, the bouquet can be grasped in one hand and held casually to the side with the arm hanging almost straight down. For an abundant bouquet of this type, the bouquet may also be carried under the arm, with the flowers facing forward and the stems pointing toward the back. The arm curves loosely around the bouquet and the hand is cupped underneath the bouquet for support. The bouquet's position should be somewhere between waist and hip level. This manner of presentation is an English style often used for garden weddings.

The colonial, cascade, crescent, wreath, and presentation bouquet styles have been and will continue to be popular because they express a timeless beauty. They also may be tailored to suit any client by using special decorations or unusual flowers. Novelty styles may be chosen by some brides to evoke a particular mood, as in the case of a Bible bouquet. The novelty designs also may be used by any member of the wedding party to emphasize the season of, or setting for, the wedding. Advanced

Notes

bouquet styles, such as the modern hand-tied or European contemporary, may be used to make a statement of uniqueness. These bouquets may be designed to create a trendy or distinguished theme. No matter what type of bouquet is chosen, the florist should know how it is to be carried and how to assist the customer with this information.

Notes, Photographs, Sketches, Etc.

Notes, Photographs, Sketches, Etc.

Corsages, Boutonnieres, and Floral Fashion Accents

Flowers are worn in weddings as accessories to the bridal party's attire. These floral fashion accessories are worn on the shoulder, wrist, waist, in the hair, or attached to a personal item, such as a purse. To create the most effective body flowers, the florist should coordinate the style of each floral piece with the color and style of the wedding attire. Whenever possible, the flowers should also be designed with the personality of the wearer in mind. For example, a typically conservative mother of the bride wearing a tailored suit would most likely prefer a simple cymbidium orchid corsage rather than an ornate cattleya orchid with an abundance of ribbon and tulle. It is important to remember that the flowers are accessories designed to complement an outfit, not compete with it.

Boutonnieres

"Boutonniere" is a French word meaning buttonhole. The boutonniere is a flower to be worn in the buttonhole of a man's jacket. Since many suit coats no longer have buttonholes, the boutonniere is typically pinned on the lapel.

The boutonniere is intended to be small and simple. It may be a single flower or a cluster of two or three small flowers with filler and foliage backing. When the boutonniere is designed larger than this, it begins to look like a corsage. Occasionally, customers will request a bow on a boutonniere. Generally, bows are used only on corsages. However, ribbon may be used to wrap the boutonniere stem using the same technique as that used to wrap a bouquet handle. The ribbon may be chosen to match the flowers or to blend with the color of the man's attire. Another popular boutonniere finish is the garden stem, in which the flowers are taped into the design at a single binding point. Individual wires are then spread out to give the look of flower stems. ***(Figure 6.1)***

Figure 6.1 Garden Stem

A number of boutonnieres are usually needed for the wedding party. These include the groom's, groomsmen's, ushers', ring bearer's, fathers', grandfathers', and minister's boutonnieres. To unify the wedding look, and simplify the process of distributing the flowers, the boutonnieres for most of the wedding party are often designed alike. However, the groom's boutonniere is usually made differently from the rest and is coordinated to match the bride's bouquet. The colors and flowers in the bridesmaid's bouquet typically dictate the boutonniere style for the male attendants.

Single Flower Boutonniere

The single flower boutonniere is frequently chosen for members of the wedding party. Roses and carnations are two of the most commonly requested flowers for this design. Medium-sized flowers are most desirable for single flower boutonnieres. Smaller flowers are better used in clusters. Large flowers are usually avoided to prevent a corsage-like appearance. ***(Figure 6.2)***

Figure 6.2 Single Flower Boutonniere

1. Wire and tape a single flower, such as a rose, and a single broad leaf, such as a camellia leaf.

2. Place the leaf behind the flower so that the tip of the leaf extends about 1/2 inch above the flower.

3. Tape the stems of the flower and leaf together.

4. Trim the stem to a length of 1 1/2 to 2 inches.

Three Flower Boutonniere

The three flower boutonniere is often used for the groom. Generally, all of the flowers used in this type of design are small so that the finished design is not too large.

1. Wire and tape three small flowers, such as stephanotis, and three small leaves, such as ivy.

2. Begin with the smallest flower in a vertical position. Place the second flower about halfway below the first

Figure 6.3a Constructing a Three Flower Boutonniere Step 2

Figure 6.3b Constructing a Three Flower Boutonniere Step 3

Figure 6.3c Constructing a Three Flower Boutonniere Step 4

Figure 6.3d Constructing a Three Flower Boutonniere Step 6

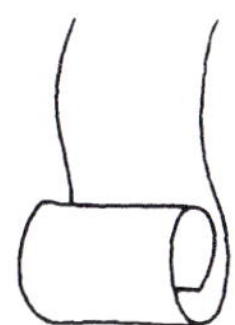

Figure 6.4a Constructing a Bow Step 1

and angle it slightly to the left. Tape the two stems together. ***(Figure 6.3a)***

3. Position the third flower about halfway below the second flower and angle it slightly to the right. Tape the flower to the boutonniere stem. ***(Figure 6.3b)***
4. Position a leaf behind the first flower so that the tip extends about 1/2 inch beyond the flower. Tape the leaf to the stem. ***(Figure 6.3c)***
5. Arch the two remaining leaves slightly, using the wire stitched through the leaf.
6. Position one leaf behind each of the remaining flowers and allow the leaves to arch to the left and right following the angle of the flowers. Tape the leaves to the stem. ***(Figure 6.3d)***
7. Add wired pieces of filler, such as baby's breath, between the flower placements, as desired.
8. Trim the boutonniere stem to a length of 1 1/2 to 2 inches.

How to Construct a Bow

Bows may be constructed in a number of ways. Corsage and bouquet bows are typically designed with #3 or smaller ribbon. The six loop bow is a standard florist bow; however, this bow can be made larger or smaller by increasing or decreasing the number of loops. Ribbon typically has a top side and an under side. For example, satin ribbon is usually shiny on one side and dull on the other. When designing a bow with two-sided ribbon, the ribbon must be twisted after each loop is made in order for the tops of the loops to be shiny.

1. Hold the end of a length of #3 ribbon between the thumb and index finger of the left hand. ***(Figure 6.4a)***
2. Use the ribbon to make a loop around the thumb and grasp the ribbon between the thumb and index finger. Be sure the shiny side of the ribbon is on the outside of the loop. ***(Figure 6.4b on page 126)***

3. Gather or pleat the ribbon between the thumb and finger.

4. Give the free end of the ribbon a half twist at the base of the loop to reverse the ribbon to the opposite side (from the dull side to the shiny side). ***(Figure 6.4c)***

5. Make a 2-inch loop by folding the ribbon over backward and gathering the ribbon between the thumb and index finger. ***(Figure 6.4d)***

6. Repeat Steps 4 and 5 on the opposite side of the bow to make a matching loop.

7. Make two more loops on each side in the same manner. ***(Figure 6.4e)***

8. Make one more half twist of the ribbon and form a large (3-inch to 4-inch) loop. ***(Figure 6.4f)***

9. Insert a #24 gauge wire or chenille stem through the center loop and tightly twist it behind the bow to secure the loops in place. ***(Figure 6.4g on page 127)***

10. Cut the large loop in half to form streamers. ***(Figure 6.4h on page 127)***

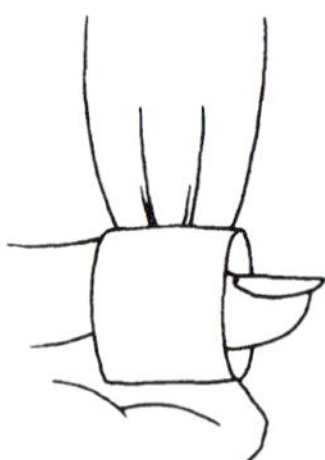

Figure 6.4b Constructing a Bow Step 2

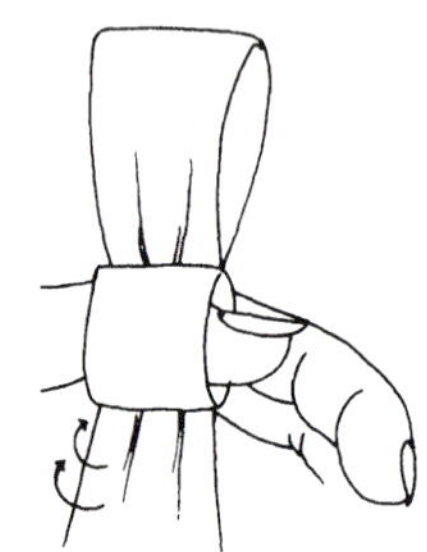

Figure 6.4c Constructing a Bow Step 4

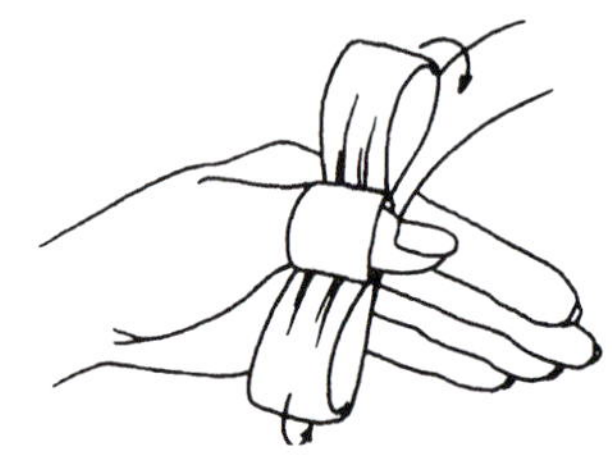

Figure 6.4d Constructing a Bow Step 5

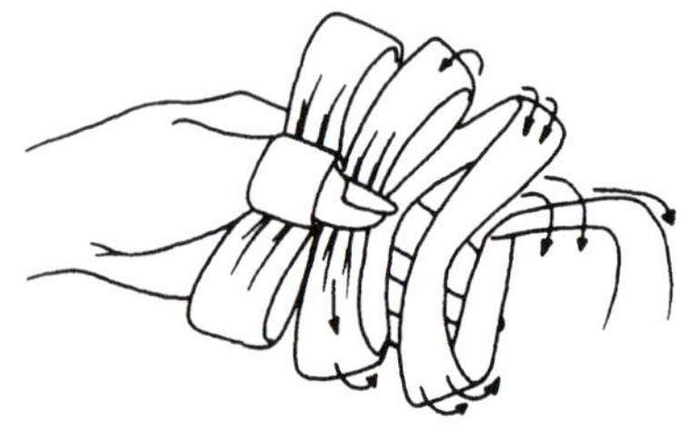

Figure 6.4e Constructing a Bow Step 7

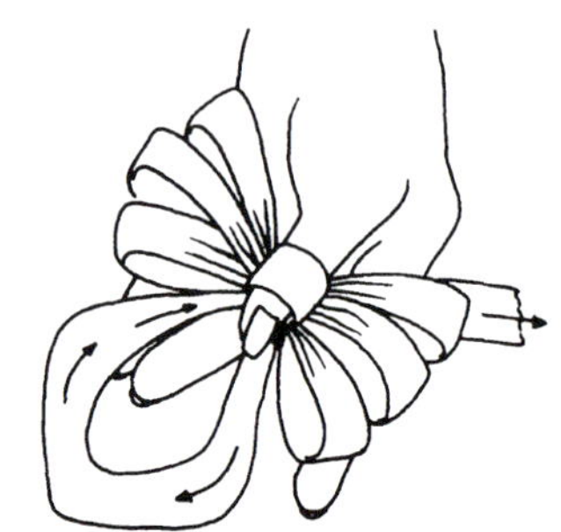

Figure 6.4f Constructing a Bow Step 8

Corsages

Corsages are traditionally designed to be worn on the shoulder; however, fashions sometimes make this a difficult place to pin a flower. Strapless gowns and sheer fabrics prevent the use of shoulder corsages altogether. Instead, women often opt for corsages worn at the waist or on the wrist. The florist can be most helpful in suggesting an appropriate corsage style if the client brings in the dress or a swatch of the fabric.

Corsages should always be designed to be as lightweight as possible in order to make them more comfortable to wear. This means using the most lightweight wire possible for every component in the design. The corsages can also be made lighter by limiting the number of flower placements in the design. Each flower should be given enough space so that it maintains its own identity. A well constructed corsage worn appropriately on a gown is a powerful, walking advertisement for the florist.

The flowers most often used in corsages are carnations, roses, gladiolus blossoms, chrysanthemums, alstroemeria,

Figure 6.4g Constructing a Bow Step 9

Figure 6.4h Constructing a Bow Step 10

Figure 6.5 Single Flower Corsage

Figure 6.6a Designing a Triangular Corsage Step 2

gardenias, and orchids. Common orchid varieties include cattleya, cymbidium, phalaenopsis, and dendrobium.

Single Flower Corsage

The single flower corsage is a popular design for wedding assistants or participants, such as the hostess or soloist. It may be designed simply by constructing a single flower boutonniere and adding a bow. Construction steps for a slightly more decorative single flower corsage follow. ***(Figure 6.5)***

1. Wire and tape a single flower and three pieces of foliage. Carnations, camellias, gardenias, and orchids are the flowers most often selected to make a single flower corsage.

2. Place one leaf behind the flower so that the tip of the leaf extends about 1/2 inch above the flower. Tape the two stems together.

3. Arch the two remaining leaves slightly, using the wires stitched through the leaves.

4. Position one leaf to the left and one leaf to the right of the flower. Tape the leaves to the stem.

5. Add wired pieces of filler around the flower, as desired.

6. Add a bow at the base of the flower.

7. Trim the corsage stem to a length of about 2 inches.

Triangular Corsage

The triangular corsage typically incorporates a variety of small flowers. Foliage and filler material are used to soften the lines and provide relief from a strict geometric appearance. This style is a popular choice for mothers and grandmothers of the bride and groom.

1. Wire and tape seven to nine small flowers and six or seven pieces of foliage.

2. Hold a single, small flower in a vertical position and place a second flower just below it, so that the two overlap slightly. Tape the two stems together. ***(Figure 6.6a)***

3. Design two more units of two flowers each, as instructed in Step 2.

4. Create a triangular shape by positioning one of the three units vertically, a second one sideways to the left, and the third unit downward and to the right (bent over the thumb). Tape the three stems together. ***(Figure 6.6b)***

Figure 6.6b Designing a Triangular Corsage Step 4

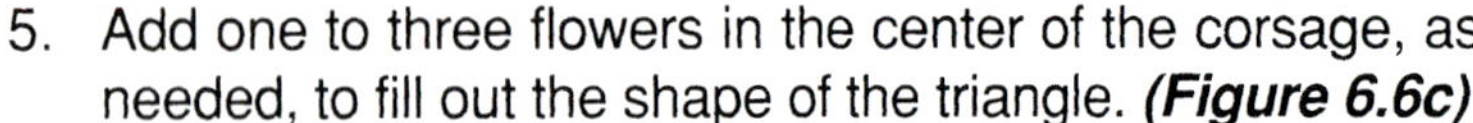

5. Add one to three flowers in the center of the corsage, as needed, to fill out the shape of the triangle. ***(Figure 6.6c)***

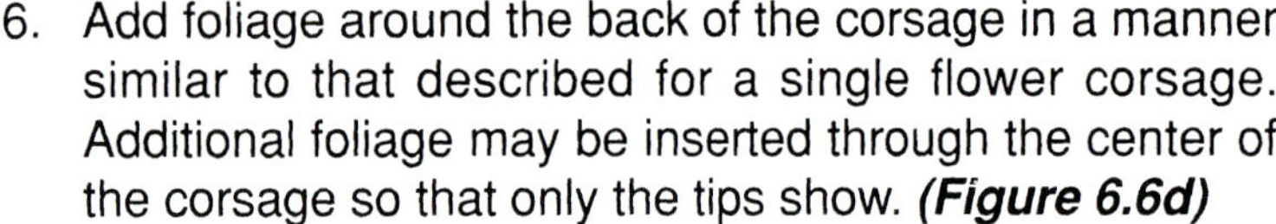

6. Add foliage around the back of the corsage in a manner similar to that described for a single flower corsage. Additional foliage may be inserted through the center of the corsage so that only the tips show. ***(Figure 6.6d)***

7. Add filler flowers, if desired.

8. Attach a bow at the base of the triangle.

9. Trim the corsage stem to a length of about 2 inches. ***(Figure 6.6e)***

Figure 6.6c Designing a Triangular Corsage Step 5

Crescent Corsage

The crescent corsage has a soft, curved line which lends a gentle, feminine quality to the design. The curve of the corsage may be styled in either direction but is particularly flattering when curved inward toward the face.

Figure 6.6d Designing a Triangular Corsage Step 6

1. Wire and tape six to eight small flowers and six or seven pieces of foliage.

2. Create two 2-flower units, as described in Step 2 of the triangular corsage instructions.

3. Position one unit vertically and the second one downward and to the right (bent over the thumb). Tape the two units together. ***(Figure 6.7a on page 129)***

4. Add two or three focal flowers in the center between the two units. ***(Figure 6.7b on page 129)***

5. Use additional flowers to connect the center flowers to the end points in a crescent shape. ***(Figure 6.7c on page 129)***

Figure 6.6e Designing a Triangular Corsage Step 9

Figure 6.7a Designing a Crescent Corsage Step 3

6. Add foliage around the back of the corsage so that the tips show about 1/4 inch beyond the flowers. Use the foliage to disguise the mechanics on the underside of the corsage. ***(Figure 6.7d)***

7. Add filler flowers, if desired.

8. If a bow is needed, it should be positioned on the lower outside curve of the crescent.

9. Trim the corsage stem to a length of about 2 inches.

Figure 6.7b Designing a Crescent Corsage Step 4

Double Spray Corsage

The double spray corsage is a popular style because of its pointed elliptical shape. It should be designed with relatively small flowers and foliage in order to keep the finished corsage a reasonable size.

1. Wire and tape about ten small flowers and six or seven pieces of foliage.

2. Begin with the smallest flower in a vertical position and tape a second flower to the right and about two-thirds of the way below the first flower.

Figure 6.7c Designing a Crescent Corsage Step 5

3. Position the next flower to the left and about two-thirds of the way below the second flower. Tape the flower to the stem.

4. Continue staggering flower placements left and right until five flowers are in position. Each flower should be slightly larger than the one above it.

5. Add the sixth flower in the same staggered manner but at a slightly downward angle. This placement should be the largest flower in the design.

Figure 6.7d Designing a Crescent Corsage Step 6

6. Add the remaining four flowers, one at a time, below the sixth flower by bending each one over the thumb and positioning them to the left or right of the previous flower. The size of these flowers should taper in the reverse of the rest so that the bottom flower is about the same size as the top flower in the corsage.

Notes

7. Add foliage to the back of the design to cover the mechanics and provide a strong background for the corsage.

8. If a bow is desired, it should be tucked into the corsage under the sixth flower.

9. Trim the corsage stem to a length of about 2 inches.

Nosegay Corsage

The nosegay corsage is a circular Victorian design. It is typically created with a variety of petite flowers and/or buds and may be designed in a pattern of concentric rings or in a mixed manner.

1. Begin with a single flower, such as a sweetheart rose, as the center flower.

2. Add a ring of flowers around the center placement and tape them at a single joining point, leaving the ends of the wires free.

3. Continue adding rings of flowers to the design in the same manner until it reaches the desired size (usually about 3 inches in diameter).

4. Add a row of foliage under the last row of flowers to disguise the mechanics and provide a background for the flowers.

5. Tape a bow of narrow ribbon to the base of the corsage.

6. Separate the individual wire stems and trim them to a length of about 2 inches to create a garden stem.

Over-the-Shoulder Corsage

The over-the-shoulder corsage is designed to rest on the top of the shoulder and cascade slightly down the front and back of the body. It is an excellent choice for weddings, because it is less likely to be damaged after a great deal of hugging. This style is particularly effective for the mother of the bride or the mother of the groom since she is typically seen from the back throughout

Notes

the ceremony. The over-the-shoulder corsage is constructed in the same manner as the double spray style with the following exceptions.

- The smallest flowers at the points of the design should be wired with a very light gauge wire in order to cascade freely over the shoulder and provide motion.

- Position the first and last two or three flowers about 2 inches below each other to create a more effective cascade over the shoulder. The design will look sparse and elongated at both ends as it is constructed, but once curved over the shoulder it will look more appropriate.

- Once the corsage is designed, it should be placed on the shoulder of an average-sized person and curved to follow the lines of the body.

Purse Corsage

Occasionally, the mother of the bride or another member of the wedding party will elect to carry a corsage on her purse rather than somewhere on her body. Generally, this type of ornamentation looks best on a small clutch hand bag. Any corsage style may be used to decorate a purse. It is important, however, to keep the design in proportion to the size of the purse. A purse corsage may be attached rather easily with corsage or safety pins. If the client does not wish the purse to be pinned, the corsage may be attached in the following manner.

1. Tape a #24 gauge wire from top to bottom with floral tape which matches the color of the purse.

2. Bend the wire in half and tape the ends of the wire to the corsage stem.

3. Bend the opposite *U*-shaped end of the wire over the clasp or down into the purse to secure the corsage in position.

Wrist Corsage

A wrist corsage is constructed by designing a lightweight corsage and attaching it to some form of bracelet-like holder.

There are a number of wristlet holders available. Some have elasticized wrist bands; others have a plastic latch similar to that of a watch band. The corsage is usually attached to these bands either with a metal clamp or ribbon. Hot glue may be applied to the corsage stem in order to better secure the corsage to the wrist band. Another type of wrist band, often considered more secure and comfortable to wear, can be created with ordinary floral products, as explained below:

Notes

1. Cut a 16-inch length of satin or velvet covered wire tubing.

2. Bend both ends in toward the center of the wire.

3. Use a piece of #28 gauge wire to bind the ends of the tubing to the center. This should create a figure *8*.

4. Tape over the binding wire with matching floral tape.

5. Tie the corsage to the taped portion of the figure *8* with ribbon.

6. To secure the band around the wrist, slip one loop of the figure *8* through the other and bend the loop backward to tighten the design on the arm.

Note: Two chenille stems may be taped together and used to form the same type of figure *8* band.

Hand-Held Flowers

Hand-held flowers evolved in response to some mothers' dislike for wearing flowers on their wedding attire. Instead, a tied collection of flowers or simple bouquet is designed and carried informally to the side. Today, a mother may carry a single long-stemmed rose with a touch of fern and ribbon streamers or a scepter of nerine lilies bound with braided ribbon. These hand-held designs may be as elaborate as a small presentation bouquet (see Chapter 5) or as simple as a cluster of blossoms. Whatever the size or style, hand-held designs generally are most effective when designed with a few interesting botanical specimens rather than a mass of everyday flowers.

Notes

Flower Girl's Basket and Ring Bearer's Pillow

Traditionally, the flower girl carries a basket filled with rose petals which she distributes down the aisle during the processional. The basket is usually decorated with ribbons and flowers that are attached to the handle with ribbon or wire. Many churches do not allow fresh flower petals to be strewn in the church. In this situation, confetti or potpourri are often used as a substitute. Also, flower girls may carry such floral decorations as petite nosegays or basquettes, floral rings and garlands, or a floral decoration attached to the child's favorite teddy bear.

The ring bearer traditionally carries a pillow that holds the bride's and the groom's rings. The pillow is often decorated with a cluster or cascade of flowers. This decoration is constructed in the manner of a corsage and is pinned or sewn securely to the pillow. Since the ring bearer is usually rather young, it is important to be sure the pinpoints are not exposed.

Floral Headpieces

Floral headpieces of various types are popular for members of the bridal party. Wired and taped headpieces are sometimes heavy and difficult to secure in the hair. Therefore, hair flowers are designed without wire as often as possible. The following are three types of hair decorations which may be constructed with glue instead of wire.

Barrettes

1. Open the barrette and hot glue a piece of ribbon to the underside of the decorative bar.

2. Glue a second piece of ribbon across the top of the barrette. The two pieces of ribbon should overlap and create a completely sealed surface around the barrette.

3. Glue a thin layer of greenery on the ribbon with floral adhesive glue. Elevate some of the greenery to give the design depth.

4. Add a bow or streamers to the barrette, if desired.

5. Begin gluing flower placements onto the center of the barrette and work toward the ends with smaller flowers, buds, and filler.

Hair Combs

1. Use hot glue to secure a piece of ribbon on the upper front and back portions of the comb (opposite the teeth). The two pieces of ribbon should overlap and create a sealed surface along the edge of the comb.

2. Follow Steps 3 through 5 for designing a barrette.

Hair Clips

1. Place a piece of waxed paper between the teeth of a hair clip. This keeps the clip from being glued together during the design of the piece.

2. Hot glue a piece of ribbon over the metal forks on each side of the clip.

3. Follow Steps 3 through 5 for designing a barrette. Be sure to add flowers around the clamp to help conceal it.

4. When all of the glue has dried, remove the waxed paper from between the teeth of the clip.

Floral Wreaths and Headbands

Floral wreaths ***(Figure 6.8)*** and headbands ***(Figure 6.9)*** are designed in exactly the same way. The difference between them is the position in which they are worn on the head. The floral wreath should be worn around the crown of the head, while the headband is wrapped straight across the forehead. These headpieces must be custom designed to fit the head of the individual. To ensure a correct fit, measure the head with a tape measure or a piece of ribbon. Place the measure gently around the top of the head, approximately 2 inches above the ear for a wreath and 1 inch above the ear for a headband. Design the headpiece to the appropriate length in the following method.

Figure 6.8 Floral Wreath Headpiece

Figure 6.9 Floral Headband

1. Tape two #24 gauge wires together end to end.

2. Bend one end of the wire into a 1-inch hook.

3. Tape the end of the hook to the wire to create a small loop.

4. Beginning at the looped end of the wire, create a garland of foliage by binding 2-inch to 3-inch long clusters to the wrapped wire with a #28 gauge wire. The stems of the foliage should face the straight end of the wire.

5. When the greenery reaches the end of the wire, bind one more cluster to the wire in the opposite direction.

6. Add flowers to the garland in a random pattern with floral adhesive glue.

7. Bend the garland into a ring and insert the straight end of the wire through the looped end. Bend 1 inch of the straight wire back over the loop to secure the ring.

8. Attach ribbon and streamers to the back of the ring to conceal the connecting point.

Bridal Veils

Figure 6.10a Bridal Veil Styles

Many traditional floral hair decorations can be designed using silk flowers, beads, and pearl sprays. When attached to a length of tulle or illusion, these headpieces become bridal veils. ***(Figures 6.10a and 6.10b and Figure 6.10c on page 136)*** The florist is often able to construct veils comparable to those sold in bridal salons but for a much lower price. The florist may also use his or her skills to create custom-made veils according to the bride's specifications. This type of personalized service enhances the florist's reputation as a complete wedding flower shop.

The simplest of bridal headpieces might be a floral wreath with a large tulle bow and streamers at the back. The floral wreath and other headpiece styles can be enhanced with more exaggerated lengths of veiling according to the bride's desires. The following materials are needed to construct a bridal veil:

Figure 6.10b Bridal Veil Styles

1. Sharp fabric scissors

2. Wire cutters

3. A yardstick and a tape measure

4. Pins

5. One double-sized (full), flat, navy blue sheet

6. Hot glue gun

7. Assorted pearls, lace, ribbons, and silk flowers

8. Hair combs

9. Cotton mercerized thread (This thread is constructed of a thin thread of nylon that is wrapped with cotton thread. It can be found at retail fabric stores.)

10. Quality sewing needles

11. Tulle or illusion - Use the following guide to determine the amount of material needed:

    - Pouf veil without blusher - 3/4 yard

    - Shoulder length veil without blusher - 1 1/4 yards; with blusher - 2 1/4 yards

    - Fingertip veil without blusher - 2 1/4 yards; with blusher 3 1/4 yards

    - Floor-length veil - This type of veil varies according to the height of the bride. Measure from the crown of the head to the floor; add 1 yard for blusher.

    - Chapel-length or cathedral-length veil - Measure from the crown of the head to the waist. Then measure from the waist to the end of the train. Add 7 inches for trimming and rounding off the bottom. Add an additional yard if a blusher is desired.

Figure 6.10c Bridal Veil Styles

Construction of a Bridal Veil

Once all needed supplies have been gathered for veil construction, establish a work area with a large, clean surface. A wide counter top, large table, or spacious floor will work well.

1. Cover the work area with a navy blue sheet. The dark colored surface makes the netting easier to see and cut.

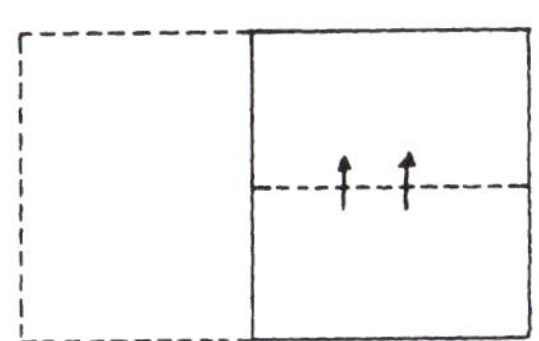

Figure 6.11a Constructing a Bridal Veil Steps 2 and 3

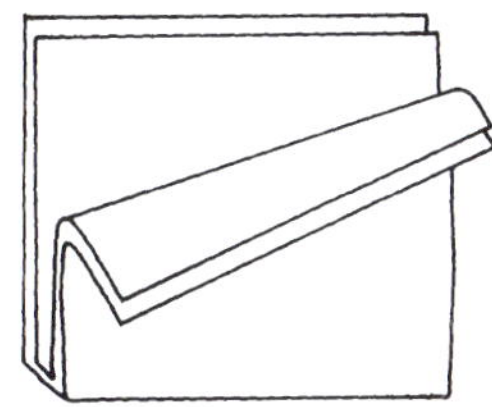

Figure 6.11b Constructing a Bridal Veil Step 3

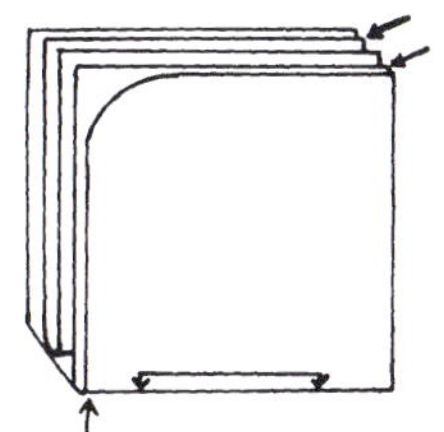

Figure 6.11c Constructing a Bridal Veil Step 4

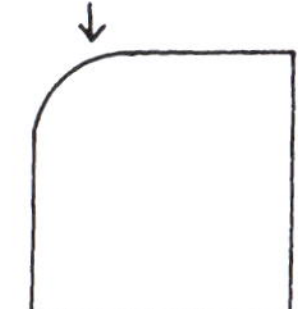

Figure 6.11d Constructing a Bridal Veil Step 4

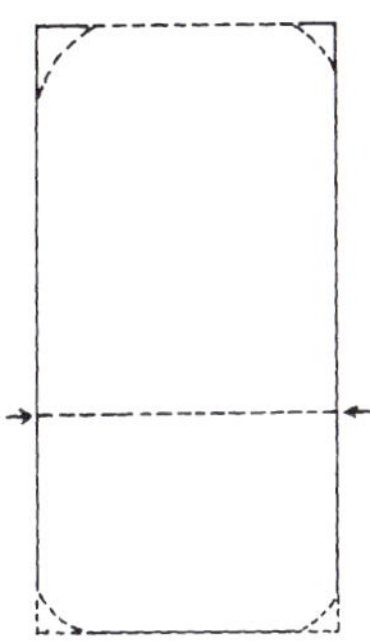

Figure 6.11e Constructing a Bridal Veil Step 7

2. To achieve a perfectly curved edge, fold the tulle in half lengthwise. ***(Figure 6.11a)***

3. Fold the tulle in half again, widthwise. (There should now be four layers of tulle lying flat on the navy blue sheet.) ***(Figures 6.11b and 6.11c)***

4. With sharp scissors, round off the lower right-hand corner of the folded net. This process should provide a gentle, curving edge for the bottom right-hand corner of the folded fabric. ***(Figures 6.11c and 6.11d)***

5. Unfold the fabric widthwise.

6. Next, unfold the fabric lengthwise.

7. Measure the amount required for the blusher from one end of the length of tulle. Place a pin on either side of the fabric at that measuring point. ***(Figure 6.11e)***

8. Double thread a needle, using four strands of thread extending from it.

9. Create a gathering thread from one pin to the other using a running stitch 1/4 inch long. Do not tie the ends of the thread.

10. Make a second gathering thread in the same way, stitching 1/4 inch below the first thread. ***(Figure 6.11f on page 138)***

11. Pull the thread tautly, gathering the fabric to a width of 2 1/2 inches. Sew a knot in the thread to secure the gather.

12. Fold the shorter end of the veil over the longer one. The shorter piece will serve as the blusher over the bride's face.

13. Position the veil with the blusher on top and place the straight edge of one or two combs along the gathered fold so that the teeth point away from the tulle.

14. Stitch the comb to the tulle and/or use hot glue to secure the comb to the veil.

15. Reverse the direction of the combs so they are underneath the tulle. This will increase the volume of the veiling and will allow the blusher to fall forward over the comb.

16. Stitch the veiling to the headpiece in several places.

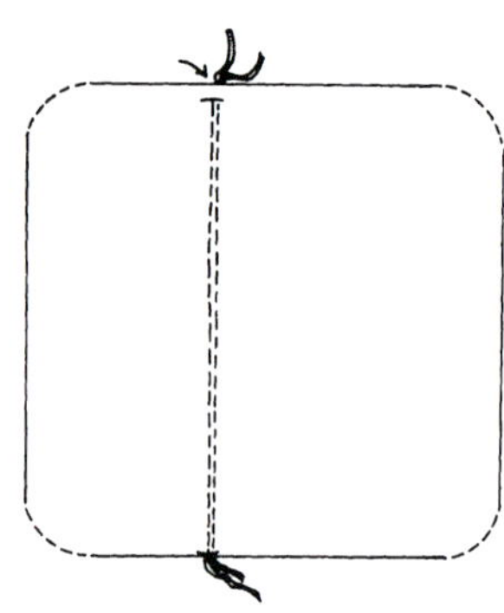

Figure 6.11f Constructing a Bridal Veil Step 10

Ribbons, Tulle, and Lace

Ribbons, tulle, and lace may be used in weddings to create added opulence and romance at a relatively low cost. The following are several effective uses for these often-requested accessories.

Ribbon

- Streamers add movement and color. Knotting at different lengths adds interest.
- Bows create focal points and add color.
- French braiding adds an interesting touch to stem ends and adds interest to bouquets.
- Loops and tails provide accents to corsages and boutonnieres.

Tulle

- Streamers add softness and color.
- Bows add a cloud-like focal point.
- Puffs add support, softness, and color.
- Casings (wrappings) create a veil over the flowers.

Lace

- Streamers add color and movement.
- Bows create a soft focal point.
- Loops and tails provide accents to corsages, boutonnieres, and bouquets.

Notes

Wearing Flowers Appropriately

Corsages and boutonnieres are traditionally worn on the left shoulder. This originated with the Victorian custom of wearing flowers over the heart.

Corsages are generally worn somewhat higher on the shoulder than boutonnieres. A corsage may be worn up and over the top of the shoulder so that it is slightly to the front of the body with the tip at about collarbone level. Corsages should be positioned to follow the natural curve of the shoulder and secured with two pins. One pin should be placed through the corsage stem. The other pin should be used higher in the corsage, among the flowers, to help prevent the corsage from rocking side to side. For garments made of delicate fabrics, a piece of cotton, folded tissue, or matching felt may be placed on the underside of the fabric to provide more bulk for the pins to grip. The pins may be stitched through the bra strap for added security. White or pearl-headed pins are typically used for corsages, but should be matched to the dress appropriately.

Boutonnieres are usually smaller and worn lower on the shoulder, near the buttonhole of the jacket lapel about 6 inches below the shoulder. Shorter, black-headed pins are usually used to secure boutonnieres, but again, the pins should be appropriately matched to the garment. For example, a groom wearing a white tuxedo should wear a white-headed corsage pin instead of a black-headed boutonniere pin. Boutonniere pins may also be inserted from the back side of the lapel so the pinhead does not show.

Wristlets are generally worn on the left wrist; however, left-handed individuals may prefer to wear them on their right. A wristlet corsage should be worn comfortably near the wristbone rather than higher on the forearm. The corsage should not be so large that it interferes with the use of the hand.

Profile sprays of flowers for the hair are usually worn on the right. In this way, the flowers are visible to the congregation as the bride or bridesmaids stand at the altar. Bobby pins are effective for pinning wired floral sprays, wreaths, or headbands into most types of hair. One or two bobby pins secured through narrow stems at each end of the spray should hold it firmly in place. This is generally more effective than pinning through the bulky center of the spray. For fine hair, twist a small section of hair around itself a few times before pinning into it. Hair combs can be secured in any type of hair by teasing a section of the hair, misting it with hairspray, and inserting the comb after the spray has dried.

The wedding party is comprised of a wide variety of individuals. Fortunately, the array of floral fashion accessories is also widely varied. This versatility allows the florist to integrate a variety of flowers into the wedding motif, yet allows individuals to maintain their personalities. However, in some cases, such as men's boutonnieres, a uniform design may strengthen the wedding look and simplify flower distribution. Circumstances, such as a dress style or fabric, may also limit the choice of an accessory. Regardless of the choice of corsage, boutonniere, or accessory, the correct position and attachment of the item is vital for the optimum effect.

Notes

Notes, Photographs, Sketches, etc.

Notes, Photographs, Sketches, etc.

Notes, Photographs, Sketches, etc.

Chapter

7

Ceremonial Decorations

When a bride and groom are to be married, ceremonial flowers are an integral part of the setting. The moment the couple exchanges vows is a very memorable occasion. Creating the proper background with flowers is essential in creating a day the bride and groom and all their guests will never forget. Well executed ceremonial decorations act as a silent advertisement for the florist since they will be viewed for 30 minutes or more by a large, captive audience.

Ceremony Location and Style

During the wedding consultation, the florist should ask a number of questions in order to develop a visual image of the site of the ceremony. This helps set the style and mood of the ceremony and allows the florist to suggest decorations which will enhance the environment, not distract from the ceremony. Questions to ask might include:

- What is the overall size of the facility or site?
- Is it a formal or informal facility?
- How high are the ceilings?
- Where will the bride and groom stand during the ceremony?
- Are there any known restrictions concerning flower use in the facility?

Often the bride does not know the answers to many of these questions. If not, the florist is wise to visit the site and gather the

Notes

specifics required. It is a good idea to take photographs of the facility and make a few notes and measurements of the area. This helps prevent confusing one church with another when several weddings are scheduled on the same day. A ceremony site checklist is provided in Appendix D for use when visiting the location of the ceremony.

Rituals and Regulations

Once familiar with the location and style of the ceremony site, the florist should check with the church official, hotel banquet manager, or another party who is familiar with restrictions or regulations concerning the use of floral decorations at the ceremonial site. For example, some churches do not allow papier-mâché containers to be used on the altar. Instead, the church will often require that decorations be designed in their own altar vases. The florist must arrange to pick up the liners for these vases from the church prior to the wedding so that the decorations may be designed at the shop. Some general rituals and regulations are common among certain religious denominations The following information should be used as a guide. Individual houses of worship may have their own requirements in addition to these.

Christian Science Weddings

- The Church of Christ Scientists is composed of laymen who are elected, not ordained. Therefore, Christian Scientists may be married in another church by an ordained minister of any Protestant faith or outside the church by any other legally authorized person.

- Floral decorations are usually kept rather simple for these services.

Eastern Orthodox Weddings (Greek Orthodox, Russian Orthodox, and Rumanian Orthodox)

- Marriage is not allowed during Greek Lent. Weddings are held most frequently on Sundays.

- The wedding service is in two parts: the betrothal service; and the order of marriage or crowning. When

Notes

the bride joins the groom after the betrothal service, the priest makes the sign of the cross three times over their heads and then gives them lighted candles which they hold through the rest of the ceremony.

- There is much emphasis on the number three, representing the Trinity. This includes putting a crown on the groom's head, and then another on the bride's head. The crowns have triple significance: honor and glory, purity, and a memorial to the Martyr's Crowns. They are exchanged between the bride and groom three times. In the Slavic Church, the crowns are gold. In Russian and Greek Orthodox churches, they can be branches, greenery, flowers, and ribbons. The crowns may be purchased as a predecorated set or made especially for the bride and groom.

Jewish Weddings

The three main divisions of the Jewish faith are Orthodox, Conservative, and Reformed. Although the marriage service is similar, more traditional rituals are followed in the Orthodox and Conservative groups than in the Reformed. There are many variations in each division, and almost every rabbi follows a slightly different form.

- Weddings do not take place on the Sabbath (sunset Friday until sunset Saturday), or on certain festival days and fasting periods.

- Flowers are usually placed on the Beama, a stage-like setting where the ceremony takes place.

- Orthodox, Conservative, and sometimes Reformed weddings are held under a canopy or Chuppah, which symbolizes the couple's new home. It is made of velvet or satin cloth, often beautifully embroidered and embellished with precious jewels, and is supported by four poles. Greenery and flowers may be used in most synagogues to decorate the canopy, and large fern baskets can be placed at both sides. It has become popular, particularly at Reform weddings, to have a floral canopy made entirely of branches, vines, greenery, and flowers.

- Additional equipment needed for the ceremony includes a small, white, covered table; two cups; one thin glass wrapped in a white napkin; and sacramental wine. This is placed under the canopy before, beside, or behind the rabbi.

- The sequence begins with a betrothal benediction followed by the ring ceremony and the reading of the ketubah, the written marriage document or "contract." After the reading is the chanting of the seven benedictions, the sipping of wine from the second cup, and the breaking of the cloth-wrapped glass (to symbolize the destruction of the temple in Jerusalem, which Jews must remember even in times of joy).

Notes

Mormon Weddings

Non-members are not allowed to enter Mormon temple for any reason. Therefore, the florist must make special arrangements with a church official for delivery and setup. This may limit the type of decorations possible for the ceremony.

Protestant Weddings

- Altar guild members must sometimes be present when decorating the altar.

- Specific sizes and placements are sometimes required for altar vases.

- The use of the church's own altar vases with liners may not be allowed due to insurance regulations.

Roman Catholic Weddings

- The Catholic marriage service follows one of several established rituals, depending on whether a nuptial mass is included. A wedding without a mass may be held in the morning, afternoon, or evening. A wedding that includes a mass is scheduled before noon.

- Marriage is not usually allowed during Lent.

- A traditional part of the service is for the bride to place a bouquet of flowers at the statue of the Blessed Virgin.

Notes

- Usually the church's own vases must be used for altar decorations.
- Papier-mâché containers are not allowed on the altar.
- Plastic and silk flowers may not be used in the church.
- Aisle runners may or may not be used depending on insurance regulations.

Designing Ceremonial Decorations

Floral decorations for the wedding ceremony may be simple or elaborate, bright or subdued, traditional or contemporary. The formality of the ceremony, the size and style of the ceremony location, and the bride's desired wedding mood all influence the type of decorations to be created. No matter what the bride chooses for her ceremonial decor, the florist must be careful to create floral decorations that will enhance, not detract from, the ceremony.

A variety of different decorations may be used for the wedding ceremony. Although it is most important to decorate the area where the bride and groom exchange vows, the site of the ceremony has a more unified appearance when the entry and seating areas are also decorated. The florist should encourage decoration of the entire ceremonial site, starting with the entryway, continuing into the vestibule or guest book area, down the aisle, surrounding the seating area, and finishing with a strong impact at the altar area.

When creating ceremonial decorations, it is important to keep in mind the distance from which the designs will be viewed. For example, in a large church, small altar decorations may be nearly impossible to see from the back half of the sanctuary. Lavender, violet, or blue flowers will recede into the background despite adequate lighting. Baby's breath becomes a blur from a short distance away and is almost invisible from greater distances. For this reason, a few bold floral designs strategically placed throughout the setting may be more effective than numerous small floral accents in every "nook and cranny."

Entry and Vestibule Decorations

From the moment guests arrive at the location of the ceremony, they should begin to feel the mood of the wedding. Floral decorations outside the ceremonial site help identify the location to guests who are unfamiliar with the area. Colorful bows with festive streamers may be tied to light posts to draw attention to a driveway or parking lot. Helium balloons or fresh foliage garlands may be attached to railings to lead guests to the entry way. A floral arch may be created to surround the doors to the church or wedding site.

Inside the ceremony location, the vestibule may be further decorated with flowers, ribbons, balloons, or plants. The entrance to the sanctuary might be framed by tall ficus trees, evergreen topiaries, a heart-shaped balloon arch, or pedestals with fresh floral arrangements. The guest book stand might be decorated with a grouping of blooming plants at the base, a small cascading spray of flowers placed on the ledge, or a simple cluster of flowers tied to the pen with a narrow ribbon. The formality of the altar decorations should be repeated in the entryway decorations. The color scheme and flower types used should be consistent, as well. Because these decorations will be viewed from close proximity, more intricate designs are appropriate.

Constructing a Foliage Garland

Garlands can be made of most any foliage, although trailing foliage, such as ivy or sprengeri, work best. The foliage can be bound together with #28 gauge paddle wire, raffia, waxed string, or heavy thread.

Figure 7.1a Constructing a Foliage Garland Step 1

1. Gather a few short pieces of foliage (about 4 to 6 inches long) and wrap the binding material tightly around the stems several times. The fullness of the garland is determined by the number of foliage stems gathered together. ***(Figure 7.1a)***

2. Make a second cluster of foliage the same size as the first. Lay the tips of the foliage about halfway over the stems of the first bunch.

3. Using the same piece of binding material still attached to the first bunch, wrap around the stems of the second bunch three or four times. One continuous piece is used to bind the entire garland, and it becomes the backbone of the design. ***(Figure 7.1b)***

4. Continue adding foliage as in Steps 2 and 3 until the desired length is reached.

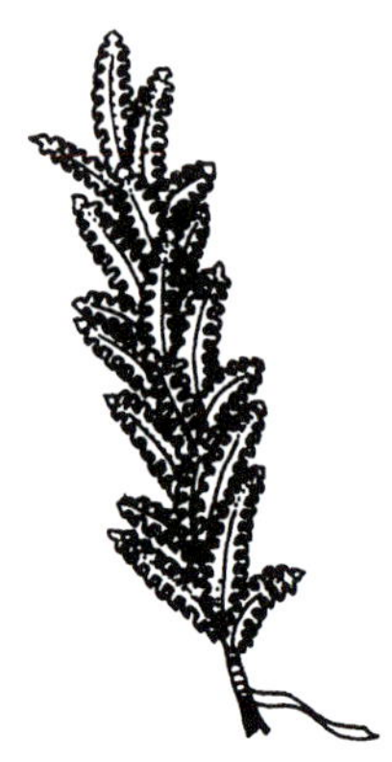

Figure 7.1b Constructing a Foliage Garland Step 3

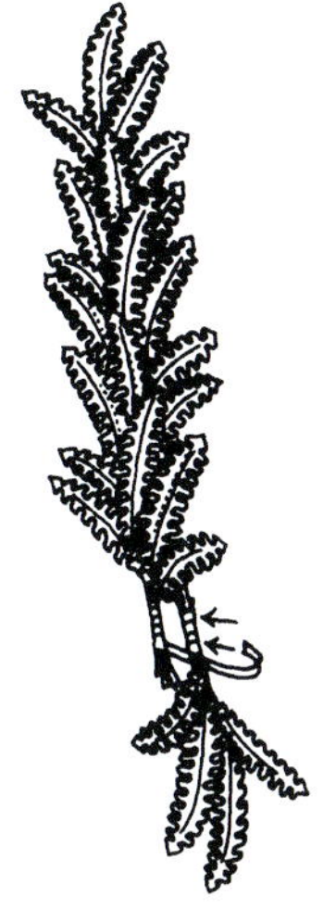

Figure 7.1c Constructing a Foliage Garland Step 7

5. To finish the garland, tie or otherwise secure the end of the binding material.

6. Gather another grouping of foliage and lay it against the end of the garland in the opposite direction.

7. Tie the grouping into place with a separate piece of binding material. ***(Figure 7.1c)***

8. Trim the stems of the last grouping and conceal them among the foliage.

9. Items may be added to the garland in the following ways:

    - Items can be wired as they would be for a corsage and then wired around the foliage stems in the garland.

    - Fresh flowers, ribbons, birds, and other accessories can be added by gluing them into the garland with floral adhesive.

    - Delicate flowers may be inserted into small water tubes and taped into the garland with corsage tape. The water tube and tape are then concealed under the foliage.

Constructing a Floral Arch

Floral arches may be used in a number of ways for the wedding ceremony. Typically, they are used around exterior or interior doorways or to "frame" the bride and groom at the altar. The "magic moment arch" is used at the back of the church or at the end of the aisle to "frame" the bride and her escort at the moment she is first seen. Standard arches may be brass, wood, wrought iron, or fiber glass. These arches may be simply decorated with ribbons and bows tied to the frame, or with floral sprays designed in floral foam cages and attached to the arch with chenille stems. For a richer effect, wilt-resistant foliage, such as salal and huckleberry, may be attached to the entire arch with wire, chenille stems, or waxed string. Ferns, blooming plants, or fresh flower arrangements are tasteful additions at the base of the arch. Due to the size of these decorations, arches must often be designed on site. A large, free-standing, foliage-covered arch, suitable for indoor or outdoor use may be constructed on site in the following way.

1. Gather the following materials:
    - Three 7-foot, 2-inch x 4-inch boards
    - Four 3-foot, 1-inch x 4-inch boards
    - Fourteen 16-penny nails
    - Twenty-four 8-penny nails
    - Two 5-gallon buckets
    - Plaster of Paris mix - enough to make 10 gallons
    - Chicken wire
    - Hammer
    - Saw
2. Lay two 7-foot, 2-inch x 4-inch boards flat on the floor on the 4 inch sides.
3. Drive four 16-penny nails into the lower 2 feet of each board. Leave approximately 3 inches between each nail. The nails should not be hammered through the board, but instead they should protrude about 2 inches from the wood. ***(Figure 7.2a)***
4. Turn both boards onto their 2-inch sides and spread them 6 feet 2 inches apart from each other.
5. Lay the third 7-foot, 2-inch x 4-inch board on its 2-inch side, perpendicular to the other two boards at the ends opposite those with the protruding nails. Line up the three boards so they meet and form a *U.* ***(Figure 7.2b)***
6. Drive three 16-penny nails into each point where the boards intersect.

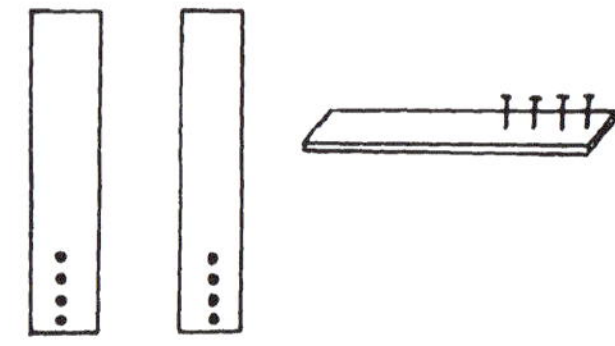

Figure 7.2a Constructing a Floral Arch Step 3

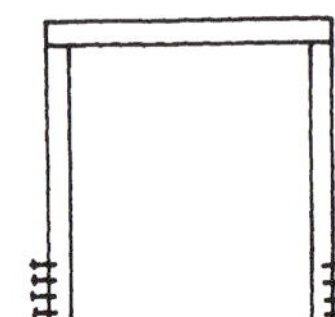

Figure 7.2b Constructing a Floral Arch Step 5

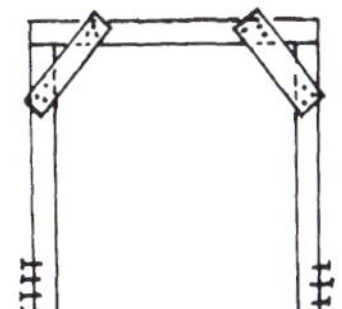

Figure 7.2c Constructing a Floral Arch Step 7

7. Create cross-braces by laying the 4-inch surfaces of two 1-inch x 4-inch boards at 45-degree angles about 2 feet away from the corners of the *U*. ***(Figure 7.2c)***

8. Use three 8-penny nails to attach the 1-inch x 4-inch boards to the 2-inch x 4-inch boards at each intersection.

9. Saw off any excess ends of the 1-inch x 4-inch boards extending beyond the *U*.

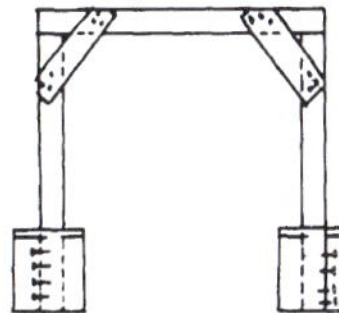

Figure 7.2d Constructing a Floral Arch Step 11

10. Turn the structure over and attach two additional cross-braces to the other side in the same manner, as described in Steps 7 through 9.

11. Stand the arch upright and position the legs in 5-gallon buckets. ***(Figure 7.2d)***

12. Mix the plaster of Paris and pour it in the 5-gallon buckets to secure the arch into an upright position. The nails extending out of the legs will help the plaster of Paris "grip" the wood and hold it securely. Be sure to hold the arch straight in the buckets until the plaster of Paris sets.

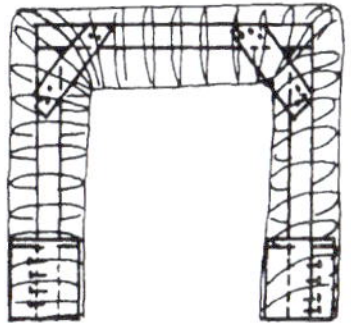

Figure 7.2e Constructing a Floral Arch Step 13

13. Wrap the entire structure from the base of the buckets, around the legs, and over the top with chicken wire. ***(Figure 7.2e)***

Figure 7.2f Constructing a Floral Arch Step 14

14. Stuff wilt-resistant foliage, such as boxwood or salal, into the chicken wire to cover the structure. ***(Figure 7.2f)***

15. Attach floral foam cages, as desired, in order to add fresh flower accents to the arch. ***(Figure 7.2g)***

Figure 7.2g Constructing a Floral Arch Step 15

Seating Area and Aisle Decorations

The area where guests are seated for the wedding ceremony may be decorated in a variety of ways. In a church, the area between the entrance and the altar is known as the nave. Decoration of the nave helps create a feeling of unity between the couple and their guests during the ceremony. Pew and aisle decorations are most commonly used in this area.

Pew Decorations

Notes

The simplest form of pew decoration is a bow. Pew bows may be designed with #9 or #40 ribbon or with a combination of different ribbon sizes and colors. Tulle can be used to create a romantic look. Long streamers, almost reaching the floor, add drama.

Although sometimes requested, it is not necessary to use bows on the end of every pew. Spacing bows every second or third pew is just as effective and often less monotonous. The bride on a budget may elect to decorate only the first one or two pews to mark family seating areas. In any case, pew bows should be attached in a manner that will not damage the pews. When making pew bows, taped wires or chenille stems should be used to secure the bows and prevent scratching of the pew.

Much to the dismay of church officials, some florists tape pew bows into place. This method tends to leave tape marks and a sticky residue on the pews. Additionally, unless large amounts of tape are used, there is a risk that some of the bows will come loose before the end of the ceremony. The following alternatives for attaching pew bows are recommended:

Attaching Pew Bows with Rubber Bands

1. Slide a rubber band horizontally over the top of the pew end. Use a rubber band that will fit snugly over the pew end and will blend with the color of the pew.

2. Slip one of the wire ends from the bow through the rubber band and twist the two wires together to secure the bow in place.

Attaching Pew Bows with Chenille Stems

For pew ends which are too wide or unusually shaped to use the rubber band method, a chenille stem can be used to create a bow holder.

1. Bend a chenille stem matching the color of the pew into a loop and twist the ends together.

2. Pull the end of the chenille loop opposite the twist to create an elongated oval.

Notes

3. Twist this same end to form a small circle.

4. Bend the chenille loop in half over the pew end and pinch it so that it clamps into place. Be sure the small circle is on the aisle side of the pew.

5. Attach the bow to the small circle by inserting one of the bow's wires through the circle and twisting the two wires together.

Roping Off Pews

Roping is sometimes desired to prevent access to certain sections of seating or to mark seating areas for family or special guests. Ribbon may be used to form roping which will blend with pew bows. This is easily achieved in the following manner.

1. Design a pew bow with one extra long streamer at least 3 feet long. This streamer will form the roping from one pew to the next.

2. Attach the pew bow to the desired pew using the rubber band or the chenille stem method.

3. Attach another pew bow to the next pew.

4. Grasp the long streamer from the first pew and drape it across to the next pew to give the desired amount of swagging.

5. Twist the end of a 3-inch piece of matching chenille stem around the streamer at the desired attachment point.

6. Tuck the end of the chenille stem into the rubber band or chenille clamp of the pew. This allows the roping to be moved back and forth for the seating of guests. It also provides for a simple breaking away of the roping in an emergency situation.

Pew Bows Accented with Flowers and Foliage

Pew bows are often accented with flowers and foliage that complement the altar decorations. A variety of devices is available which provides either a water tube or floral foam cage in

Notes

which to design various types of pew ends. When planning elaborate pew decorations, it is essential to visit the church and test the attachment of these devices to the pews. Often the shape and size of the pew end prohibits the use of these holders and custom-designed mechanics become necessary. When wilt-resistant materials are used, a water source may not be required. In this case, flowers and foliage may be tied together in a bunch and secured to the pew with ribbons.

Pew ends are typically designed as one-sided arrangements and may be round, oval, upright, cascading, or asymmetrical in shape. They should be designed in proportion to the size of the pew so that guests may easily be seated without interfering with the decorations. A simple pew decoration with a delicate wedding motif might include a base of leatherleaf (baker fern), trails of cascading ivy, a bow with streamers in the center, and a cloud of baby's breath for the finishing touch.

Aisle Candelabras

Candlelight wedding ceremonies are sometimes enhanced with the use of aisle candelabras. While these decorations add majesty to the aisle, they must be used with caution. Aisle candelabras typically contain a single candle. In order to use them safely, glass globes or hurricanes should be used to enclose the flame. Candles should not extend above the globes. Despite these safety precautions, fire codes and insurance restrictions frequently prohibit the use of these decorations. Battery-operated candles may be used as an alternative in most cases.

To decorate aisle candelabras with flowers and foliage, various floral foam cages may be used. Foam bouquet holders may be secured to the posts of the candelabras with waterproof tape wrapped around the handles. Slender, cascading styles are most appropriate on aisle candelabras to follow the lines of the post and prevent flowers from protruding into the aisle. This style also helps ensure that floral materials will be away from the candle's flame. The floral decorations may be designed before or after the candelabra is set into position. Most aisle posts clamp or slip over the top of the pew. Candelabras should not scratch or mar the pew in any way. To prevent such damage, a piece of #40 velvet ribbon can be folded in half and placed between the clamp and the pew. An additional security measure is the placement of a green or blooming plant at the foot of the candelabra post. This helps prevent guests from tripping over or toppling the post and also adds a decorative accent.

Aisle Runners

The aisle runner is used in the wedding ceremony to provide a clean surface for the bridal party to walk upon. After all of the guests have been seated, the ushers pull the aisle runner from the front of the aisle to the back. The wedding party then begins its entrance down the aisle.

Aisle runners may be linen, "lace," or plastic. Linen runners are a permanent aisle cloth made of heavy fabric. They may be used on a roll or in a neat stack which unfolds as it is pulled down the aisle. A linen aisle runner must be professionally cleaned, which is usually rather costly and contributes to the high rental price of this item. "Lace" aisle runners are disposable versions of the linen runner. They are made of a fibrous material with a heavy, paper-like texture and typically with a floral or lace pattern. Plastic aisle runners are usually the least expensive. They may be white, pastel, or brightly colored. The "lace" and plastic runners both come on rolls and are available in a number of lengths.

Attaching Aisle Runners

It is important for the florist to attach the aisle runner securely to the floor in order to ensure the proper use of the runner. If the runner is not pulled tightly or straight to the end of the aisle, there is a risk that guests will trip or fall over the buckled cloth. For this reason, many churches restrict the use of aisle runners. Ushers should be instructed on pulling an aisle runner down the aisle. Rolled runners usually come with a cord which has been fed through the cardboard roll and tied together. The ends of this cord should be untied by the florist to allow the runner to roll freely. By tying a single flower or a satin bow to the ends of the cord, the ushers can easily locate them. The pull corners of linen aisle runners can also be easily located by attaching similar decorations to the cloth with safety pins.

Securing an Aisle Runner to a Tile Floor

1. Center the runner at the front of the aisle.

2. Unroll or unfold the runner about 1 foot.

3. Using wide (2-inch) runner tape or duct tape in a color matching the cloth, tape the sides of the runner. Begin taping about 1 inch over the end of the cloth and tape down the edges approximately 8 inches. ***(Figure 7.3a)***

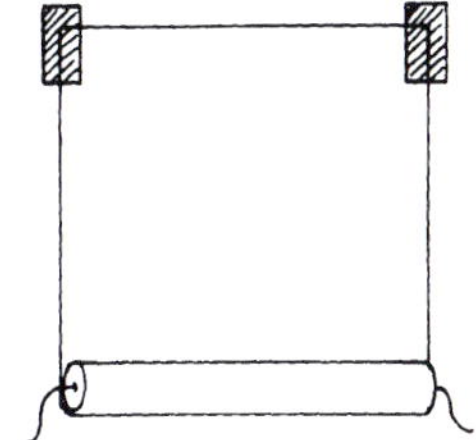

Figure 7.3a Securing an Aisle Runner to a Tile Floor Step 3

4. Tape the end of the runner from one side to the other making sure to overlap the tape applied in Step 3. ***(Figure 7.3b)***

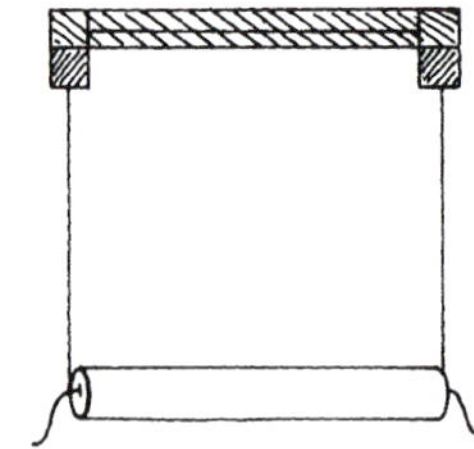

Figure 7.3b Securing an Aisle Runner to a Tile Floor Step 4

Securing an Aisle Runner to a Carpeted Floor

1. Center the runner at the front of the aisle.
2. Unroll or unfold the runner about 1 foot.
3. Secure each corner of the runner by inserting pearl-headed corsage pins almost horizontally through the runner and into the carpet. Use two pins in a crisscrossed manner with the heads of the pins along the end. ***(Figure 7.4a)***
4. Use three or four additional pins along the end of the runner. Insert the pins so that they follow the runner's edge. ***(Figure 7.4b)***
5. Add a pair of crisscrossed pins on each side of the runner about 10 inches from the end so that the heads of the pins are along the edge. ***(Figure 7.4c)***

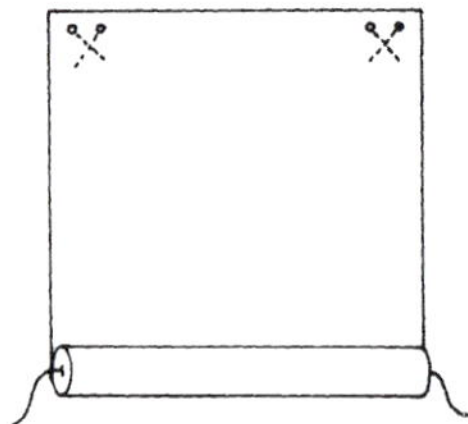

Figure 7.4a Securing an Aisle Runner to a Carpeted Floor Step 3

Securing an Aisle Runner to Steps

1. Attach the end of the runner at the desired point as directed for tile or carpet.
2. Pull the runner down the steps and secure the sides of the runner at the base and edge of every step, using either tape or pins. ***(Figure 7.5 on page 159)***
3. Leave the remainder of the runner at the base of the steps to be pulled by the ushers.

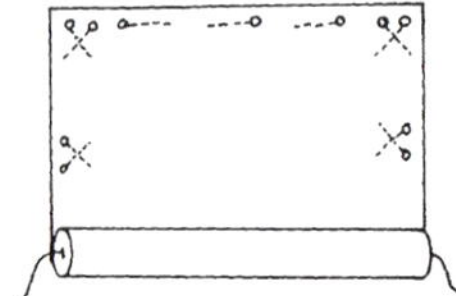

Figure 7.4b Securing an Aisle Runner to a Carpeted Floor Step 4

<u>Additional Seating Area Decorations</u>

A formal wedding with an emphasis on floral detailing might include additional decorations in the seating area. These decorations might include special touches on window sills, such as floral garlands, upright arrangements, or groupings of votive candles. The interior entry or perimeter of the seating area might be enhanced with crystal vases of flowers raised on pedestals. Green or blooming plants might also be used. If the aisle is

Figure 7.4c Securing an Aisle Runner to a Carpeted Floor Step 5

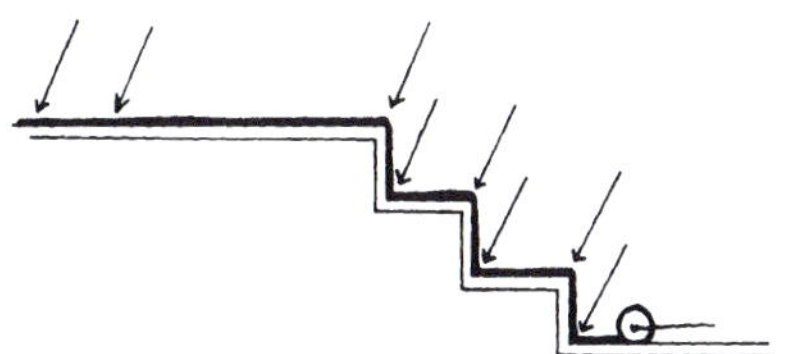

Figure 7.5 Aisle Runner Secured to Steps

especially wide, colorful plants might be placed on the floor at the base of every other pew. The decorations in this area should blend with those in the entry and on the altar to unite the entire floral picture.

Altar Decorations

Since the altar is the focal point of the wedding ceremony, it is critical for the decorations in this area to have a strong impact. A number of different floral decorations can be created to enhance the area where the bridal party stands. These decorations should be large enough to be seen by the wedding guests, but not so large that they interfere with church fixtures or ceremony proceedings. Since these decorations are viewed from long distances, intricate detail in the design is less important. Instead, the use of large flowers, bright colors, and showy ribbons is most effective. It is also advisable to create altar arrangements tall enough to be visible above the heads of the bridal party.

Altar Table

The altar table is a key area of decoration for most wedding ceremonies. The florist is often required to use the church's altar vases for these designs. The vases, which are usually a matched pair, may sit directly on the altar table or on pedestals next to the table. In either case, the floral arrangements designed in these vases should not compete with the other decorations on the altar table. Flowers should never be taller than, or interfere with, a standing cross. At the same time, the flowers should not be equal in height with, or in close proximity to, altar candles. Paired altar vases may be designed identically or as mirror images of each other.

A single arrangement is often used in the center of a large altar table. This may be a bold, upright mass design or a long, low centerpiece. When a unity candle is used as part of the wedding ceremony, it is sometimes incorporated into a low altar table centerpiece. A large pillar candle is inserted into the center of the design and two taper candles are either positioned to the sides of the pillar in the arrangement or at the ends of the centerpiece in candleholders. The tapers are lit at the beginning of the ceremony, and the bride and groom each use a taper to light the center pillar candle simultaneously. This ritual symbolizes the uniting of the two spirits, individuals, or families as one. Another possibility is to have each mother light one of the tapers used later by the couple to light the unity candle. The mothers usually light the tapers after being shown to their seats and before the actual ceremony begins. Besides giving the mothers an active part in the ceremony, their acts also symbolize the joining of the two families.

An additional item that is sometimes placed on the altar table is a presentation flower or bouquet for the parents. This may be as simple as a single rose or as elaborate as a full hand-tied bouquet. These flowers may be laid on the altar table prior to the ceremony and are typically carried by the bride and groom and presented to the parents at some point after the exchange of vows.

Figure 7.6a Free-Standing Altar Baskets and Stands

Free-Standing Altar Arrangements

Free-standing altar arrangements are often used in addition to altar table decorations. They may also be used in place of these decorations when church regulations prohibit flowers on the altar table. Standing wicker baskets or brass stands, as shown in ***Figures 7.6a and 7.6b***, provide an adaptable means of elevating flowers near the altar. Another option is to create a structure in which a tall, columnar floral arrangement can be designed. A number of methods can be used to design such a piece as long as it is stable. The following method works well and provides a structure that may be used repeatedly:

Figure 7.6b Free-Standing Altar Baskets and Stands

Designing a Columnar Altar Arrangement

1. Cement a 5-foot, 2-inch x 2-inch board into a 2-gallon bucket.

2. Hammer two 1/2-inch finishing nails into two opposite sides of the board at 1-foot intervals starting from the top. Angle the nails slightly downward as they are hammered. ***(Figure 7.7a)***

3. Starting 6 inches from the top, hammer additional nails on the remaining two sides of the board in the same manner as in Step 2. ***(Figure 7.7b on page 161)***

4. Hang soaked floral cages on the nails using the hole in each handle. ***(Figure 7.7c on page 161)***

5. Green the structure by inserting foliage into each of the cages. Blend the foliage to fill the gaps between the cages.

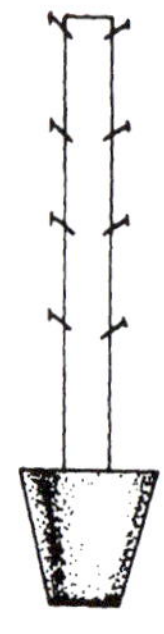

Figure 7.7a Mechanics for a Columnar Altar Arrangement Step 2

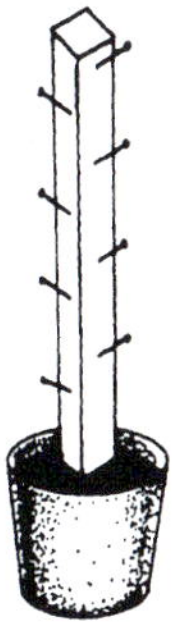

Figure 7.7b Mechanics for a Columnar Altar Arrangement Step 3

6. Add flowers, as desired, to create a columnar form.

7. Finish the base of the design by concealing the bucket in one of the following ways:

    - Group plants, such as ferns, around the bucket.

    - Set the bucket in the center of a large, plastic plant saucer. Place floral foam inside the saucer around the bucket and continue the columnar design to the floor.

Figure 7.7c Mechanics for a Columnar Altar Arrangement Step 4

Plants may also be used on the altar to soften the architecture and create a more intimate setting. Upright foliage plants, such as ficus trees or areca palms, are effective in churches with high ceilings. Palm stands can also be used for this purpose. The metal frames of these stands have small openings at the ends of "stems" which branch out from the base, as shown in ***Figure 7.8***. Two or three palm fronds are inserted into each of the openings to create a faux palm plant. These "plants" are easy to assemble and transport and may be reused by replacing the palm fronds.

Boston or sprengeri ferns are useful on pedestals. They may also be used on the floor at the bases of candelabras or standing baskets.

Shrubs and small evergreen trees are useful on large altars. They may be used individually, in clumps, or as a hedge. Balled and burlapped plants can be disguised at the base with fabric gathered around the ball and tied with ribbon. Any of these plants can be used as rental items.

Topiaries are another type of free-standing decoration that are popular for weddings. Evergreen shrubs trimmed into topiary forms may be used with floral foam cages tucked into the branches and floral accents added. The florist might subcontract these shrubs from a local nursery.

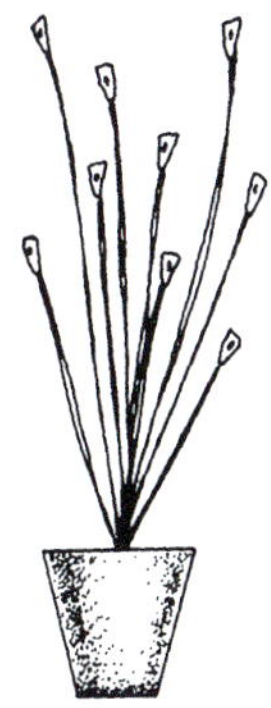

Figure 7.8 Palm Stand

Designing a Fresh Flower Topiary

1. Use plaster of Paris to anchor a 3-foot to 5-foot PVC pipe or tree limb (2 inches in diameter) into a 2-gallon bucket.

2. Soak an OASIS® Corso™, turn it upside down, and wrap the open flaps over the top of the pipe or limb. Press the foam slightly into the post. ***(Figure 7.9a)***

Figure 7.9a Mechanics for a Topiary Step 2

3. Use waxed string or wire to secure the flaps tightly around the post. ***(Figure 7.9b)***

4. Green the foam in a globular form proportioned to the length of the post.

5. Add flowers to conform to the round shape.

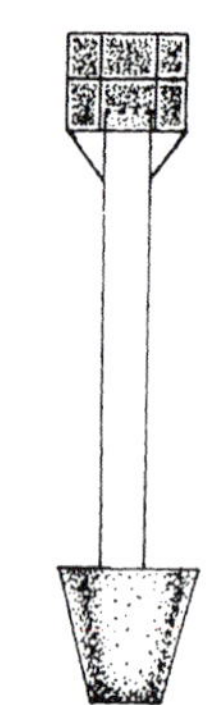

Figure 7.9b Mechanics for a Topiary Step 3

Candelabras

Candelabras are popular altar decorations, particularly for evening weddings where the glow of the candlelight provides a romantic setting. There are many different types of candelabras ranging from three-branch to as many as twenty-five branch styles. They are also available in a variety of shapes including the standard seven-branch inverted-*V*, the fan, the diagonal, the spiral, the entwined hearts, and the double ring. ***(Figures 7.10a and 7.10b and Figure 7.10c on page 163)*** Some candelabras are designed with holders for glass hurricanes which enclose the candles' flames. If candelabras are used with open flames, they should be placed toward the back of the altar away from ceremony activity. It is also important to position them away from drafts so the candles will burn evenly. Many churches have their own candelabras which may be used for the wedding ceremony. Usually, the bride will obtain permission for the florist to decorate them. However, the florist should consult a church official to determine an acceptable means of attaching the decorations. Some florists own several different types of candelabras in order to offer a number of choices to their clients. The interior of the ceremony site and formality of the wedding typically dictate which types of candelabras will be most appropriate.

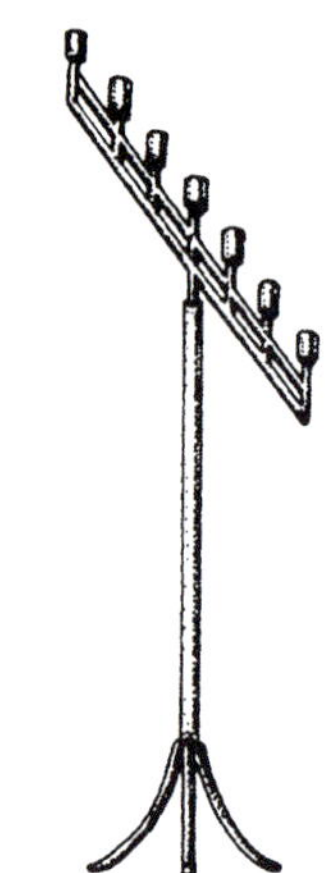

Figure 7.10a Candelabras

The candles used in altar candelabras should be of high quality in order to prevent excessive wax dripping and to allow for the longest possible burning time. Refrigerating the candles also helps them burn more slowly. Plastic drip cloths should be placed under candelabras to prevent wax from dripping on the floor. Dripless candles may be used instead of standard wax tapers in order to alleviate problems with wax dripping. These devices are made with a metal casing in the shape of a candle. Inside the casing, a spring mechanism pushes a thin wax candle up to the top as it burns. The metal casings may be used repeatedly, with the filler candles replaced with each use. Battery-operated candles are yet another option, particularly suited for use in churches with strict insurance or fire regulations. Wax candles of all types will light more easily during the ceremony if they are lit in advance and allowed to burn for about 1 minute.

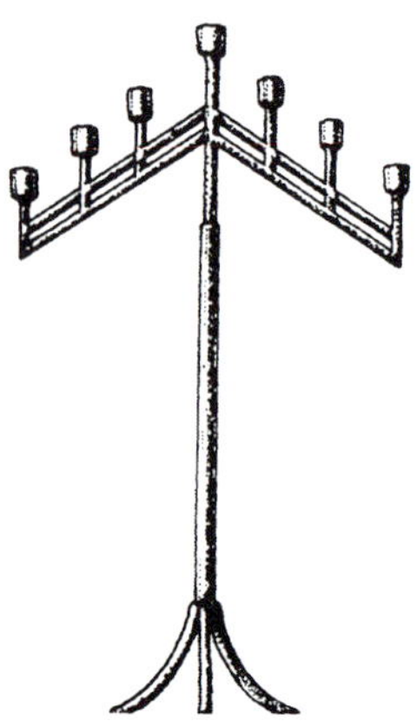

Figure 7.10b Candelabras

Figure 7.10c Candelabras

Tips for Removing Candle Wax

- Use a non-stick cooking spray to coat the candle holders prior to use. Votive candle cups may be prepared the same way. Hardened wax is easily peeled off the surface after each use.

- Place glass votive cups or other non-metal candle holders on a paper towel in a microwave oven. Warm them for about 30 seconds at a low temperature. Thin layers of wax will be melted off. Thick wax will be softened enough to pry off.

- To remove wax from a carpet, place a brown paper bag over the wax and press a low heat iron over the bag. The wax will adhere to the bag and be lifted from the carpet.

Decorating Candelabras

The simplest decoration for a candelabra is a bow with streamers. Typically, these bows are made with #40 ribbon to achieve a large bow that is visible from a distance. If the bow is secured with a chenille stem or taped wire, it may be attached to the candelabra by wrapping the wire around the center post. Alternatively, an extra pair of short streamers may be attached to the bow and used to tie the bow to the candelabra. Either of these methods is preferable to using tape which could leave a sticky residue.

A combination of foliage and ribbon may be used to give more impact to the center of a candelabra. Hardy foliage, such as salal, sprengeri, and leatherleaf, may be tied together with spool wire or waxed string in a single or double ended swag-like design. The decoration is then attached to the candelabra with chenille stems and a bow added to cover the tied stems. For a more formal design using less hardy foliage, a foam bouquet holder or a floral foam cage can be used. Taped #20 gauge wire or chenille stems can be used to attach the holder at the center of the candelabra post just below the candle cups. The foliage can be arranged in a cascading fashion or in a line that follows the shape of the candelabra. However, vertical placements should be avoided to keep the foliage away from the candles.

Fresh flowers may be designed in candelabras with floral foam, as well. The technique is the same as for all foliage designs, but a larger foam cage may be required to accommodate a large number of stem insertions. The oval, *T*-shape, and crescent designs, as shown in ***Figures 7.11a, 7.11b, and 7.11c***, are popular choices for candelabra decorations. The center area of each of these designs can be accented with focal flowers or left open for the addition of a bow. Whenever possible, elaborate candelabra decorations should be designed in place to ensure proper fit to the structure. It is also helpful to design candelabra decorations with the candles in place. This helps keep the flowers and foliage a safe distance from the candles' flames.

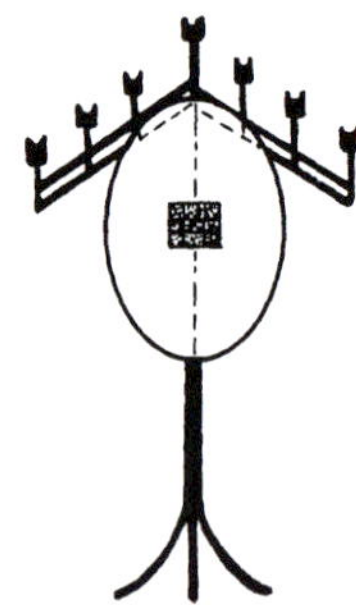

Figure 7.11a Candelabra Decoration Styles

Kneeling Benches

The kneeling bench ***(Figure 7.12 on page 165)*** is often a key feature around which much of the wedding ceremony takes place. Traditionally, it is positioned so that the bride and groom face the altar as they kneel upon the bench in prayer. In many modern ceremonies, however, the bench may be positioned so that the bride and groom face the congregation or even face each other using a profile kneeling bench. Decorations for the kneeling bench are somewhat limited due to the manner in which it is used. Bows, greenery, and/or flowers on the sides are usually the only suitable decorations for a kneeling bench used in the traditional way. These same decorations, a garland, or a spray of flowers across the front may be used on a bench positioned to face the congregation. A profile bench may be decorated on the narrow front panel with a cascade of flowers, foliage, or ribbon. Generally, no decorations are attached to the knee or elbow pads to provide the maximum amount of room for the bride and groom.

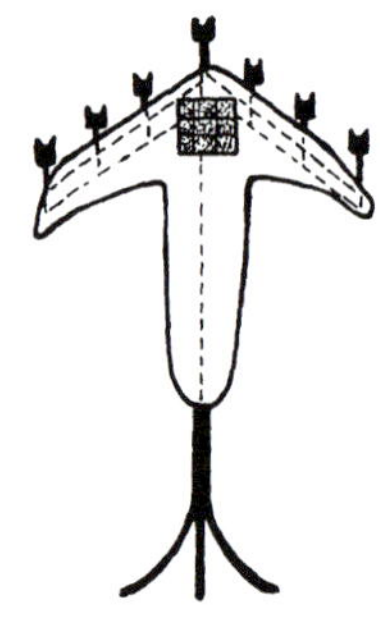

Figure 7.11b Candelabra Decoration Styles

Methods for attaching kneeling bench decorations vary according to the style of the bench. Metal or wrought iron benches usually allow designs to be wired on with chenille stems or taped wires. OASIS® IGLU® holders or other foam cages can easily be attached in this way. Decorations are often more difficult to attach to wooden kneeling benches. Some decorations must be tied on with ribbon or secured with waterproof floral tape. Water tubes may be substituted for foam cages to reduce the weight and bulk of the design. Some florists rent their own kneeling benches for weddings to ensure the possibility of attaching the desired decorations.

Chuppah

A chuppah ***(Figure 7.13 on page 165)*** is a special structure used as the focal point for the Jewish wedding ceremony. It consists of four poles and a roof-like canopy across the top. The chuppah is usually provided by the synagogue. Sometimes a portable chuppah, which includes a canopy held by four of the

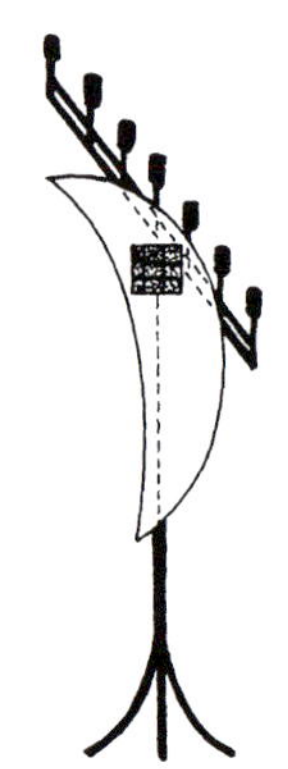

Figure 7.11c Candelabra Decoration Styles

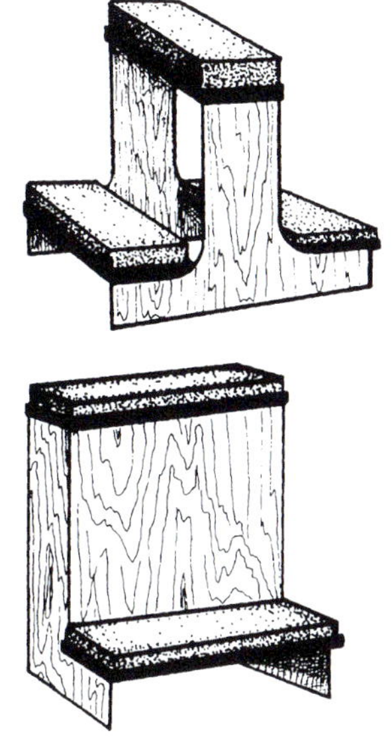

Figure 7.12 Kneeling Benches

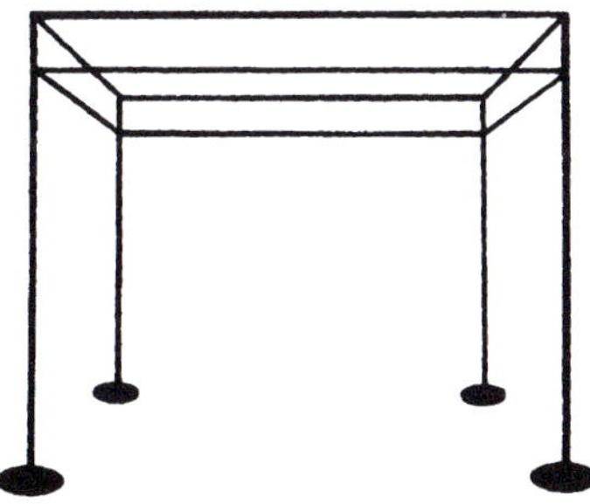

Figure 7.13 Chuppah

couple's relatives is used. Since this is not a fixed structure, little, if any, decoration is advisable. Sometimes a rather simple chuppah is used with a plain fabric or lattice top. In this case, elaborate decoration of the top and pole is encouraged. A casket saddle provides an effective means of creating a large spray for the top of the canopy. Flower and foliage garlands are good choices for enhancing the poles. A lavish chuppah with a richly embellished canopy is sometimes used for large formal weddings. Extensive floral decoration of the rooftop is usually discouraged so that it will not compete with the beauty of the fabric. Garlands on the poles or large floral arrangements at the bases may be suitable alternatives.

If the florist must provide the chuppah for a Jewish wedding ceremony, a sound structure can be built with a simple frame of birch branches. Poles can be cemented into buckets and a canopy created with cross branches connecting the poles. If screws are used instead of nails to assemble the structure, it can be easily disassembled and reused. Floral foam cages can be attached to the connecting points and sprays of flowers designed in the wedding colors.

Creating an Altar

Couples being married in locations other than a church or synagogue often look to the florist to help create a ceremonial atmosphere. Particularly important is the establishment of an altar-like area where the exchange of vows will take place. When considering the surroundings of a ceremonial site, the florist should look for special features around which the wedding may be centered. A home wedding might be staged in front of a fireplace mantel or picture window. A garden wedding might take place in a gazebo or around a fountain. In a country club or hotel ballroom, a plain wall may be the only background available. In any case, flowers, plants, ribbons, and props can turn each of these settings into a lovely wedding atmosphere.

To enclose a large space or focus attention on a particular area, props and large plants can be used. Arches, candelabras, and pedestals with arrangements help create a romantic wedding atmosphere. Chairs can be grouped into pew-like rows with an aisle down the center. Ribbon can be used to rope off areas meant only for the wedding party or family members. Low risers can be used to create a stage-like platform for the bride and groom. Since decorations for these settings need not follow the rules of any particular church or religious denomination, an endless array of possibilities exists for using flowers to enhance the surroundings.

Dressing Room Decorations

Notes

When the bridal party dresses at the ceremony location, a floral arrangement or necessity basket in the dressing room is a lovely way to create a more comfortable, homey atmosphere. A whimsical bouquet of flowers in a basket is an excellent choice to help provide a relaxed mood in the room. A necessity basket, including often-forgotten items such as bobby pins, hairspray, nail files, breath mints, and aspirin, is also a welcome addition. The florist might suggest this item be sent by the groom or groom's parents.

Car or Carriage Decorations

For the most lavish of weddings, the ceremonial decorations may be continued with the going-away car or the limousine. Bows may be attached to the antenna, door handles, or front and back bumpers using chenille stems. Flowers and foliage may be added in the form of garlands attached to these same fixtures. Sprays of flowers may be designed on the hood, roof, or trunk of the car using a floral foam cage with a suction cup attachment. These decorations should be designed in a low fashion to avoid impairing the driver's visibility and to prevent extensive damage from the wind. When floral foam cages are attached, the vehicle should be driven only at slow speeds. Carriage decorations may be designed and attached in a fashion similar to decorating a car. Additional options for decorating a carriage include wrapping the spokes of the wheels with ribbon, adding flowers and ribbon to the horse's mane and tail, and providing a boutonniere for the carriage driver.

Balloon Release

An exciting finale to the ceremonial proceedings is a balloon release. The guests are each given a helium balloon as they leave the church. When the new couple exits, the balloons are released simultaneously. The result is a festive display of colorful globes floating freely in the sky. This rather simple decoration is a great replacement for the tradition of throwing rice, which has been disallowed by many churches.

Floral decorations are the key ingredient in softening a ceremonial site and enhancing the look and feel of a wedding. The choice of decorations should be selected based on the color,

Notes

style, formality, and location of the wedding. Churches and other ceremony locations often impose restrictions which limit the decorative possibilities. Creativity and imagination are required to devise distinctive floral arrangements for the unique situations of each individual ceremony. Plants, props, ribbons, and garlands can all be used in addition to flowers to decorate the ceremony site from the exterior entry to the altar. While designing ceremonial decorations, the florist must not lose sight of the true focus of the wedding. The solemnness of the ceremony and the emphasis on a personalized setting for the exchange of vows should be kept in mind as every flower is selected and put into place.

Notes, Photographs, Sketches, etc.

Notes, Photographs, Sketches, etc.

Reception Decorations

Chapter

8

A wedding reception is a time to celebrate with family and friends. The atmosphere created for the reception should be based upon the bride's selected wedding theme. This theme might be orchestrated with color, food, favors, props, or novelties, as well as with flowers. The florist should help unite all of the elements of the reception in order to maintain this established theme. A close working relationship should be established with the caterers, bakers, and other professionals commonly hired to provide reception services. Colors, props, and other needs can then be coordinated among the professionals involved to create a memorable event for the new couple and their guests.

The formality of the wedding should be carried through to the reception. A formal wedding would most likely involve a sit-down dinner in a country club or hotel banquet room. A semiformal wedding might involve a buffet-style meal at a restaurant or hall. An informal wedding might involve a buffet-style meal, hors d'oeuvres, or simply cake and punch in a garden or a family member's home. There are as many different types of receptions as there are brides. Therefore, the florist must be flexible and creative in designing the appropriate floral atmosphere for the given situation.

Traditional Reception Locations and Decorations

The reception room, whether in a restaurant, hotel, country club, or other location, can easily continue the wedding's theme with appropriate decorations in the entry and interior. Large plants, such as ficus trees, can be used to soften the harsh interiors of some halls. Plants also help create a cozier atmosphere in very large ballrooms. For an evening reception, twinkle lights can be strung through the tall plants to create a

Notes

magical, romantic mood. Tall columns with ferns or arrangements above eye level add volume to a room. The columns can be very effective when tall trees are not available. Low pedestals with plants or arrangements might be used on each side of the doorway to frame the entry. Support pillars can also be made less noticeable by placing tall plants around them.

Balloons can be used to create a festive or sophisticated look. For an elegant evening reception, black, white, or clear balloons could be used to fill the ceiling above the dance floor. Long, silver mylar streamers could be tied to the balloons and allowed to hang down to create a shimmery look. These streamers should be out of reach of most guests, approximately 7 to 8 feet above the floor. For a festive look, balloons could be used to create arches, hearts, pillars, gazebos, topiaries, and even free-standing mosaic walls.

The amount of decoration needed around the entry and interior of the reception room will be determined by the room's size and ceiling height, the number of guests, and the floor plan. The goal should be to provide enough decorations to enhance the environment and maintain the wedding theme without making the room crowded and uncomfortable.

A florist should visit the reception site to become familiar with the physical needs of the room. The floor plan for the tables, bandstand, and dance floor can usually be obtained from the catering director or location manager. A checklist, such as the traditional reception location checklist provided in Appendix D of the book, should be taken to the location to assist in planning.

Installation Tips for Traditional Receptions

- Work closely with the catering director or location coordinator.
- Schedule, in advance, the required times for installation and tear down.
- Work with a floor plan whenever possible.
- Secure all decorations with the guests' safety in mind.

Transition Flowers

Some brides find that their budget will not allow them to have lavish decorations for the ceremony and the reception. In this situation, the florist might suggest the use of transition flowers. This allows the bride to use some of the ceremonial decorations

Notes

at the reception, as well. Depending on the situation, the bride might transport the decorations from the ceremony to the reception, or the florist might provide this service for an additional fee. If transition flowers will be used, often the design of these pieces will need to be altered in some way. Transition flowers and suggested uses are provided in Table 7.

TABLE 7

TRANSITION FLOWERS AND SUGGESTED USES

Ceremony Use	Reception Use	Design Tips
Tall altar arrangements	Buffet table decoration	Tall altar arrangements may require being designed in a round, rather than one-sided, style for use on a two-sided buffet table at the reception.
Long, low unity candle arrangement	Head table centerpiece	The unity candle arrangement may be used as a head table centerpiece, either as is, with the side tapers removed, or with all of the candles removed and replaced with flowers.
Standing candelabras	Cake or head table accents	Standing candelabras might be used on either side of the cake or head table. The florist might suggest changing the color of the candles for a different look.
Table candelabra arrangements	Head table arrangements	Table candelabras used on the altar can be used as head table arrangements. The florist might suggest changing the color of the candles for a different look.
Aisle candelabra arrangements	Guest table centerpieces	Arrangements designed in aisle candelabras using floral foam block or cages may be removed and placed in plant saucers for use as table centerpieces. The globe and candle may be removed and replaced with flowers for a different look, if desired.
Pew bows	Table skirt decorations	
Window sill arrangements	Station-buffet table arrangements	
Standing basket or pedestal arrangements	Cake or head table accents or receiving line markers	

Cake Decorations

The bride's cake can come in many configurations. Round layers are the most popular. Square-shaped layers are effective depending on the decorations applied. Other shapes, such as heart-shaped cakes, are less common and sometimes expensive. The top layer on a round cake can be 6 to 8 inches in diameter. Square cakes usually have a 9-inch top. Each tier of the cake is about 2 inches larger than the one above it.

Wedding cakes can be decorated in a variety of ways, as shown in ***Figures 8.1a, 8.1b, and 8.1c***. Porcelain figures or blown glass cake tops are popular alternatives to the traditional plastic bride and groom. These may be accented with silk or fresh flowers. Floral decorations can also be added between the layers and around the base of the cake. The style of the cake will determine the amount of decoration needed. A cake with very intricate detailing in the icing should not be heavily decorated with flowers. The cake knife and server can be given an added touch by simply tying flowers onto the handles with narrow ribbon. These pieces might also be trimmed to match the toasting glasses.

Floral cake tops are a popular choice for brides and, as such, should be encouraged by florists. These cake tops can be made in lace-trimmed cake top cups, OASIS® IGLU® Holders, 4-inch plant trays, or even spray paint can lids. When decorating cakes, the florist should be cautious about the type of flowers used and the chemical sprays used to treat the flowers during growing and processing. Some react when the flowers are used on or around the cake. Special care should also be taken to prevent floral foam holders from leaking or dripping water on the frosting of the cake.

Figure 8.1a Cake Decorating Ideas

Figure 8.1b Cake Decorating Ideas

How to Make a Floral Cake Top

1. The cake top should be constructed the day before the wedding to allow water dripping to cease.

2. Cake tops for multi-tiered cakes should be designed on top of an overturned bucket or other raised surface to help create the design from the proper viewpoint.

3. Soak the floral foam and fill the holder.

4. Cut out a paper circle the same diameter as the cake and place the cake top holder in the center of the circle.

Figure 8.1c Cake Decorating Ideas

Notes

5. Green the holder so that an all-around design can be created. Keep the greenery within the boundaries of the paper circle. Place the foliage at the rim of the container at a slightly downward angle to help ensure a smooth transition between the cake and the cake top.

6. Insert the flowers carefully. Only small-stemmed materials should be used due to the limited amount of floral foam in the holder. Generally, the flowers should remain within the boundaries of the paper circle for the best proportion to the cake's size. Any style can be created depending on the cake's style and the reception theme.

7. Do not re-soak or add water to the holder unless the cake top is constructed several days in advance.

Options for Adding Flowers Between Cake Layers

Separations between cake layers sometimes include a plastic plate with four pillars. Other cakes may be separated by pillars which are inserted directly through the cake. It is important to contact the baker to determine the style and the length of the pillars. Different methods may be used to add flowers between the cake layers:

- If the florist will be setting up the cake decorations, flowers may be added between the layers by simply laying the materials on the plastic separator plate. For cakes without separator plates, the florist should place an acrylic disc, mirrored plate, or paper doily under the flowers to keep them off the icing. Begin with a thin layer of foliage and then place flowers in the desired pattern on top of the foliage. Flowers and foliage should overlap somewhat to help unify the grouping.

  Note: If wilt-sensitive flowers are used with this method, water tubes will be needed and should be hidden under the foliage.

- If the baker will be setting up the cake decorations, the flowers should be wired and taped and designed in a corsage-like manner. The corsage stem should be trimmed closely so that the decoration lies flat on the

Notes

separator plate. To save time, flowers may be glued to broad-leaved foliage, such as salal, instead of wiring and taping the unit together.

- For cakes with tall pillars, vertical stem placements may be desired. In this case, a small piece of soaked floral foam (approximately 2 inches x 2 inches) may be wrapped in green floral foil and attached to the separator plate with double-faced tape. Flowers may be carefully designed within the foam, and additional flowers and foliage may be layered around the foiled foam to conceal it.

Cake pillars may also be decorated more lavishly. Small foliage, such as ivy, is most effective. The decorations may be wired at the top of the pillar with a #28 gauge wire or tied with an 1/8-inch ribbon. The material is then spiralled around the pillar and secured at the base in the same manner. Gluing the decorations to the pillar is faster and less tedious; however, a florist should purchase his own pillars for this purpose, rather than damaging those of the baker.

Options for Decorating the Base of the Cake

- A garland of foliage and flowers can be created and wrapped around the cake base. (See Chapter 7.) The florist requires the circumference of the cake in order to design this decoration.

- Layering loose flowers and foliage around the cake provides a quick base finish and allows design flexibility.

- Pre-constructed clusters of flowers may be placed around the base of the cake. When these clusters are used along with clusters between the layers, the total look is unified.

Cake Decorating Tips

- The florist is liable for a cake if he decorates it without the baker's assistance.

- An acrylic mirror or similar acrylic base should be placed under a figurine when placing it on a cake. This will prevent it from shifting in the frosting and falling off the cake.

- The cake top and other decorations should be designed in direct proportion to the size of the cake, as well as the diameter of each individual layer.

- It is best not to insert fresh flowers into the frosting of a cake unless they were specifically grown for human consumption.

The cake table may have one or both cakes placed on it at the reception. The serving pieces and napkins should be on the table along with the cake. A table skirt decoration would be a perfect complement to the table.

Punch and Champagne Table

The punch or champagne table is an area of high visibility and activity. Thus, a table skirt decoration is an excellent choice for this table. If a champagne fountain or punch bowl is used, it may be decorated around the base, similarly to the cake. Most fountains have a container built into the top specifically to hold flowers. This decoration may be designed similarly to the cake top, but must be properly proportioned for the size of the fountain. For very formal receptions, the guests' champagne glasses might be decorated with bows and silk flowers tied on the stem. The bride's and groom's toasting glasses might have more elaborate or special decorations. Lace bows or fresh flowers tied on with thin satin ribbons are lovely accents.

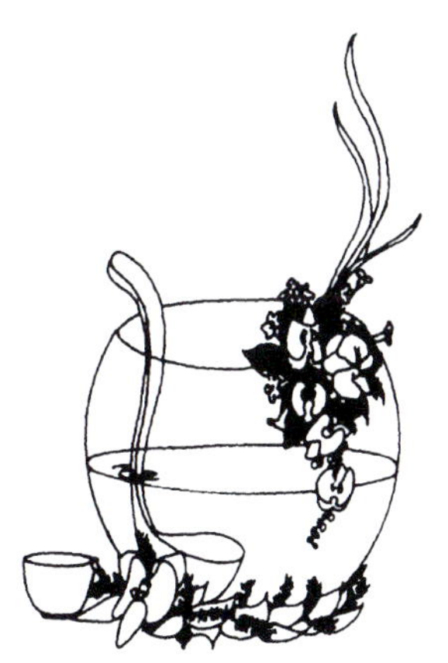

Figure 8.2a Punch Bowl Decorations

Figure 8.2b Punch Bowl Decorations

Punch and Champagne Table Decorating Tips

1. Obtain the top container for the fountain, or fit a cup or liner into it, so that the top arrangement can be made at the flower shop.

2. Obtain the proper number of glasses several days in advance if the guests' glasses are to be decorated.

3. Avoid designing a fountain top arrangement in place, especially if the fountain has already been filled with punch or champagne. If the top must be designed in place, cover the fountain with plastic to prevent flower pieces from dropping into the fountain wells.

4. Decorations may be added to the rim of a punch bowl or fountain in different ways. ***(Figures 8.2a and 8.2b)***

Notes

- Wire and tape wilt-resistant flowers and design them in a corsage-like cluster that can be bent over the edge of the bowl. The "stem" of the cluster should be positioned on the outside of the bowl and bent to press against it.

- Glue flowers, foliage, and other decorations onto a hair clip and attach it to the edge of the punch bowl. Be sure the entire hair clip is concealed by the decorations.

- Bend a taped #18 gauge wire in half, dip the ends in glue, and insert them into the edge of an OASIS® IGLU® Holder. Once the glue has dried, bend the wire over the edge of the punch bowl, making the IGLU® outside the bowl. Flowers may be designed in a cluster, cascade, or upright position.

Buffet Tables

A buffet table is most often constructed with a series of 8-foot tables. Some locations may create other styles of buffet tables, such as the serpentine style or buffet-station style. A serpentine table resembles a series of connected *S*'s. They are usually about 2 feet wide. Stations are separate tables set up around the room with different parts of the menu on each table. It is important to know whether the guests will serve themselves from one side or from both sides of the buffet.

Effectively utilizing flowers is important no matter what serving style is chosen. Skirt treatments work well on a buffet table that is rectangular. The serpentine style is not as well suited for this trim.

Any of the table arrangements can utilize tall designs. Inexpensive plastic containers may be used to construct a multitude of structures. For example, a plastic birdbath can be weighted at the base and painted the desired color to create a raised container with a large amount of design space. Experiment with plastic risers, cylinders, and trays to create the size of structure best suited for the table. Mechanics are very important when creating a well balanced and self-supporting structure.

A serpentine table is sometimes difficult to decorate due to its narrow width and unusual shape. Serving from a serpentine table almost always takes place on both sides. Decorations in sets of three look best on this style of table. One arrangement in the center of the table and one on a pedestal at each end can be very

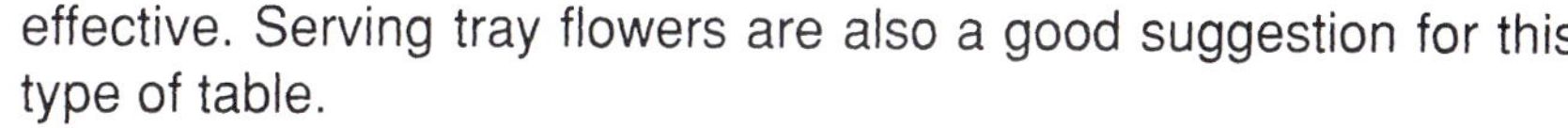
effective. Serving tray flowers are also a good suggestion for this type of table.

Smaller designs are best for station-style serving. Each table can utilize a different design as long as they blend with the overall theme. Small structures can create different looks to accent what the station is serving. Station-style buffet tables are usually easier to decorate because they typically measure at least 8 feet long.

Tips for Creating Elevated Table Designs

Simple tray and riser structures need only be glued together with hot glue. Special care must be taken when creating large elevated structures with risers, trays, and cylinders. The following tips will help create effective buffet structures. ***(Figures 8.3a and 8.3b)***

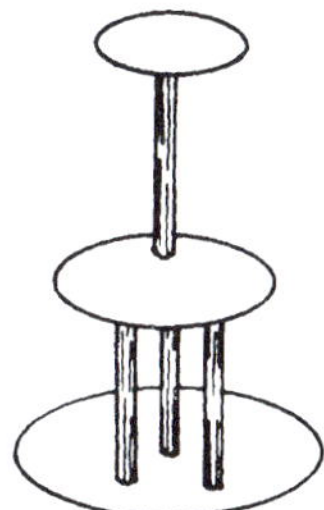

Figure 8.3a Elevated Table Designs

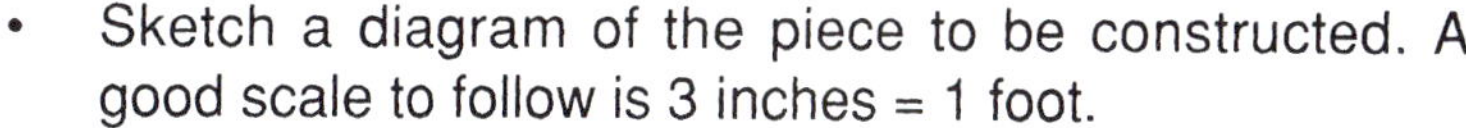

- Sketch a diagram of the piece to be constructed. A good scale to follow is 3 inches = 1 foot.

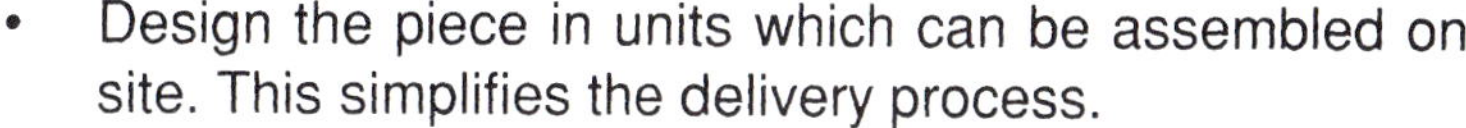

- Design the piece in units which can be assembled on site. This simplifies the delivery process.

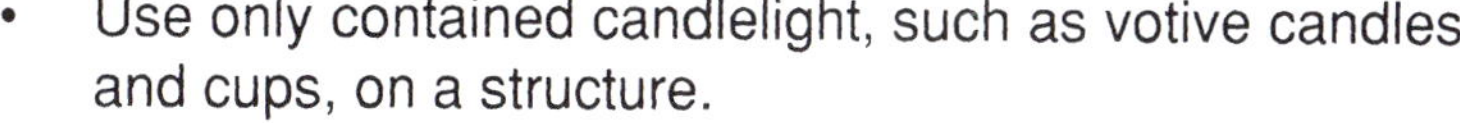

- Use only contained candlelight, such as votive candles and cups, on a structure.

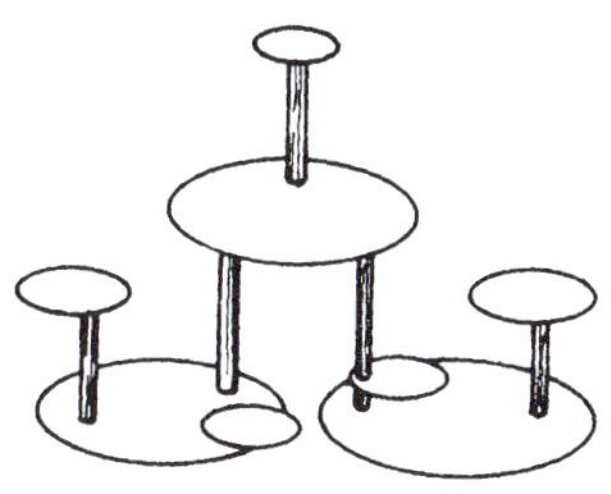

Figure 8.3b Elevated Table Designs

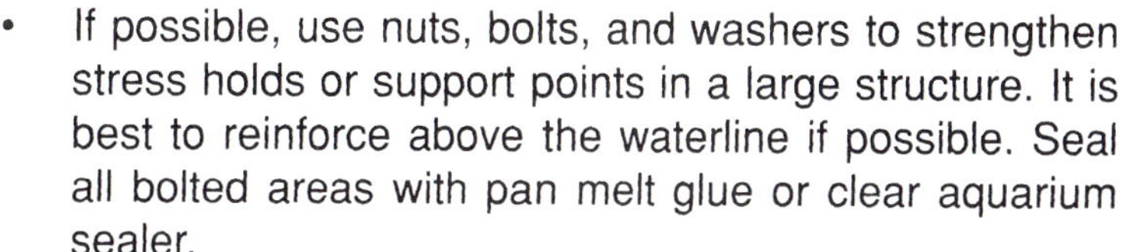

- If possible, use nuts, bolts, and washers to strengthen stress holds or support points in a large structure. It is best to reinforce above the waterline if possible. Seal all bolted areas with pan melt glue or clear aquarium sealer.
- Elevated designs can be created out of baskets for a garden wedding. These structures are wired and hot glued together for security. It is best to weight the base basket for stability.
- Keep the structure physically and visually balanced during construction.
- Use floral foam IGLU® Holders or cylinders to create small floral accents in multiple locations on the structure.
- Remember that the overall effect of a modular piece is more important than that of the individually designed areas of the arrangement.

Head Tables

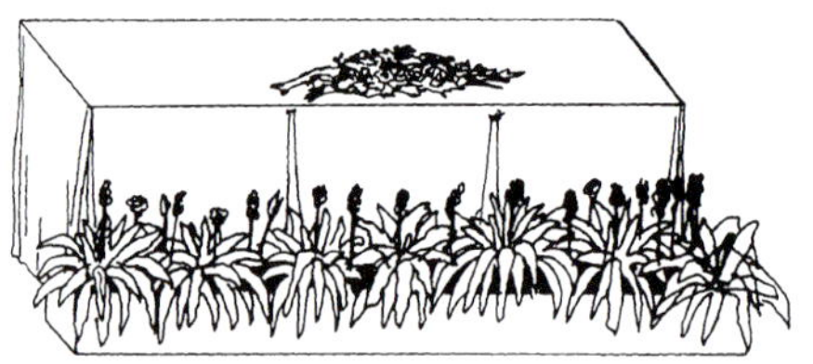

Figure 8.4 Head Table Decorations

People seated at the head table will want to see their guests, so it is important not to block their view with floral decorations. Tall plants or a balloon display behind the table can create an effective background. When the head table is placed on a raised platform, a window box or hedge effect can be created by lining ferns and blooming plants in front of the table on the platform as shown in ***Figure 8.4***. Appropriate table skirt decorations help complete the theme.

Low arrangements, heavy garlands, or elevated designs may be used on the table top itself. A less expensive option for brides on a budget is to decorate the head table with the bridesmaids' bouquets. These could be grouped at the corners with a centerpiece in the middle of the table, or evenly distributed on a bed of foliage along the front edge of the table for maximum effect.

The length of the head table depends on the size of the bridal party. A general rule of thumb is 2 feet of space per place setting. Thus, if ten people will be seated at the table, a 20-foot table is needed. Since most tables are 8 feet long, the caterer will probably use three tables to make a 24-foot table.

Guest Tables

The theme created with the cake, flowers, head table, and other major decorations should be carried through to the dining tables. The size and shape of the tables will often determine the type of decorations needed. The seating capacity of different table types is shown in Table 8.

TABLE 8

SEATING CAPACITY OF DIFFERENT TABLE TYPES

Table Type/ Size	Number of Seats
24-inch cocktail table	Two to four
34-inch square card table	Four
8 foot x 3 foot table	Eight to ten
60-inch round table	Eight
72-inch round table	Ten
80-inch round table	Twelve

Notes

Decorations for cocktail tables should be kept small. Simple designs such as bud vases, candles with floral accents, small potted violets, or bubble bowls are appropriate. Flower heads or glitter can also be scattered over the tablecloth for a whimsical effect.

Square card tables are large enough to use small centerpieces or plants with decorative trims. Long rectangular tables might be decorated with narrow centerpiece garlands running down the center or groupings of small vases with unique flower specimens.

Large receptions with tables lined up end to end or smaller receptions using 8-foot tables in configurations, such as a *U*-shape or *T*-shape, require controlled use of flowers due to limited table top space. For simple decorations on a limited budget, helium balloons with festive streamers may be used by tying the balloons to a small decorative sandbag covered with mylar.

Round tables offer unlimited possibilities for decorating with flowers. Mirrors, candles, fabrics, and tulle may be used singly or in combination to create exciting table tops before the design is placed in position. Elevated containers work perfectly on round tables, especially when the designs coordinate with those used on the buffet table. In addition, baskets filled with a mixture of annuals are effective for a garden reception. For a formal reception, five-branch candelabras are elegant accents on round guest tables.

Tips for Decorating Guest Tables

- In order for guests to see across the table, keep the decorations below 12 inches or above 18 inches in height.
- All structures should be very stable due to the high level of activity at and around the table.
- For a reception with a large number of tables, design three different arrangement styles and heights to create volume and interest. For example, for a reception with thirty tables, ten designs might be 14-inch vertical arrangements, ten might be 20-inch topiaries and another ten might be 26-inch tall cascading designs.
- Work with the catering director to coordinate salt and pepper shakers, sugar bowls and creamers, and other table accessories into the floral setting.

Children's Tables

Notes

At some receptions, children are grouped at tables separately from the adults. Novelty table arrangements can be used to help entertain these special guests. For example, tables may be covered with heavy paper and crayons placed at each place setting. Smiling faces may be created with wiggly eyes and chenille stems glued into the middle of the flowers in the centerpieces. Large branches with individual candies attached can be added to the centerpieces to create festive candy trees. No matter what the decoration, the overall appearance should blend well with the total wedding theme. (Note: Never use candles of any kind on children's tables.)

Gift Table

The gift table is usually long and narrow. The average gift table is 8 by 3 feet wide. Since the table is primarily used to hold gifts, a skirt decoration is advisable. An appropriate "add-on" sale for this table could be a decorated basket or box for wedding cards. Ribbon, tulle, silk flowers, balloons, or fresh materials may be used to decorate this container.

Wedding Card Basket and Box Tips

- Wire or hot glue fresh or artificial material to the basket handle or edge.
- Wrap a box in decorative wedding paper. Finish the slit for the cards by folding paper inside the lid and securing with glue or tape.
- Pressed flowers or other decorations may be applied to a card box with rubber cement or floral adhesive glue.
- Elaborate card baskets or boxes may be provided as a rental item for brides on a budget.

Guest Book Table

The guest book is typically placed at the entry to the reception room. If a table is used, a table skirt decoration and/or a small flower arrangement is advisable. A guest book pedestal might be

Notes

decorated with a plant grouping at the base, a garland of flowers across the top and cascading over the side, or with a simple accent of flowers attached to the pen.

Seating Table

At formal weddings, it is customary to have a seating table prepared with place cards for the guests in alphabetical order. This table is placed just prior to the guest book table or immediately outside the dining room. Sometimes this table is combined with the guest book table, thus requiring only a simple decoration. A table skirt decoration or small arrangement is an appropriate decoration for this table. A candelabra is also acceptable.

Table Skirt Decorations

Table skirt decorations provide appealing accents to the skirting on reception tables, such as the cake table, gift table, buffet table, punch and champagne table, guest book table, and the head table. Ribbon, tulle, and garlands can each be used to create different impressions. Garlands of ribbon braids, beads, and other material may be pinned on the skirt,t as well.

Attaching Bows to Table Skirts

Bows are a popular adornment for table skirts, particularly on the cake and bride's tables. These decorations are usually pinned to the skirting, and must be well attached so they will remain in place as guests pass by the tables.

1. Curl the bow's wire around two fingers to create a pin curl. The wire used to secure the bow should be taped. Chenille stems may also be used.

2. Weave a corsage or straight pin through the pin curl and into the fabric of the skirt or tablecloth to secure the bow in place.

Attaching Garlands to Skirting

Fresh or artificial flowers and foliage garlands are beautiful accents to any table skirt. To swag the table properly, the garland should be one and a half times the length of the table. A longer piece of garland can be used if the swag will be closer to the floor. Attachment of the garland to the table is done in the following manner.

1. Twist a taped wire around the garland, creating a pin curl as described for bows.

2. Twist the wire below the pin curl to secure the loop.

3. Weave a corsage or straight pin through the pin curl and into the fabric of the skirt or tablecloth. For heavy garlands, two or more pins may be necessary at each pinning point to secure the garland in place.

Clothes pins and drapery hooks also make good attachment tools. Bows can be glued to clothes pins which are then used to clip garland to the skirting. Drapery hooks may be attached to the table skirt as shown in ***Figure 8.5*** and may be used for securing garlands to the table in an inverted position.

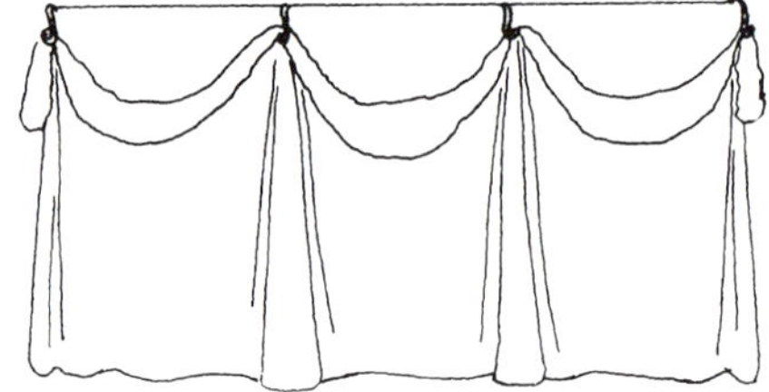

Figure 8.5 Drapery Hooks Used to Attach Table Skirt Decorations

Creating a Braided Ribbon Garland

Ribbons are a good choice for creating inexpensive garlands. A variety of ribbon colors and sizes may be combined to create different looks. For a more elaborate effect, ribbons can be braided into a garland and used to swag a table skirt in a similar manner to fresh flower garlands. The following steps are used to create such a garland.

1. For braiding, use ribbon lengths two times the length of the table. This should be enough ribbon to swag the table and allow for shrinkage during the braiding process.

2. Align three equal lengths of #40 ribbon and wrap a taped wire around them at one end.

3. Attach the wire to a fixed structure, such as a doorknob. This allows the ribbon to be pulled tautly during the braiding process.

4. Braid the ribbon by crossing the right ribbon over the center ribbon. The right ribbon then becomes the center ribbon.

Notes

5. Cross the left ribbon over the center ribbon. The left ribbon then becomes the center ribbon.

6. Continue working back and forth, crossing the right and then the left ribbon over the center ribbon.

7. Braid to the end of the ribbon and secure the end with a taped wire.

8. Attach the braided ribbon to the skirt or tablecloth in the same manner as a garland.

Creating Tulle Festoon

Tulle is a popular wedding embellishment for bouquets, corsages, and pew ends. It is also a good choice for table festoons because of its natural draping quality. Abundant layers of tulle give the best overall effect. Narrow tulle or broad bridal illusion may also be used.

1. Gather the tulle with a taped wire or chenille stem and pin it into the fabric in the same manner as a bow. Heavy festooning will require more than a single pin.

2. The festoon may be left plain or finished by:

   - Creating tulle puffs or bows and attaching them at the gathering points.

   - Garlanding ribbon or pearl strands into the festoons.

   - Pinning fine ribbon loops and streamers at each gathering point and gluing flowers into the center.

   - Dotting the tulle with sequins or pearls glued in a scattered pattern.

   - Stringing twinkle lights among the festoons.

   - Attaching floral foam cages at each gathering point and designing floral or foliage accents within them.

Candelabras

Floor candelabras can be used to decorate the areas beside the cake and head tables. These may be transition designs that are moved to the reception from the ceremony, or they may be designed specifically for the reception.

Table top candelabras may be used on almost any type of table at the reception. Most often they are used on the head table. They may also be used on the cake and punch tables, as well as the gift and seating tables. Table top candelabras come in many different styles. ***(Figures 8.6a and 8.6b)*** The most commonly used styles are those with three or four branches. Other styles may have one to twelve branches on them.

Floral foam adapters which fit into the candleholders simplify the process of designing these decorations. Cascading styles are particularly appropriate in table top candelabras in order to keep the flowers away from the candles' flames. Most often, table top candelabras are designed with flowers radiating from the center. However, multi-branched candelabras may also be designed in a more asymmetrical pattern, with floral sprays radiating from more than one location within the candelabra.

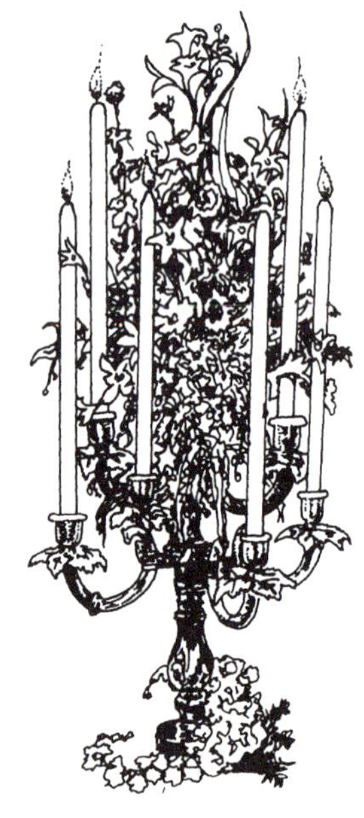

Figure 8.6a Table Top Candelabra

Tips for Using Candelabras

- Candelabras may be cleaned and shrink-wrapped after each use and/or polished prior to each use. The shrink-wrap helps protect the silver in packing, and also keeps fingerprints off the candelabras.
- Handle silver candelabras with clean rubber or fabric gloves, or hold them with a plastic bag to prevent fingerprints and smudges. The "used" shrink-wrap may also be used in handling the candelabras, and in making the candles fit tightly in them.
- Be sure the floral foam adapter is in the candleholder securely. If it is loose, floral tape may be wrapped around the base to tighten the fit. (Floral clay may also be used if the candelabra belongs to the florist.)
- Design the arrangement with all the candles in place. Remove them for delivery purposes. It is best not to remove any candles which have been inserted into the floral foam.

Figure 8.6b Table Top Candelabra

Notes

- If the candles do not fit the holders tightly, simply wrap floral tape around their bases. Tape that matches the candle's color is best.

- If the candles will be burning for a long period of time, 24-inch candles are recommended.

Receiving Line Flowers

A receiving line is usually part of a formal or semiformal reception. The receiving line may be located in a number of different locations within the reception hall. Depending on the setup, decorations such as a floral arch might be suggested to frame the bride and groom within the line. When the arch is positioned in front of a plain wall, the area becomes a perfect setting for picture-taking, as well. Pedestal arrangements or tall plants might be placed at each end of the line for a totally finished appearance.

Dance Floor and Bandstand

Understandably, the bandstand and dance floor are areas of much activity. Floral decorations in this area can be effective, but they must be secure and stable. It is wise to keep all decorations at least 2 feet away from the edge of the dance floor rather than directly on the dance surface. If decorations are at eye level or higher, the likelihood of an accident is lessened greatly. Bandstand decorations should not interfere with the band's activity on stage or with the guests' views of individual band members. Large plants or arrangements on pedestals are effective ways to frame the dance floor and bandstand areas. Balloons can also be a festive addition for these areas.

Powder Room Flowers

Flowers in the powder room are the perfect finishing touch to a carefully planned reception. This attention to detail is quickly recognized and appreciated by the wedding guests. A simple arrangement or vase of flowers in the wedding colors is appropriate. A necessity basket, containing such items as small soaps, lotions, and towelettes, is also a thoughtful gesture. The florist can decorate a basket edge or handle with flowers and ribbons in the wedding colors and allow the bride to provide the necessities, or the basket can be sold as a complete unit.

Guest Favors

Favors, such as scrolls, sachets, satin roses with jordan almonds, or specially packaged chocolates, are a delightful gift of thanks for each guest. Brides often desire very special, personalized options for their favors. The creative florist can often design the perfect novelty favor for a client using readily available items. The way in which a favor is packaged is as important as the favor itself. Miniature bags or boxes tied with narrow ribbons in the wedding colors make any favor seem special.

Favors may be placed in a basket or hung on a tree on the gift table. Alternatively, the favors may be placed at each guest's place or presented to guests as they enter the reception room.

Easy Ideas for Guest Favors

- Sachets of potpourri or small candies can be gathered in the center of two crisscrossed, 8-inch lengths of tulle, tied with a thin ribbon bow, then decorated with matching silk flowers glued to the tulle. ***(Figure 8.7a)***

Figure 8.7a Guest Favors

- Small boxes of chocolates can be tied with a thin ribbon bow. Just before delivery, a fresh flower could be tucked under the bow.

- Parchment scrolls with a wedding poem could be printed or written in calligraphy, rolled up, secured with a lace ribbon, and decorated with a cluster of dried baby's breath or tiny silk blossoms. ***(Figure 8.7b)***

Figure 8.7b Guest Favors

Food Tray Flowers

Loose flowers laid on a serving tray add a special touch to the food, as well as the reception. Small clusters of filler flowers can also be effective when the theme is one of romance or garden elegance. It is suggested that only flowers grown specifically to be eaten or used as food decoration be placed among the food items. These types of flowers are sometimes available through specialty produce stores.

Service Personnel's Flowers

A well coordinated, formal reception often includes flowers for the service personnel. The waiters, waitresses, hostess, and

Notes

other personnel who service a wedding reception enjoy feeling that they are part of the affair. Boutonnieres and small single flower corsages can put a genuine smile on their faces, along with increasing the service the bride and her guests receive. Everyone enjoys feeling special, including the servers at a wedding reception. When appropriate, the florist should use the service persons' flowers in creating a uniform reception look.

Bride's Toss Bouquet

A bride's toss bouquet is typically used when the bride desires to keep her silk bouquet or is having her fresh bouquet preserved. A toss bouquet can be as simple as a few flowers and baby's breath tied with a ribbon, or as elaborate as a duplicate of the bride's original bouquet. This bouquet should be delivered in its own box to the reception location. It can be placed at the bride's place at the head table or given to the wedding coordinator.

Going Away Corsage and Boutonniere

The going away corsage and boutonniere can be made of silk or fresh flowers. The bride can enjoy the silk corsage as a keepsake, as well as using it for special days after the wedding. Fresh flowers are short, sweet remembrances worn by the bride and groom as they leave for their honeymoon. Either way this final touch can be an add-on sale or a gift to the bride and groom from the florist. Occasionally, the going away corsage is incorporated into the bride's bouquet.

Home Receptions

Decorations for the home reception can vary greatly. The size and decor of the home will dictate the type of floral decorations needed. It is most advisable to visit the home in advance to survey the areas where the reception will take place. A home reception checklist is provided in Appendix D for this purpose.

The exterior and interior entries should be decorated to provide an inviting atmosphere upon the arrival of guests. The ambience from the front door through the rest of the house should be warm and congenial. In the main reception area, floral decorations might include the coffee table, piano, or mantel arrangements. Stairways are another key area which could benefit from decorations, particularly if guests will be using the stairs. Banisters may be swagged in a variety of ways, or plants

Notes

can be placed on individual steps all the way to the top of the stairs. Chandeliers can be effectively decorated with garlands, flowers, ribbon, or tulle, as long as the materials are kept a safe distance from the lights. Other areas of the home which guests might enter will benefit from small, impromptu-looking designs, such as a casual vase of flowers on the kitchen window sill.

Installations Tips for Home Receptions

- Be cautious when placing arrangements on the furniture in a client's home. Use trays or pads to protect furniture from water damage.

- It is best to use taped wire to install decorations on a wood banister. Matching ribbon may also be tied onto the banister and the wire attached over it for added protection.

- Bring extra flowers so that small impromptu vases can be designed upon special request.

Garden Receptions

Garden receptions offer special challenges due to unpredictable weather conditions. Floral decorations must be designed to withstand rain, heat, and wind, as well as the precarious nature of uneven ground surfaces. Centerpieces may need extra weight to prevent them from tipping over in the wind. Sand, gravel, rocks, cement, or plaster may be used, depending on the size of the container. Delicate flowers may need to be avoided to prevent wilting in the heat. A garden reception checklist is provided in Appendix D.

Faux Garden with Cut Flowers

Ultimately, the garden should be in peak bloom for a garden reception. In the event that blooming occurs too early or too late, cut flowers in water tubes may be inserted in the soil around the plants. Potted blooming plants may also be worked into the garden beds concealing the pots with layers of sheet moss. Entire gardens of cut flowers and plants can be created to camouflage bare areas. Garden props, such as trellises or gazebos, may be rented to help give a sparse garden more personality. Here are tips on how to create a faux garden.

- Secure blocks of soaked floral foam to the ground by inserting two hyacinth stakes through the foam and into the ground. The stakes should go into the ground at least 3 to 4 inches.

- Create a garden in the foam. Remember to design it in the manner which plants grow. Most flowers should be grouped by variety and have their blooms about the same height. For example, gladioli should be positioned in a tall, upright manner, while marigolds should be grouped in a low, shrub-like fashion.

- Cover any exposed foam with damp moss or wood chips to blend the design with the rest of the garden.

Note: A false garden can be created in containers if installation time will not permit on-site construction.

Tent Decorations

Garden receptions often include tents to provide protection from possible inclement weather. Tent poles may be decorated with fabric festoons, balloons, or foliage garlands to create different effects. The poles can even be turned into large palm trees. The inner roof of the tent may be decorated with hanging plants, arrangements, or covered with a layer of helium-filled balloons. It is important to secure all hanging arrangements or plants with a taped #18 gauge wire, to prevent them from falling in the event of high winds. When planning decorations for tent poles, the florist should contact the tent company to determine the diameter of the poles. Also, the use of fireproof or fire code approved materials is recommended when decorating the tent.

How to Festoon Tent Poles with Fabric

Festoons of draperies are a popular look in home interiors. This decorating idea can be used skillfully for weddings in order to conceal tent poles or other posts at the ceremony or reception. Cotton, satin, or other fabrics in solid colors or prints can be used to achieve the desired look.

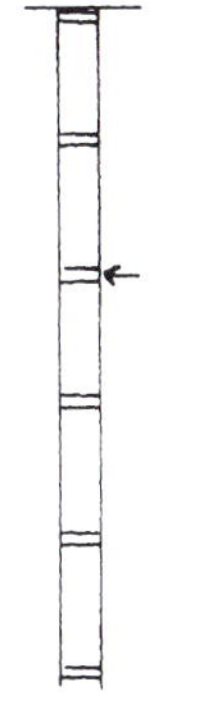

Figure 8.8a Festooning a Tent Pole Step 1

1. Apply strips of double-faced tape around the poles, beginning at the top and then at equal intervals, approximately every 2 feet. ***(Figure 8.8a)***

2. Cut the fabric to a length about one and a half times the length of the pole.

3. Wrap the fabric around the top of the pole. Gather it evenly and secure it to the tape with a taped wire.

4. Pull up the fabric to create a puffy effect at the next taped location on the pole. Secure the fabric with a taped wire. Work in the same manner until the base of the pole is reached. ***(Figure 8.8b)***

Figure 8.8b Festooning a Tent Pole Step 4

5. Complete the bottom of the pole with the balance of the fabric. Trim any excess fabric to avoid having fabric lying on the ground.

How to Attach a Garland to a Tent Pole

Tent poles and other posts can be decorated quickly by wrapping them in garlands of foliage, flowers, ribbon, or fabric. The length of the garland needed will depend on how closely together it will be wrapped. Generally, one and a half times the length of the pole is sufficient for a barber pole effect. ***(Figure 8.9a)*** To fully wrap and cover a pole, a garland at least two times the length of the pole is needed. ***(Figure 8.9b)***

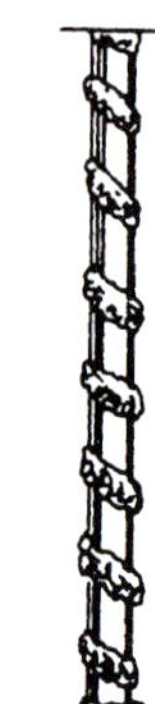

Figure 8.9a Attaching Garland to a Tent Pole

1. Securely attach the end of the garland to the top of the pole and cross frame using a taped wire. Hide the attaching point with a bow or similar treatment.

2. Wrap the garland around the pole to the base.

3. Attach the end of the garland to the base of the pole with another taped wire.

How to Create a Palm Tree on a Tent Pole

An exotic look can be achieved on tent poles and other narrow posts by turning them into imitation palm trees. This procedure must be completed on site and can be rather time consuming. Thus, a sufficient labor charge should be added onto the price of these designs in order to ensure profit.

Figure 8.9b Attaching Garland to a Tent Pole

1. To create a trunk, wrap the poles from top to bottom with sheets of polyester fiberfil from the fabric store. Use waxed string to secure the fiberfil in place. Next,

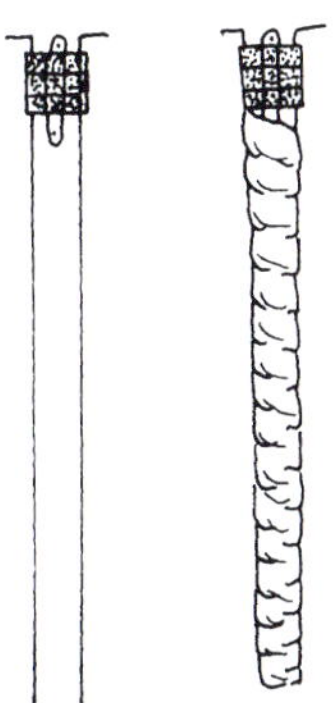

Figure 8.10a Creating a Palm Tree on a Tent Pole Steps 1 and 2

Figure 8.10b Creating a Palm Tree on a Tent Pole Step 4

wrap natural-colored paper ribbon over the fiberfil. Straight pins or raffia may be used as needed to hold the paper ribbon in place. The overall effect should be that of a plump tree trunk. ***(Figure 8.10a)***

2. Securely attach one or two floral foam cages to the top of the tent pole. Use the crosspoles to help secure the cages in place so that they cannot slip down the pole. One cage is needed for a half or corner tree, and two cages are needed for an all-around tree. ***(Figure 8.10a)***

3. Moss the floral foam cage to hide the mechanics.

4. Insert palm fronds, such as emerald fern, to create the tree top. The number of fronds needed will vary from thirty-five to seventy-five (one and a half to three bunches), depending on the desired size of the tree. ***(Figure 8.10b)***

Floating Pool Arrangements

A florist might suggest using a floating arrangement as a decoration whenever a reception area features a pool. The mechanics of this type of design are important since the arrangement will not have a stable surface to rest upon. A floating pool arrangement must also have perfect balance to avoid tipping or sinking.

There are two methods used to keep a design floating in a pool. The first method uses a dense Styrofoam™ funeral wreath or child's life preserver, and sheet Styrofoam™. This type of float will support only a small amount of weight, approximately 15 pounds. The second method of constructing a pool float uses acrylic sheeting and bubbles. It can be designed to hold as much weight as desired and should be used as a rental item because of the cost of construction.

How to Construct a Styrofoam™ Pool Float

1. Cut a piece of 2-inch sheet Styrofoam™ to fit over the top of a Styrofoam™ funeral wreath or a child's life preserver ring. (For example, if the ring is 18-inches in diameter, cut out an 18 inch circle of foam.)

2. Attach the Styrofoam™ circle to the life preserver ring with pan melt glue. Be neat, but use plenty of glue to assure a good bond.

3. Attach a design tray to the center of the foam circle in the same manner.

4. Tape or glue soaked floral foam onto the container.

5. Create the desired arrangement, making sure to cover the exposed Styrofoam™ with flowers and foliage. Keep the design balanced during assembly, and, if possible, test float the design in the flower shop before delivery.

How to Construct an Acrylic Pool Float

1. Have the following materials made by a plastics company:

    - Three 8-inch or 10-inch acrylic half-bubbles with a 1-inch lip. This size bubble should support an arrangement weight 35 to 65 pounds. Larger or smaller bubbles can be used, depending on the weight of the arrangement to be floated. ***(Figure 8.11a)***

    - One piece of 3/8-inch acrylic sheeting cut into an equilateral triangle large enough to accommodate all three bubbles on its surface. All three points of the triangle should have a hole drilled through it 3 inches from the edge. These will be used to anchor the float in the pool. All pieces should have their edges flamed for a smooth surface finish. ***(Figure 8.11a)***

Figure 8.11a Constructing an Acrylic Pool Float Step 1

2. Seal the lips of the three half-bubbles to one side of the triangle with clear aquarium sealer. Allow the sealer to dry for about 5 days.

3. Turn the float over and allow it to rest on the bubbles. Attach a design tray or a group of smaller trays to the triangle with floral clay.

Figure 8.11b Constructing an Acrylic Pool Float Step 4

4. Tape or glue in the floral foam and create the arrangement. ***(Figure 8.11b)***

5. Any type of structure can be created on this type float as long as it is balanced.

How to Install and Anchor a Floating Pool Arrangement

There are two methods used to secure a floating arrangement in a pool. The first method requires the florist to get into the pool. Although this may be an inconvenience, it is necessary when the anchoring lines must be out of sight or out of reach of the guests.

Method A:

1. Fill a fine, mesh bag with enough clear marbles to anchor the arrangement into position.

2. Tie the bag closed with nine pieces of 60-pound test fishing line measured to a length about 1 foot longer than the depth of the pool.

3. Attach the nine pieces of fishing line to the float at three equidistant points. Three pieces of fishing line will be tied at each point.

4. Carefully place the pool float in the water with the anchor at the pool's edge.

5. Get in the pool and hold the anchor as the float is slowly pushed into the desired position.

6. Hold the fishing lines close to the top and release the anchor.

The second method of installing a floating pool arrangement requires two people. However, neither person must get into the pool.

Method B:

1. Use 60-pound test fishing line in lengths that are 5 feet longer than the longest point across the pool. Use three lengths of line for each hole in the acrylic float or two lengths for the Styrofoam™ ring.

Notes

2. Attach the fishing line to the float at three equidistant points.

3. Carefully place the floating pool arrangement in the water from the side of the pool, while holding the lines. Pull on the lines to position the arrangement.

4. Securely tie the lines to ladders, diving board supports, or any other fixed object that is secure and away from foot traffic around the pool. Three concrete blocks may even be wrapped like wedding presents and used at locations to tie down the pool float. These must be placed at the edge of the pool in three different locations.

The wedding reception offers a multitude of ways to decorate with flowers. The many activities associated with a reception, including eating, dancing, picture-taking, gift-giving, and tossing a garter and bouquet, can all be enhanced with special floral touches. The focal point of all this activity is typically the wedding cake. This particular item should be given the special attention it deserves by accenting it, and the table it rests upon, with the appropriate floral treatments. The bride's table is another key area requiring an exaggerated use of flowers. Transition flowers, such as the unity candle arrangement, may be the perfect choice for brides on a budget. Accessories can also help achieve character in floral decorations. Balloons lend a festive mood, mirrors add elegance, and candles add romance. With so many possibilities for decorations, the florist must be careful to coordinate each detail. Unity in combining the freshest flowers with original design ideas will make the desired impression on the bride and all her guests.

Notes, Photographs, Sketches, etc.

Notes, Photographs, Sketches, etc.

Notes, Photographs, Sketches, etc.

Packaging, Delivering, and Servicing Weddings

Chapter 9

To each bride, her greatly anticipated wedding day is one of the most special times of her life. The beautiful packaging of the wedding bouquets, the prompt and efficient delivery of the flowers, and the reassurance that a professional wedding consultant is servicing the wedding, all contribute to a happy wedding and a satisfied client. These three factors greatly influence the florist's reputation for quality products and professional service.

Packaging

Beautiful packaging is the crowning touch to artistically designed wedding flowers. Creative finishing touches add an air of romance and beauty. These touches also demonstrate to the bride that the florist has professionally created her wedding flowers with care, sensitivity, and artistry.

Wedding Bouquets

Bouquets may be placed in appropriate boxes, set on a layer of waxed tissue or shredded cellophane, or encased in a large plastic bag. Alternatively, the bouquet handles could be placed in a layer of white Styrofoam™ on the bottom of the box. If a standard white cardboard wedding delivery box is used, all corners of the lid and box should be stapled for strength. Alternatives to the standard white cardboard box are a dressmaker's box, a similar utility box of appropriate dimensions without advertising or other printing, or a large floral wholesaler's cut flower delivery box. These boxes can be made more attractive for delivery by creatively decorating them with gift wrap, wallpaper, colored foil, vinyl, or ribbons. These trims may be fastened with cellophane tape, double-faced tape, adhesive, staples, or hot glue. A sheet of clear cellophane may be attached across the top of the box to create a "window" for viewing the bouquets. The box can then be closed. The box may be finished with a matching colored ribbon and accented with a dainty, complimentary corsage. A label should be added, and poetry, or a similar romantic embellishment may be included for a special romantic touch. Wedding box labels may be color-coded with waterproof markers to reduce confusion and simplify delivery on days when more than one wedding is scheduled. The label should clearly identify the recipient of the flowers, the individual's relationship to the bride, such as "Aunt Mary Smith," the location and time of delivery, and the name of the bride and groom (i.e., Anderson/Lancaster Wedding).

Special delivery packaging for delicate bouquets may be created in the following ways:

- Glue two boards of white Styrofoam™ together with hot melt glue and encase them in a custom-made wooden box, suitably decorated. The bouquet handles are then inserted into the foam for delivery.

- Use hot melt glue to secure PVC on acrylic tubing into an appropriate base of wood or Styrofoam™. The base and tubes of the unit can be spray painted with a neutral tint. The bouquets are then placed in tubes for delivery and presentation. For added protection, the bouquets may be wrapped in cellophane or encased in a cellophane bag.

- Ice chests of white Styrofoam™ make ideal bouquet boxes in extremely hot weather. Pre-cooling the chest and placing a frozen cooler block inside the chest will keep the bouquets cool for an extended period of time. The bouquets can be set on waxed tissue or shredded cellophane for added protection.

Corsages and Boutonnieres

Corsages and boutonnieres may be packaged in a fashion similar to bouquets. Smaller boxes are better suited for smaller design sizes. Individual corsage and boutonniere boxes may be used or several pieces may be placed in a single rose box. The designs may be set on a layer of shredded cellophane or waxed tissue or may be placed in individual cellophane corsage and boutonniere bags. The lid of the box is then labeled, tied with ribbon, and, if desired, accented with a romantic sentiment.

Notes

Notes

Delivery

It is of the utmost importance that all wedding flowers be delivered on time, professionally, and efficiently. A delivery schedule is provided in Appendix B to assist floral personnel in the successful delivery of wedding flowers.

Color-Coding

Many florists use a color-coding system to ensure the most efficient execution of their wedding orders. The initial wedding planner, its file, and all pre-made delivery boxes, floral stock, and rental equipment are color-coded with either a colored sticker or waterproof marker. This allows immediate identification of all materials for that specific wedding. Completed floral bouquets and other wedding flowers are stored in their color-coded delivery boxes in the cooler. This allows for easy identification by all personnel.

Delivery Tips

The following tips will ensure a more efficient and professional wedding delivery.

1. Provide delivery personnel with the following items:

    - A duplicate copy of the wedding planner, in Appendix B, without prices.

    - A completed delivery schedule, in Appendix B, that clearly states all deliveries to be made and the time and location of each delivery.

    - A list of all rental equipment that will be delivered for the wedding, the location, the time of the delivery, and when the equipment is be picked up. A duplicate copy is kept by the florist as a reminder to pick up the items.

2. Do not load the wedding flowers into the delivery vehicle early, especially in extremely hot or cold weather.

Notes

3. Make sure all boxes of flowers, all church and reception flowers, and all rental equipment for the wedding are clearly labeled to avoid any confusion and to ensure prompt and efficient delivery.

4. Ensure that the delivery vehicle has a full tank of gas, that money is provided for tolls, as needed, and that there is a clear understanding of all locations of delivery. A map of the town or city in the delivery vehicle is helpful.

5. Provide a tool kit for delivery personnel and send a student designer with the delivery crew to repair decorations, as needed.

Tool Kit for Wedding Decorating

The following items should accompany wedding deliveries to allow for quick and easy setup of the ceremony and reception decorations:

- Florist's snips, wire, corsage pins or carpet tape for securing the aisle carpet, and a yardstick for smoothing the aisle carpet.

- Dropsheet to work on and collect debris during setup; plastic garbage bags for debris; portable hand vacuum for church and reception carpets; small whisk broom and dustpan.

- Drip sheets to place under candelabras.

- Matches or lighter to light church or reception candles.

- Hammer, nails, and paddle wire.

- Corsage and boutonniere pins.

- Extra flowers and foliage of the same type as those used in the church and reception flowers for emergency repairs.

- Floral tape, floral adhesive, double-faced tape.

- Hyacinth stakes and wooden picks.

Notes

- Hot glue gun and glue sticks.
- Extra ribbon and floral foam.
- Flower shop business cards to offer wedding guests who inquire about the floral designs.
- Paper towels, tissues, first aid kit.
- Refreshments for the crew if it is going to be a lengthy setup.
- Watering can to replenish water in large arrangements.

Servicing Weddings

Weddings are usually serviced by a wedding consultant, who is either contracted by the florist or a professional employed by a department store or dress shop. The florist might train such a person, pay him an agreed upon fee, and in turn, charge the client. This person could be a student designer, or a church or service club member. He should be a person of good grooming and one who projects a calm, friendly, and professional manner. The purpose of a wedding consultant is to reassure the bride's family that a trained person will oversee the coordination of all the details of the wedding day. The florist might offer the client a printed list of extra services which the bridal consultant offers, the prices for each, or a package price. The client may then select the desired services. It is advisable to have the client sign a contract for the services he or she desires and to give a copy to the client. This clarifies what the florist's responsibilities are and helps avoid misunderstandings. Services a consultant might be responsible for include:

- Distributing the bouquets at either the home or ceremony location.
- Distributing personal flowers at the church and pinning on corsages and boutonnieres.
- Assisting in the photography session by adjusting the bridal train or offering guidance in the correct manner of holding the bouquets.

Notes

- Assisting in the church decorating, including lighting candles and laying the aisle carpet.

- Assisting the bridal party with their gowns.

- Adjusting the bride's veil and train before she proceeds down the aisle.

- Assisting in the removal of any church flowers to be transported to the reception.

- Assisting in the correct and efficient placement of reception flowers.

- Receiving gifts at the reception and displaying them appropriately on the gift table.

- Assisting the bride in changing into her honeymoon attire, taking charge of the wedding gown, and pinning on the going-away corsage and boutonniere of the wedding couple.

Service Kit for the Wedding

The consultant usually carries a kit to assist in servicing the wedding. This kit should be attractive, neutral in color, and unobtrusive. It might contain the following:

- Hair spray, bobby pins, and combs.

- Pins (straight, safety, corsage, and boutonniere).

- Scissors, needle and thread, extra buttons, and static guard.

- Extra pair of nylons.

- Disposable training pants for a young flower girl in case of an emergency.

- Tissues and makeup.

- Aspirin and a first aid kit.

Notes

The service a bride receives on her wedding day will determine if she will recommend the florist to others. When the wedding party sees a friendly professional aiding them with their attire and floral accessories, assisting in the distribution and placement of the flowers, and helping with any last minute details, they will realize how vitally important a good florist can be. Another significant factor in the wedding party's opinion of the florist is the packaging of the flowers. If the flowers are fresh and intact, clearly labeled, and attractively wrapped, they will make an excellent impression. Prompt delivery and setup of the wedding flowers is the final key to pleasing the wedding client. The wise florist will take advantage of this opportunity to generate good will by delivering finely wrapped wedding flowers and providing the necessary related services with pride. If all flowers and decorations are in place early, the bride and her family will be reassured that they have chosen the perfect florist for their special event.

Notes, Photographs, Sketches, etc.

Notes, Photographs, Sketches, etc.

Glossary

Acrylic - Transparent plastic made from a resin, usually available in a variety of thicknesses and colors in 4-foot x 8-foot sheets. The resin may also be molded into various shapes, such as bubbles. Acrylic forms do not normally shatter and splinter, as glass does.

Basquette - A bouquet carried by the flower girl or young member of the bridal party. It is designed to resemble flowers in a basket without the use of a basket.

Bent Neck - A cut rose disorder in which the flower droops or "nods;" bent neck involves a weakening of the neck or stem just under the flower head and may be caused by excessive drying during handling.

Biedermeier - A round, tightly spaced bouquet style, often with patterned flower placements or rings of flower placements.

Blockage - Clogging of water and food-carrying capillaries in cut flower stems with microorganisms, debris (dust and soil particles), small plant hairs, stem contents, and trapped air.

Blusher - The effect created by a flower or flowers when enclosed within a piece of tulle or translucent fabric.

Body Flower - Floral designs that are worn on the body, such as corsages, boutonnieres, and floral hair clips.

Botanical Specimen - Flowers of particular uniqueness or beauty used as individual specimens or focal flowers in a design.

Boutonniere - A single flower or group of flowers worn on the left lapel of a man's suit or tuxedo.

Care and Handling - Procedures used to prolong the life of cut flowers, foliage, and green and blooming plants.

Cash Discount - A discount incentive that encourages early payment for merchandise purchased on credit; specifically, a percentage reduction of the invoice price for payment before the 30-day free credit period expires.

Calyx - The outermost part of a flower which surrounds the petals, usually green and leaf-like.

Cellophane Wrap - A clear plastic-like wrap which comes in sheets or on rolls in varying widths. Used in packaging or wrapping flowers, arrangements, etc.

Chain of Life - A special program developed to promote the use of care and handling procedures; these procedures are often collectively referred to as "Chain of Life Procedures."

Chancel - The section of a church containing the altar and seats for the clergy and choir.

Chuppah - A four-posted, canopy-like structure under which the Jewish wedding ceremony takes place.

Citric Acid - A chemical naturally found in citrus fruits that influences (lowers) pH. It is used to prevent water stress problems, such as rose bent neck, by maximizing water uptake.

Clutch Wiring - A wiring method used to secure clusters of flower stems. Also referred to as the wrap-around method.

Clutch Bouquet - A casual gathering of flowers tied with ribbon or string for a garden-picked look.

Conditioning - The process of preparing flowers for shipping, storage, or arranging by cutting stems and allowing uptake of conditioning solution; may be referred to as "hardening off."

Co-Op Advertising - Advertising done in cooperation with another business or other businesses to share costs.

Corolla - The first set of protective petals on a flower, located between the calyx and other petals.

Corolla Tube - The tube portion of a flower between the calyx and the petals, such as in stephanotis and hyacinths.

Corsage - A flower or group of flowers worn by a woman. The design is usually placed on the left shoulder.

Depreciate - The decline in value of an item over time.

Direct Mail - Promotional mail pieces sent directly to customers or potential customers.

Dummy Cakes - Realistic-looking, artificial cakes made for display purposes.

Encore Wedding - Any wedding after the person's first wedding (from second marriage on).

Ethylene - An odorless, colorless gas produced by all plants, flowers, and fruits, as well as, many microorganisms; also in combustion engine exhaust (including truck and auto exhaust). Ethylene is also called the "aging hormone" because it stimulates the aging process in flowers and plants, causing petals to drop, leaves to fall off, and fruits to ripen.

European Contemporary Bouquet - A modern bouquet style with an upright thrust, an emphasis on strong lines, and minimal flower placements featuring unique botanical specimens.

Faux - The French word for false.

Festoon - A suspended chain or garland of flowers, foliage, or fabric.

Filler Flowers - Small blooms used to fill space between major flowers in an arrangement and to add color or volume. For example, baby's breath, statice, acacia or feverfew.

Finishing Off - The final step or steps in completing an arrangement, bouquet, or other floral design, such as finishing off the back of an arrangement with foliage to conceal the mechanics.

Finishing Sprays - Sprays used after designing to protect fresh flowers and prolong life.

Floral Foam Adapter - A container with a rubber plug on the underside, designed specifically for use in candelabras in place of candles.

Formal - A wedding that is usually extravagant, often having engraved invitations, lavish decorations, a large bridal party, opulent bridal attire, and an elaborate reception.

Gardenia Collar - A backing of leaves made of plastic or natural leaves stapled to a small round disk of wax cardboard. It is used to protect and support the gardenia's petals.

Glamellia - A composite flower made of florets assembled into the shape and appearance of a camellia.

Greening - The act of inserting foliage, usually into floral foam, to cover mechanics while adding color and texture to a design.

Groomsmen - The groom's attendants.

Growth Regulator Treatments - Special hormone containing solutions used to prevent specific problems, such as leaf-yellowing on alstroemeria, lilies, and chrysanthemums; treatment should be used by growers to get maximum effect.

Hairpin Wiring - A wiring method used for multi-flowered stems or fern-like foliage. The wire is bent into the shape of a hairpin before using.

Hand-Tied Bouquet - A bouquet of flowers arranged in the hand and secured by tying or binding the stems with string.

Hardening Off - See "conditioning."

Hard Goods - Any non-living item, such as supplies and mechanics.

Hook Wiring - A method of wiring used for flowers with hard, disc-like centers. The wire end is shaped like a hook and anchored into the flower's center.

Informal - A simple wedding with the ceremony taking place at any location (city hall, for example) with a small wedding party (frequently some attendants and the best man), a few relatives and close friends at the reception, and simple attire.

Insertion Wiring - A wiring method used for flowers with firmly attached heads, such as asters. The wire is inserted up through the stem into the flower's center.

Ketubah - The written marriage document or contract read during a Jewish wedding ceremony.

Logo - A stylized symbol (figure and/or letter) that represents a business and is used on letterhead, business cards, etc.

Longevity - See "vase life."

Magic Moment Arch - The term coined by the late Jerry Maston, AIFD, PFCI, to refer to the floral arch or decorated entrance through which the bride will enter before proceeding down the aisle for the ceremony. The "magic moment" refers to the instant when the groom first turns to see the bride prior to her procession down the aisle.

Mylar - A thin, shiny, foil-like material which is used to make decorative balloons. It may also be purchased in sheets or rolls and may be used in design, packaging, and display.

Networking - Interacting with related businesses to share information and services.

Non-Perishable Goods - Any non-living goods (perishable), including all hard goods.

Nosegay - A bouquet style in a round shape with flowers closely spaced. Also called a colonial bouquet.

Paddle Wire - A special form of floral wire in one continuous piece wrapped around a small wooden paddle.

PVC Pipe - A pipe of varying dimensions which is made of polyvinyl chloride; often used to increase height in a design.

Pierce Wiring - A wiring method for flowers with a thick calyx. The wire is pierced through the calyx from one side to the other.

Pistil - The female, seed-bearing, part of a flower.

Poly-Foil - Aluminum foil that has been strengthened with a layer of translucent plastic bonded to one side. Usually available on rolls in a variety of embossed patterns and colors.

Pre-Booking - Ordering specific products in advance, particularly for holidays. Pre-booking periods vary greatly. There is often a discount incentive for the retailer to pre-book.

Pre-Cooling - The act of refrigerating an item, such as a box, which will be used to hold items, such as bridal bouquets or body flowers. The box is refrigerated to maintain the lowest temperature needed to keep such items from fading in extreme heat.

Preservative - A mixture of ingredients to keep flowers alive longer by providing "food" or an energy source in the form of sugar, lowering pH (acidity), keeping the water- and food-conducting system working, and reducing stem contamination by bacteria and fungi; may also be called floral preservative, cut flower food, or fresh flower food.

Processional - The ceremonial proceeding of the wedding party up the aisle at the beginning of the ceremony.

Profit Margin - Net return after all expenses have been deducted from sales.

Promotions - All activities involved in selling the business's services, including advertising and publicity. Special programs may be created to promote a specific product, flower, or design (i.e. a rose promotion).

Quantity Discount - Discount for large-volume purchases (such as a 10 percent discount for buying ten or more cases).

Raffia - A natural, grass-like material available in long strands. It may be used for basket weaving or as an accessory in design.

Receiving Line - The line in which certain bridal party members and parents stand to receive guests' greetings and congratulations after the ceremony; may be held in the church vestibule or at the reception.

Recessional - The ceremonial proceeding of the wedding party down the aisle at the end of the ceremony.

Retail Price - The actual price charged to the consumer.

Reversed-Out Print - The reverse of black printing on a white page; print is reversed out of a black or dark background so it will be more noticeable.

Sanitation - The practice of controlling microorganisms; effective sanitation means washing and disinfecting with cleaning agents rather than plain water or dishwashing soap.

Seasonality - Indicates when a fresh flower product is "in season" or in peak supply; a product may be available from other parts of the world, but is not naturally "in season" or in great supply.

Seating Table - A table used at the entrance of a formal wedding which holds place cards in alphabetical order.

Semiformal - A wedding that is less lavish than a formal wedding, often held in a small church, chapel, or home, having a small wedding party and guest list, simple attire, and decorations.

Service Charge - An added fee for providing a service (such as renting a tent).

Service Club - An organization that provides community service, such as the Jaycees or Lions Club.

Sexton - A church employee or officer who takes care of the church property.

Sheet Moss - A natural, green moss sold either fresh or dried in loose, irregular sheets.

Splinting - A wiring method used to strengthen flower stems by inserting a wire into the calyx and wrapping it gently around the stem to the base.

Stamen - The pollen bearing, male part, of a flower made of the filament and the anther.

Standing Order - An agreement with a supplier to receive the same quantity of product repeatedly within specific periods of time (such as two cases per week); there is usually a discount incentive for placing a standing order.

Stitch Wiring - A wiring method typically used for broad-leaved foliage. The wire is pierced into the leaf, over the rib, and back out the other side of the rib.

Storage Potential - Indicates a fresh flower product's response to storage; flowers with minimal storage potential can only be stored for one or two days, while those with good potential can be stored five to seven days, and those with excellent potential may be stored for a week or more under the proper conditions.

STS (Silver Thiosulfate) - A treatment that protects flowers against ethylene damage and greatly extends their vase life; used only on ethylene-sensitive varieties, such as carnations, follow-up treatment with a preservative is essential.

Subcontracting - Contracting jobs or projects out to specialty companies or other businesses (such as electricians or caterers).

Synagogue - The meeting place for Jewish religious services and ceremonies.

Table Skirt - A fabric attached to the edge of the table to give the appearance of a tablecloth that extends to the floor.

Target Marketing - Marketing strategy directed at a specific group.

Tight Bud - The stage at which flowers are showing color but petals are not unfurling; some growers prefer to harvest in the tight bud stage to minimize flower damage during shipping; flowers commonly harvested in the tight bud stage include carnations and roses.

Topiary - A special type of floral design resembling a tree. The trunk of the design is typically topped with an arrangement of flowers in an ornamental shape, such as a ball or cone.

Trade Discount - Discount offered at a cost below the suggested retail price.

Trade Fair - A gathering of companies to show products or explain and demonstrate services, usually related to a certain trade, in designated areas or booths.

Transition Flowers - Arrangements or decorations that are used during a wedding ceremony, then moved to the reception site.

Tulle - A stiff netting used for veils, dresses, and design accents.

Vase Life - The useful life of a cut flower after harvest; may also be referred to as longevity, lasting quality, or keeping quality.

Vestibule - The area in a church between the outer door and the interior of the building.

Wax Tissue - Tissue paper that has been coated with a thin layer of wax to prevent the absorption of water when wrapping floral products.

Wedding Consultant - A person specializing in planning and coordinating weddings from ceremony through reception, including invitations, clothing, flowers, and more.

Wholesale Price - The price charged by the wholesaler to the retailer.

Wilt-Sensitive - Flowers that quickly wilt and become limp when shipped or held out of water; these flowers should be unpacked and processed first when a shipment arrives and stored for minimal time periods.

Wire Gauge - The measurement used to determine the degree of thickness of wire.

Wrap-Around Wiring - See clutch wiring.

Appendix A

Bridal Fashion Terminology

Silhouettes:

A-Line

***A*-Line** - Full, flowing skirt without substantial gathering at the waist.

Balloon Skirt

Balloon Skirt - *(also Bubble Skirt)* Full, inflated skirt of any length, curving up and under at the hemline.

Bouffant - *(also Ball Gown)* Very full, gathered skirt. Traditional style for many bridal gowns.

Empire Line - A-line skirt with high waist gathered under the bustline.

Mermaid

Mermaid - Form-fitting, sheath-type gown which flares out at the knees.

Sheath - Tight, body-hugging style from the shoulders to the ankles. No waistline.

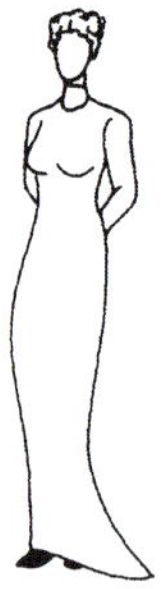

Sheath

Tiered - Full skirt with layers of ruffles or lace flowing from the waist to the hemline.

Tiered

Lengths:

Ballerina - *(also Ballet length or Waltz length)* Hemline falling to the ankles.

Ballerina

Cocktail - Hemline to the knee or just below.

Cocktail

Floor - Hemline just reaching the floor.

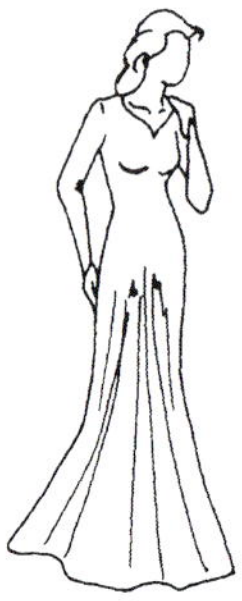

Floor

Intermezzo

Intermezzo - Hemline knee length or shorter in front, tea length in back.

Intermission

Intermission - Hemline knee to calf length in front, floor length in back.

Tea

Tea - Hemline falling to mid-calf.

Trains:

Butterfly

Butterfly - A train which dips inward at the center edge.

Cathedral

Cathedral - Extending up to 3 yards from the waist.

Chapel

Chapel - Extending 1 1/3 yards from the waist.

Court

Court - Extending 1 foot beyond the sweep train.

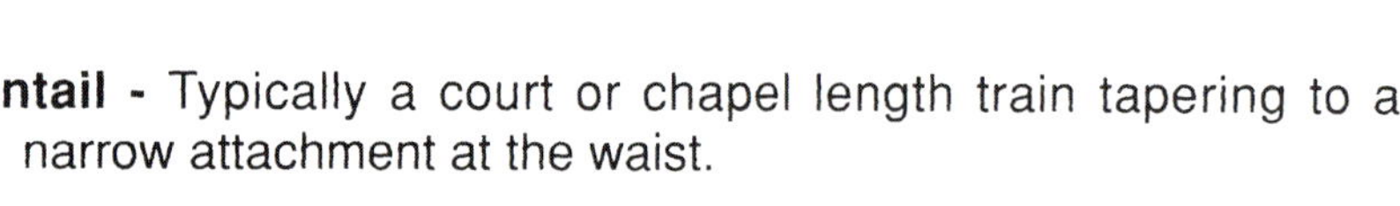

Fantail - Typically a court or chapel length train tapering to a narrow attachment at the waist.

Fantail

Monarch - *(also Extended Cathedral train)* Train extending 1 to 3 feet beyond a Cathedral train.

Monarch

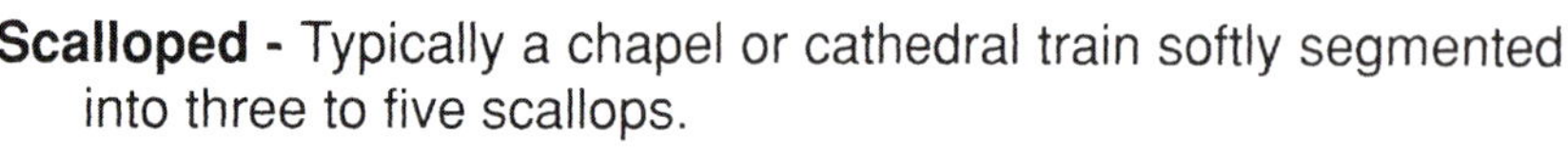

Scalloped - Typically a chapel or cathedral train softly segmented into three to five scallops.

Scalloped

Sweep - *(also Brush train)* Slight train just brushing the floor. Train sometimes worn by the bridesmaids.

Sweep

Watteau

Watteau - Train extending from the shoulders rather than the waistline.

Waistlines:

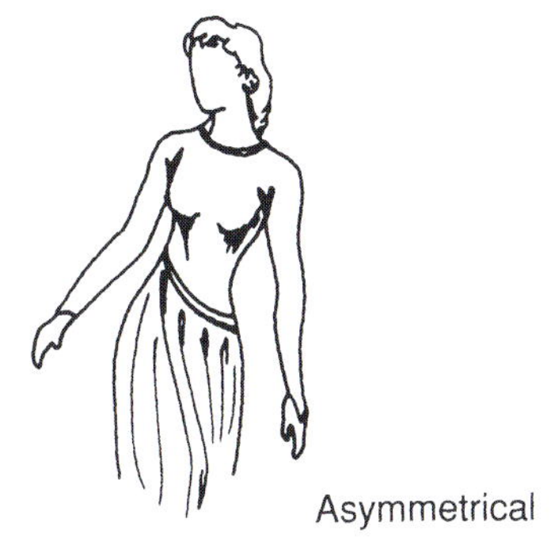
Asymmetrical

Asymmetrical - Natural waistline on one side, falling to hip level at the other.

Basque

Basque - *(also Princess waistline)* Natural waistline in the back, dipping to a *V* in the front.

Dropped

Dropped - Elongated bodice with waistline dropping to hip level.

Natural

Natural - Bodice ending and skirt beginning along a natural line at the waist.

Peplum - Ruffle or flounce at the waistline. May be extended down the back of some gowns.

Peplum

Necklines:

Fichu - A ruffle, lace, or other fabric worn across the bustline, creating a broad *V* neckline.

Fichu

Jewel - *(also Round neckline)* Neckline gently rounded close to the neck.

Jewel

Off-the-Shoulder - Skimming from the edge of one shoulder, across the bustline, to the other shoulder.

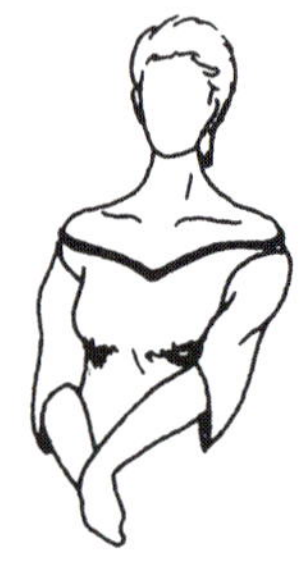
Off-the-Shoulder

Portrait Collar - *(also Bertha Collar or Shoulder Wrap)* Cape-like collar worn off-the-shoulder like a wrap.

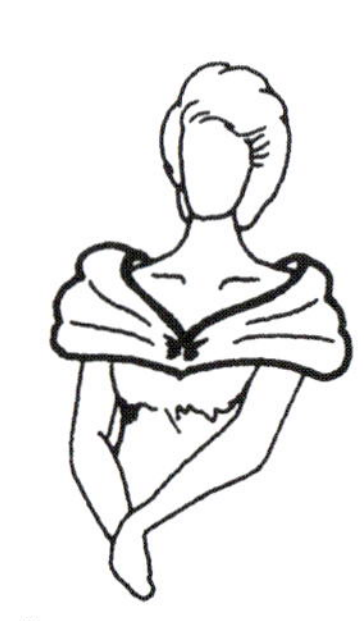
Portrait Collar

Queen Anne

Queen Anne - Open sweetheart outline with high collar at the nape of the neck.

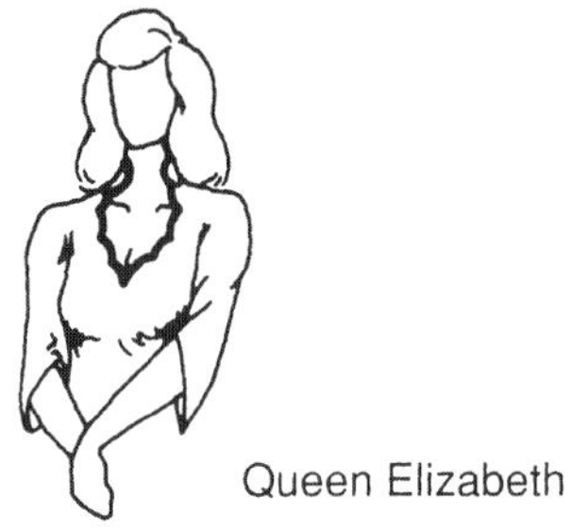

Queen Elizabeth

Queen Elizabeth - Open-*V* neckline with high collar at the nape of the neck.

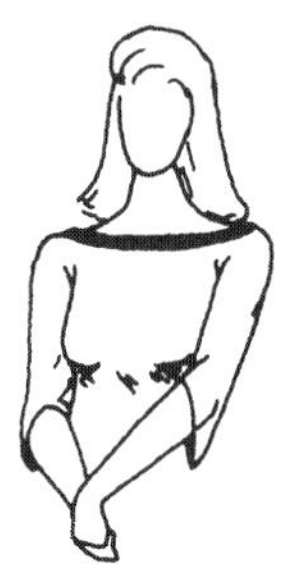

Sabrina

Sabrina - *(also Bateau or Boat neckline)* Gently flowing, almost straight across the collarbone to the shoulders.

Scoop

Scoop - A low, *U*-shaped, open neckline.

Square

Square - Open neckline skimming straight across the bustline for a squared-off look.

Sweetheart - Open neckline worn on the shoulder, softly draping into a heart shape at the bustline.

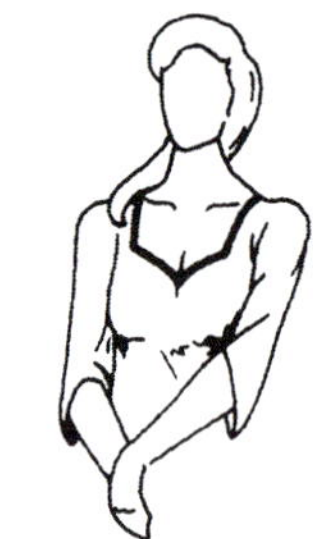
Sweetheart

***V* Neckline -** Dipping to a *V* at the front and/or back.

V Neckline

Victorian - Wedding Band or high collar, often with an illusion (net) yoke and sweetheart bodice.

Victorian

Sleeves:

Bishop - Loose, billowy sleeve gathered to a wide cuff at the wrist.

Bishop

Cap - Small sleeve extending slightly over the shoulder's edge.

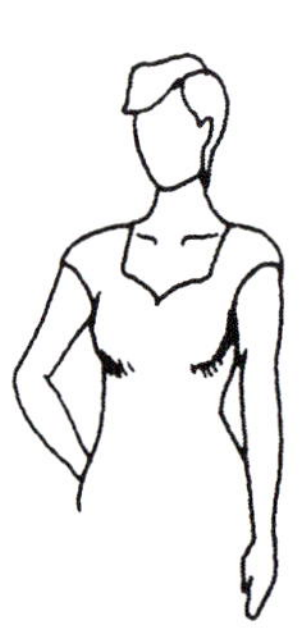
Cap

Dolman

Dolman - *(also Batwing)* Draping, cape-like sleeve extending from the bodice, between the shoulder and waistline, and fitted at the wrist.

Fitted

Fitted - Close fitting sleeve from shoulder to wrist.

Juliet

Juliet - *(also Elizabethan)* A long, fitted sleeve with a rounded puff at the shoulder.

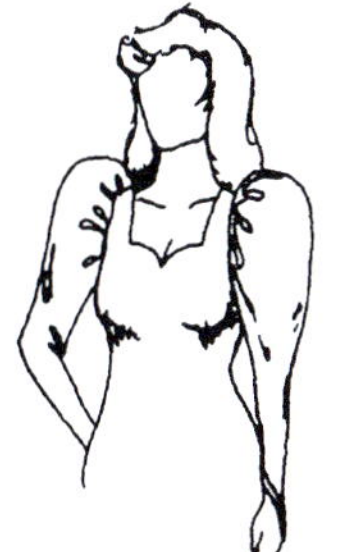
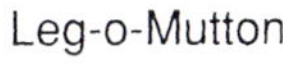
Leg-o-Mutton

Leg-o-Mutton - Full and rounded at the shoulder, tapering toward the elbow, fitted from below the elbow to the wrist.

Pouf

Pouf - *(also Puff)* Short sleeve with gently rounded puff, often rising above shoulder level.

Princess - *(also Balloon or Melon)* Full, oversized, globular sleeve, from the shoulder to above the elbow.

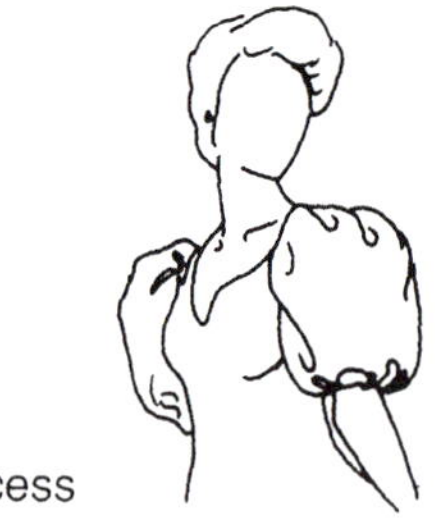

Princess

Shirred - Gently puckered or gathered between the shoulder and the elbow. May be short or long.

Shirred

Headpieces:

Derby Hat - A small picture hat with a rounded crown and upturned brim.

Derby Hat

Floral Wreath - *(also Circlet, Halo, or Point Band)* Ring of flowers and beads worn on the crown of the head or across the forehead, often coming to a point in front.

Floral Wreath

Juliet Cap - *(also Teardrop)* Small, curved cap worn close to the head, often tapering to a point in front.

Juliet Cap

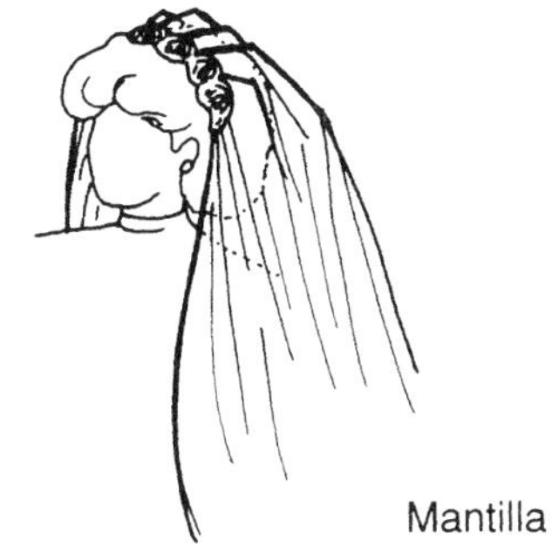
Mantilla

Mantilla - Wide, lace band or oversized comb worn toward the back of the head, with veiling attached.

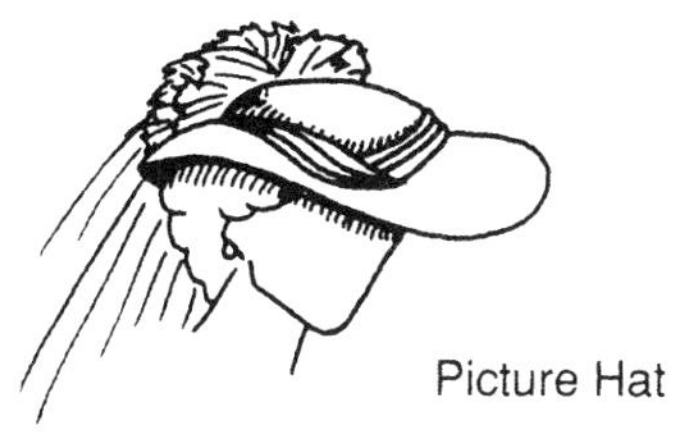
Picture Hat

Picture Hat - *(also Garden Hat)* A broad-brimmed hat with a low, rounded crown.

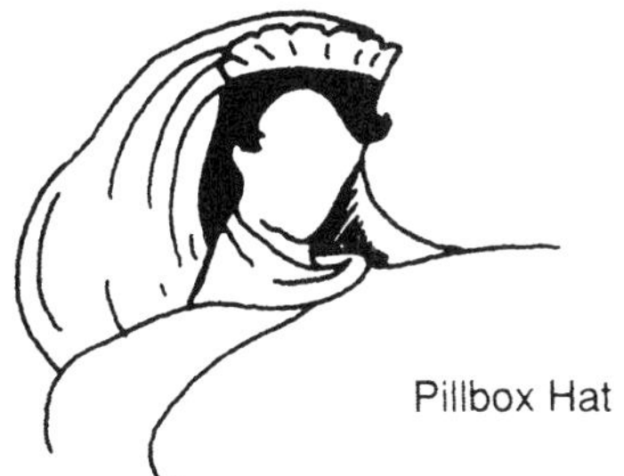
Pillbox Hat

Pillbox Hat - Small oval, round, or square hat with straight sides and a flat top.

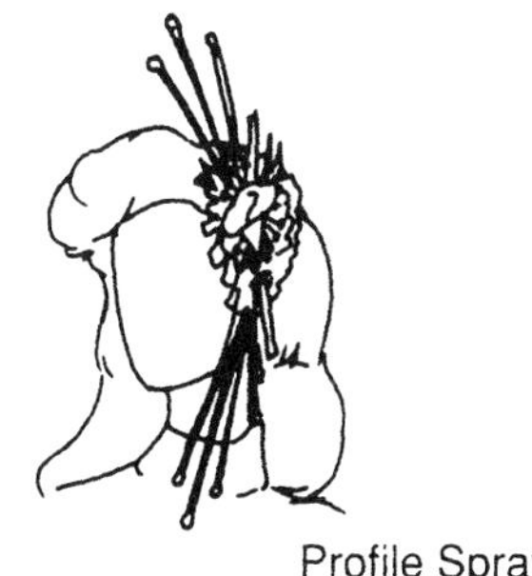
Profile Spray

Profile Spray - *(also Profile Comb)* Beaded, silk floral cluster worn on the side of the head.

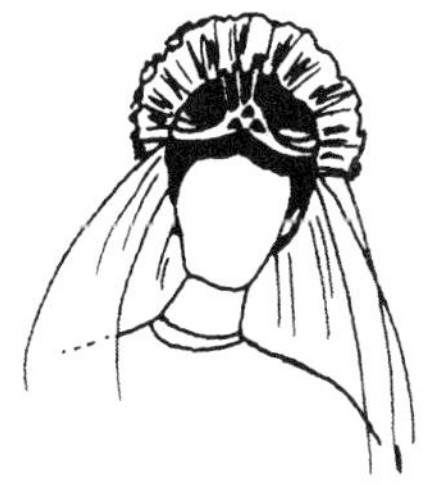
Tiara

Tiara - Crown-like headpiece worn high on the head.

Appendix B

Wedding Planner

GENERAL INFORMATION

Bride's Name ______________________

Address ______________________

____

Phone: Home ______________________

Work ______________________

Day of Wedding ______________________

Groom's Name ______________________

Address ______________________

____

Phone: Home ______________________

Work ______________________

Day of Wedding ______________________

Wedding Date ______________________

Time ______________________

Location ______________________

Address ______________________

____

Party Responsible for

Opening the Church ______________________

Phone ______________________

Reception Date ______________________

Time ______________________

Location ______________________

Address ______________________

____

Phone ______________________

Party Responsible

for Payment ______________________

Address ______________________

____

Phone ______________________

Special Instructions ______________________

____

____

____

____

____

____

FLOWER DETAILS

BOUQUETS

Price

Bride:

Sketch of bridal gown silhouette

Sketch of bridal bouquet

Gown Style & Color ______________________

Bouquet Style ______________________ $ ______

Colors ______________________

Flowers ______________________

Construction Technique ______________________

Veil/Headpiece ______________________ $ ______

Throw Bouquet ______________________ $ ______

Going Away Flowers ______________________ $ ______

Presentation for Mothers ______________________ $ ______

Presentation/Virgin Mary ______________________ $ ______

Maid/Matron of Honor:

Sketch of maid/matron of honor dress silhouette

Sketch of maid/matron of honor bouquet

Dress Style & Color ______________________

Bouquet Style ______________________ Price Each $ ______ $ ______

Colors ______________________

Flowers ______________________

Construction Technique ______________________

Headpiece ______________________ Price Each $ ______ $ ______

Bridesmaids:

Price

Sketch of bridesmaid's dress silhouette

Sketch of bridesmaid's bouquet

Number __________

Dress Style & Color __________

Bouquet Style __________ Price Each $ ______ $ ______

Colors __________

Flowers __________

Construction Technique __________

Headpiece __________ Price Each $ ______ $ ______

Junior Bridesmaids:

Sketch of junior bridesmaid's dress silhouette

Sketch of junior bridesmaid's bouquet

Number __________

Dress Style & Color __________

Bouquet Style __________ Price Each $ ______ $ ______

Colors __________

Flowers __________

Construction Technique __________

Headpiece __________ Price Each $ ______ $ ______

Candlelighter:

Price

Number ____________

Dress Style & Color ____________________

Flowers Style ____________ Price Each $ ________ $ ________

Colors ____________________

Flowers ____________________

Construction Technique ____________________

Headpiece ____________ Price Each $ ________ $ ________

Flower Girl:

Number ____________

Dress Style & Color ____________________

Bouquet Style ____________ Price Each $ ________ $ ________

Colors ____________________

Flowers ____________________

Construction Technique ____________________

Headpiece ____________ Price Each $ ________ $ ________

CORSAGES

Bride's Mother:

Dress Style & Color ____________________ $ ________

Flowers Style ____________________

Colors ____________________

Groom's Mother:

Dress Style & Color ____________________ $ ________

Flowers Style ____________________

Colors ____________________

Grandmothers:

Name ____________________ $ ________

Dress Style & Color ____________________

Flowers Style ____________________

Colors ____________________

Name ____________________ $ ________

Dress Style & Color ____________________

Flowers Style ____________________

Colors ____________________

Grandmothers (cont.):

Price

Name ______________________________ $ ________

Dress Style & Color ______________________________

Flowers Style ______________________________

Colors ______________________________

Name ______________________________ $ ________

Dress Style & Color ______________________________

Flowers Style ______________________________

Colors ______________________________

Stepmothers:

Name ______________________________ $ ________

Dress Style & Color ______________________________

Flowers Style ______________________________

Colors ______________________________

Name ______________________________ $ ________

Dress Style & Color ______________________________

Flowers Style ______________________________

Colors ______________________________

Other Corsages:

Hostesses ______________ (No. _____ @ $ ______ ea.) $ ________

Cake Server(s) ______________ (No. _____ @ $ ______ ea.) $ ________

Punch Server(s) ______________ (No. _____ @ $ ______ ea.) $ ________

Gift Attendant(s) ______________ (No. _____ @ $ ______ ea.) $ ________

Guestbook Attendant ______________________________ $ ________

Service Personnel ______________________________ $ ________

Rice Bag Attendant(s) ______________ (No. _____ @ $ ______ ea.) $ ________

Favors Attendant(s) ______________ (No. _____ @ $ ______ ea.) $ ________

Soloist(s) ______________ (No. _____ @ $ ______ ea.) $ ________

Musician(s) ______________ (No. _____ @ $ ______ ea.) $ ________

Other(s) ______________ (No. _____ @ $ ______ ea.) $ ________

BOUTONNIERES

Price

Tux Style ______________________ Color ______________________

Groom ______________________ $ ______

Best Man ______________________ $ ______

Groomsmen ______________________ (No. ______ @ $ ______ ea.) $ ______

Ushers ______________________ (No. ______ @ $ ______ ea.) $ ______

Fathers ______________________ (No. ______ @ $ ______ ea.) $ ______

Grandfathers ______________________ (No. ______ @ $ ______ ea.) $ ______

Step-Father(s) ______________________ (No. ______ @ $ ______ ea.) $ ______

Candlelighter(s) ______________________ (No. ______ @ $ ______ ea.) $ ______

Musician(s) ______________________ (No. ______ @ $ ______ ea.) $ ______

Soloist(s) ______________________ (No. ______ @ $ ______ ea.) $ ______

Minister(s) ______________________ (No. ______ @ $ ______ ea.) $ ______

Ringbearer ______________________ $ ______

Host(s) ______________________ (No. ______ @ $ ______ ea.) $ ______

Other(s) ______________________ (No. ______ @ $ ______ ea.) $ ______

CEREMONIAL DECORATIONS

Setup Time ______________

Sketch of layout of ceremony

Style ______________________________________

Colors ______________________________________

Flowers ______________________________________

CEREMONIAL DECORATIONS (cont.)

Price

Main Altar ______ $ ______

Unity Candle Flowers ______ $ ______

Side Arrangements ______ $ ______

Candelabra ______ $ ______

Kneeling Bench ______ $ ______

Arch ______ $ ______

Plant Rentals ______ $ ______

Pew Decorations ______ (No. ______ @ $ ______ ea.) $ ______

Aisle Candelabra ______ $ ______

Aisle Carpet ______ $ ______

Guestbook Table ______ $ ______

Others ______ $ ______

RECEPTION DECORATIONS

Setup Time ______

Cake $ ______

Cake Top ______

Number of Tiers ______

Number of Inserts ______

Flowers ______

Base of Cake ______

Candelabra $ ______

Candle Color ______

Number ______

Flowers ______

Table Garland ______ $ ______

Centerpieces ______ $ ______

Guest Table ______ (No. ______ @ $ ______ ea.) $ ______

Arrangements ______ (No. ______ @ $ ______ ea.) $ ______

Balloons ______ $ ______

REHEARSAL DINNER

Price

Date ______________________ Time ______________________

Location ______________________

		Price
Head Table	______________________	$
Centerpieces	______________________	$
Corsages	______________________	$
Favors	______________________	$

PAYMENT INFORMATION

Payment Terms ______________________

____

Balance Due ______________________
(date)

Signature ______________________

Date ______________________

	Bride's Cost	Groom's Cost*
Sub Total	$	$
Tax	$	$
Total	$	$
Deduct Deposit	$	$
Balance	$	$

*Groom's costs are outlined in red boxes.

Delivery Schedule

Wedding Date ____________________

Bride's Name ____________________ **Groom's Name** ____________________

Bride's Phone # ____________________ **Groom's Phone #** ____________________

REHEARSAL DINNER

Date ____________________

Time ____________________

Delivery Time ____________________

Place ____________________

Address ____________________

Contact Person ____________________

Phone # ____________________

Notes ____________________

Flowers ____________________

Equipment ____________________

Other ____________________

CEREMONY

Date ____________________

Time ____________________

Delivery Time ____________________

Place ____________________

Address ____________________

Church Custodian ____________________

Phone # ____________________

Notes ____________________

Flowers ____________________

Equipment ____________________

Other ____________________

RECEPTION

Date ________________
Time ________________
Delivery Time ________________
Place ________________
Address ________________
Contact Person ________________
Phone # ________________
Notes ________________

Flowers ________________
Equipment ________________
Other ________________

ADDITIONAL COMMENTS

Appendix C

Wedding Agreement

Acceptance

I accept the proposal by ______________________________, hereinafter called "Florist," as detailed in my Wedding Planner and authorize Florist to proceed with the plans as described therein.

Any changes to this proposal must be agreed to in writing by both parties and any addition or variations will be billed for in addition to the contract amount. Where specific varieties of flowers are defined, Florist reserves the right to make substitutions whenever market conditions affect their availability, but will maintain the integrity of the proposed color scheme and will use flowers of equivalent value.

I enclose a payment of $__________________________ as confirmation, with the balance of $____________________ to be payable on or before ______________.

Signed ______________________________________ Date ________________________
(Customer)

Signed ______________________________________ Date ________________________
(Customer)

Payment Received ______________________________ Date ________________________

Flowers Delivered ______________________________ Date ________________________

Flowers Received ______________________________ Date ________________________

Rental Contract

This Contract is made and entered into by and between ______________________________, hereinafter called "Florist," and __________ ________________________, hereinafter called "Customer," for the rental of certain equipment as listed on Exhibit "A" attached hereto and made a part hereof. Said equipment shall be

(√) __________ picked up by Customer on __________,

(√) __________ delivered by Florist on ______________,

and shall be

(√) __________ returned by Customer on __________.

(√) __________ retrieved by Florist on ______________.

In the event the equipment is not returned on the date stated above, Customer shall pay an additional rental charge of $________ per day to Florist. A deposit of $_________ is required and must be paid before pickup or delivery. This deposit is refundable in full upon the return in good condition of each piece of equipment and upon payment in full of all rental charges. At the time of pickup or delivery, the equipment has been inspected by Customer and is in the following condition: ______________________

____

____

____.

A cleaning fee of $__________ per item of equipment will be charged if the equipment is returned without having been properly cleaned.

Customer shall pay the value of any missing equipment as listed on Exhibit "A". If any equipment is damaged, Customer shall pay the cost of repair or the difference in value of the equipment in its damaged condition, whichever is a lesser amount.

Executed this ____________ day of __________________________, 19_____.

______________________________	______________________________
Florist	Customer Signature
By ___________________________	______________________________
	Customer Signature
Date _________________________	Address _______________________
	Phone (__________) _____________
	Date __________________________

Exhibit A to Rental Contract

Equipment/Supplies:	**Value:**
____________________	$ __________
____________________	$ __________
____________________	$ __________
____________________	$ __________
____________________	$ __________
____________________	$ __________
____________________	$ __________
____________________	$ __________
____________________	$ __________
____________________	$ __________
____________________	$ __________
____________________	$ __________
____________________	$ __________
____________________	$ __________
____________________	$ __________
____________________	$ __________
____________________	$ __________

____________________ Florist	____________________ Customer
By ____________________ Authorized Signature	By ____________________ Authorized Signature
Date ____________________	Date ____________________

Subcontracting Agreement

This Contract and Agreement is made and entered into by and between ____, hereinafter called "Florist," and ____, hereinafter called "Subcontractor," for services which will be rendered on ______________________________________ for ______________________________. The services to be rendered by Subcontractor are as follows:

____

____

____

____

____

____

____

____

____

For the performance of this service, Florist will pay Subcontractor the sum of $__________. A deposit of $__________, equalling _____% of the total price, has been made to Subcontractor by Florist on this day, leaving a balance due of $________, which amount shall be paid by Florist no later than ten (10) days after the event date stated above. In the event of a cancellation of the need for services of Subcontractor described above, Subcontractor shall retain the deposit as payment in full, and Florist shall have no further liability under this Contract.

If Subcontractor requires services of other parties to complete the services specified above, said services shall be the sole responsibility of Subcontractor and Subcontractor shall hold Florist harmless from any claims asserted by said parties. The relationship of the parties hereto shall be that of independent contractors and not that of principal/agent or employer/employee.

EXECUTED this _____ day of ________________, 19 ______.

________________________ Florist	________________________ Subcontractor
By: ____________________ Authorized Signature	By: ____________________ Authorized Signature

Appendix D

Wedding Supply Checklist

_____ **Aisle runner**
- _____ plastic
- _____ lace

_____ **Candles**
- _____ tapers
- _____ votive
- _____ unity
- _____ memory

_____ **Candle Hardware and Accessories**
- _____ altar candelabra
- _____ table top candelabra
- _____ aisle candelabra
- _____ unity candelabra
- _____ drip cloths
- _____ bobeches for standard tapers

_____ **Design Extras**
- _____ twinkle lights
- _____ balloons for release and decoration

_____ **Foam and Accessories**
- _____ wet foam bricks
- _____ dry foam bricks
- _____ bouquet holders
- _____ lace bouquet backings
- _____ cages or other holders

_____ **Design Accessories**
- _____ design bowls
- _____ glue
- _____ floral tape
  - _____ stem
  - _____ waterproof
  - _____ aisle runner tape
- _____ ribbon and lace
- _____ tulle
- _____ water tubes
- _____ wire
  - _____ paddle
  - _____ boxed
- _____ dropcloths

_____ **Floral Preservative**

_____ **Finishing Sprays**

_____ **Floral Coloring**
- _____ paint
- _____ tints
- _____ specialty (pearlized, glitter, etc.)
- _____ dyes (dip or absorption)

_____ **Accessories Used in Making Flowers to Wear and Carry**
- _____ chenille stems
- _____ corsage stems
- _____ corsage leaves
- _____ lace fans
- _____ lace parasols
- _____ silk flowers
- _____ pearl sprays and beads
- _____ rhinestone sprays
- _____ wristlets
- _____ hair combs
- _____ corsage pins
- _____ boutonniere pins
- _____ boxes and bags for packaging

_____ **Bridal Party Accessories**
- _____ bridal garter
- _____ guest book and pen
- _____ ring bearer pillow
- _____ flower girl basket and tissue petals
- _____ toasting set for bride and groom
- _____ cake serving set
- _____ cake top
- _____ accessories for rice bags or favor bags

_____ **Wedding Hardware and Design Pieces**
- _____ wedding arch
- _____ kneeling bench
- _____ pew clips
- _____ baskets and stands for altar pieces

Fresh Flower Market and Inventory Control Checklist

Flower	Varieties Color	Supplier	Quantity Needed	Quantity Ordered	Cost	Date Ordered	Date Received
Alstroemeria							
Anthurium							
Aster 'Monte Casino'							
Bells of Ireland							
Bird of Paradise							
Bouvardia							
Calla							
Camellia							
Carnations, Standard							
Carnations, Miniature							
Chrysanthemums, Standard China Fuji Other							
Chrysanthemums, Spray Pompon Daisy Spider Button							
Cornflower							
Delphinium							
Freesia							
Gardenia							
Gerbera							
Ginger							
Gladiolus							
Gypsophila (Baby's Breath)							
Heather							
Heliconia							
Iris							
Lilac							
Lily, Hybrid (Asiatic)							
Lily, Rubrum (Oriental)							
Lily-of-the-Valley							

Flower	Varieties Color	Supplier	Quantity Needed	Quantity Ordered	Cost	Date Ordered	Date Received
Marguerite Daisy							
Marigolds							
Nerine							
Orchid, Spray Arachnia Cymbidium Dendrobium Oncidium							
Orchid, Single Cattleya Cymbidium Japhet Phalaenopsis							
Peony							
Phlox							
Poinsettias							
Protea							
Queen Anne's Lace							
Roses							
Snapdragons							
Star of Bethlehem							
Statice							
Stephanotis							
Stock							
Tuberose							
Tulip							
Wax Flower							
Zinnia							
Other							
Greens							

Tips: Keep the following in mind when ordering:

1. What stage of development are the flowers in? (Allow time for opening if flowers are in bud stage.)
2. Have the flowers been shipped and held dry? (Allow time for a "recovery period" to take up water.)
3. Who is the grower and what is the country of origin? (This influences packaging and previous treatment.)

Ceremony Site Checklist

Location ______________________________ **Address** ______________________________

Contact Person ______________________________ **Phone Number** ______________________________

Make the Following Observations:

_____ Overall facility size

_____ Size of altar or Beama

_____ Steps present (total number)

_____ Special architectural features

_____ Color of surroundings (walls, carpet)

_____ Windowsills (size and number of windows

_____ Aisles (size, number, and length)

_____ Pews (number and type of pew end)

_____ Lighting

_____ Type and size of windows

_____ Ceiling heights

_____ Formality

_____ Church decorations in place (holiday poinsettias, lilies, etc.)

_____ Props available (candelabra, etc.)

_____ Altar cloth color (if changed for wedding)

_____ Electrical outlets

Check the Following with an Authorized Official:

_____ Amount of sunlight at time of day of ceremony

_____ Fire regulations

_____ Flower restrictions

_____ Candle restrictions

_____ Aisle runner restrictions

_____ What to do with flowers after the service

_____ Setup time

_____ Tear down time

Traditional Reception Location Checklist

Bride ____________________ **Location** ____________________

Date __________ **Time** __________ **Address** ____________________

Contact Person ____________________ **Phone Number** ____________________

Estimated travel time between ceremony location and reception location __________

Reception Site Specifications:

Room size ____________________ Ceiling height ____________________

Make a sketch of the room on the back of this sheet.

On the sketch, mark all of the following:

- Entries, exits, and windows
- Support pillars
- Band and dance floor locations
- Location of all electrical outlets, if applicable

Colors and style of room decor ____________________

Plants and flowers used at the location as permanent decorations ____________________

____

____

Location of delivery entrance ____________________

Cleanup is set up with contact person ____________________

Date ____________________ Time ____________________

Other notes ____________________

____

____

____

____

____

Home Reception Checklist

Bride ______________________ **Location** ______________________

Date ____________ **Time** ________ **Address** ______________________

Host or Hostess ______________ **Phone Number** ______________

Exterior Decorations:

Color and style of the house ______________________

Surrounding blooming plant colors ______________________

Decorations are needed for:

- Front gates ______________________
- Fence ______________________
- Doorway ______________________
- Entrance area ______________________
- Other ______________________

Interior Decorations:

- Entryway ______________________
- Staircase ______________________
- Living room ______________________
- Dining room ______________________
- Family room ______________________
- Kitchen ______________________
- Powder room ______________________
- Other ______________________

Other floral requirements ______________________

Serving table locations ______________________

Special requests of host/hostess ______________________

Setup time ______________ Tear down time ______________

Garden Reception Checklist

Bride ______________________ **Location** ______________________

Date ______________ **Time** __________ **Address** ______________________

Contact Person ______________________ **Phone Number** ______________________

Size of garden area ______________________

Condition of surrounding plants ______________________

Colors of blooming plants in area ______________________

Make a sketch of the area or yard on back.

Include the following items:

- Gazebo or arch location ______________________
- Dance floor and bandstand ______________________
- Other applicable structures ______________________
- Electrical outlet locations, if applicable ______________________
- All table locations ______________________
- Other ______________________

Special measurements and locations for false gardens ______________________

____

Tent rental company name and phone number ______________________

____

Installation time ______________________

Tear down time ______________________

Other notes ______________________

____

____

____

____

Bibliography

Ardman, Harvey, and Gisele Nadeau. The Woman's Day Book of Weddings. New York, New York: The Bobbs-Merrill Company, Inc., 1982.

"Bridal Shop Talk." Bride's and Living for Young Homemakers. August/September, 1986, 250.

Bullock, Alice-May. Lace and Lace Making. New York, New York: Larousse and Co., Inc., 1981.

Caplin, Jessie F. The Lace Book. New York, New York: The Macmillan Company, 1932.

Hardingham, Martin. The Fabric Catalog. New York, New York: Pocket Books, 1978.

Hixon, Bill. A Manual for a Treasury of Bridal Bouquets. Japan: Toppan Printing Co., Ltd., 1972.

Holstead, Christy. Care and Handling of Flowers and Plants. Alexandria, Virginia: Society of American Florists, 1985.

John Henry Company. Tips 'n Techniques for Wedding Designs. Lansing, Michigan: The John Henry Co., 1979.

Levinson, Jay Conrad. Gorilla Marketing. Boston. Houghton Mifflin Co., 1984.

McClure, Joan, and eds. of McCall's. McCall's Engagement and Wedding Guide. New York, New York: The Saturday Review Press, 1972.

McLean, Lynn Larry. Professional Floral Commentator's Workshop, 1985. San Antonio, Texas.

O'Hara, Georgiana. The Encyclopedia of Fashion. New York, New York: Harry N. Abrams, Inc. Publishers, 1986.

Piccione, Nancy. Your Wedding. Englewood Cliffs, New Jersey: Prentice-Hall, Inc., 1982.

Roberts, Edna H. How to Know Laces. New York, New York: Dry Goods Economist, 1925.

Saxtan, John H. Fresh Flower Book. Lansing, Michigan: The John Henry Company, 1986.

Stewart, Martha. Weddings. New York, New York: Crown Publishers, Inc., 1987.

Sulivan, Robertson, and Staby. Management for Retail Florists. 1980.

1985 Budget Guide. Springfield, Virginia: International Exhibitors Association, 1985.

Index

Wiring Chart

Flowers

Flower Type	Wiring Method	Wire Gauge	Comments
Alstroemeria	pierce or spiral	26	fragile
Aster	insertion	24	weak neck
Astilbe	spiral	24	
Bouvardia	hairpin hook or spiral	24-26	cotton base recommended
Carnation-miniature	pierce	24-26	
-standard	cross-pierce	24	
Cornflower	pierce	24	
Chrysanthemum-standard	hairpin hook	24	shatters easily
Daffodil	pierce	24-26	cotton base recommended
Daisy	hairpin hook	24	
Delphinium-stem	hairpin hook	26	except large hybrid varieties
-floret	hairpin hook	24	very fragile, wilt-sensitive
Freesia-stem	wrap-around or spiral	26	
-floret	pierce	26	
Fuji	hairpin hook	24	
Gardenia	pierce or spiral	24	fragile, cotton base recommended
Gerbera	hairpin hook	24	
Gladiolus floret	cross-pierce	24-26	
Gypsophila/Baby's Breath	spiral or hairpin	26-28	
Heather	spiral	24-26	
Hyacinth-stem	spiral	22	
-floret	hairpin hook	26	
Iris	pierce	24-26	
Liátris	spiral	24	
Lilac	spiral	22	
Lily	pierce	24	remove pollen from stamen
Lily-of-the-Valley	hairpin hook or spiral	28	cotton base recommended
Nerine Lily-floret	pierce	26	
Orchids:			
Cattleya	pierce	24	
Cymbidium	pierce	24	
Cypripedium/Paphiopedilum	spiral	24	
Dendrobium-blossom	hairpin hook	26	
-stem	wrap-around	22	
Japhet	pierce	24	
Phalaenopsis	hairpin hook	26	
Pompon	hairpin hook or insertion	24	
Ranunculus	hairpin hook	26	
Rose-standard	pierce	24	fragile
-sweetheart	pierce	24	
-spray	spiral	26	
Star of Bethlehem-stem	spiral	24	
-floret	hairpin hook	26	
Stephanotis	hairpin hook	26	fragile
Statice	hairpin hook	24	
Tulip	pierce	24	
Yarrow	spiral	24	cotton base recommended
Wax Flower	spiral	26	

Foliages

Foliage	Wiring Method	Wire Gauge	Comments
Bear Grass	spiral	24	
Camellia	hairpin hook	26	
Eucalyptus	spiral	24	
Fern	hairpin hook	26-28	
Galax	stitch	26	
Italian Ruscus	spiral	26	
Ivy	spiral or hairpin hook	26	
Ming Fern	spiral	24-26	